ECONOMIC HISTORY

FOREIGN FINANCE IN CONTINENTAL EUROPE AND THE UNITED STATES, 1815–1870

FINANCE, MONEY AND BANKING

FOREIGN FINANCE IN CONTINENTAL EUROPE AND THE UNITED STATES, 1815–1870

Quantities, Origins, Functions and Distribution

D.C.M. PLATT

Routledge
Taylor & Francis Group
LONDON AND NEW YORK

First published in 1984

Published in 2006 by
Routledge
2 Park Square, Milton Park, Abingdon, Oxfordshire, OX14 4RN
711 Third Avenue, New York, NY 10017

First issued in paperback 2014

Routledge is an imprint of the Taylor & Francis Group, an informa business

British Library Cataloguing in Publication Data
A CIP catalogue record for this book
is available from the British Library

Foreign Finance in Continental Europe and the United States, 1815–1870
ISBN 0-415-38205-X (volume)
ISBN 0-415-37850-8 (subset)
ISBN 0-415-28619-0 (set)

ISBN 978-1-138-87981-2 (pbk)
ISBN 978-0-415-38205-2 (hbk)

Routledge Library Editions: Economic History

Foreign Finance in Continental Europe and the United States, 1815–1870

Quantities, origins, functions and distribution

D. C. M. PLATT

London
GEORGE ALLEN & UNWIN
Boston Sydney

George Allen & Unwin (Publishers) Ltd,
40 Museum Street, London WC1A 1LU, UK

George Allen & Unwin (Publishers) Ltd
Park Lane, Hemel Hempstead, Herts HP2 4TE, UK

Allen & Unwin, Inc.,
9 Winchester Terrace, Winchester, Mass. 01890, USA

George Allen & Unwin Australia Pty Ltd,
8 Napier Street, North Sydney, NSW 2060, Australia

First published in 1984

British Library Cataloguing in Publication Data

Platt, D. C. M.
Foreign finance in continental Europe and the United States 1815–1870.
1. Investments, Foreign – Europe – History
2. Capital investments – Europe – History
3. Investments, Foreign – United States – History
4. Capital investments – United States – History
5. Europe – History – 1815–1871
6. United States – History – 1815–1861
7. United States – History – 1849–1877
I. Title
332.6'73'094 HD5422
ISBN 0–04–330336–6

Contents

Preface

This book, in its different incarnations, has been some years in preparation and writing, during which I have incurred more debts than I can remember, or properly acknowledge. Such is the level of specialisation these days that I have been compelled to ask for the assistance of a specialist for each section and sub-section of the typescript; I am immensely grateful to them all for sparing me from multiple blunders. So far as I can claim to be a specialist myself, it is for Latin America, and I regret to say that I have written myself out of my own book. Early chapters on Argentina and Mexico merely proved the insignificance of foreign finance for the period. The same was true for chapters on Canada and Portugal. None-the-less, it is sometimes useful to prove a negative, and the abandoned chapters, other than that on Canada, are now published separately – in *Historia Mexicana* (for Mexico), in the *Journal of Latin American Studies* (for Argentina), and in the *Revista de Historia Economica e Social* (for Portugal).

I was fortunate to be able to use the archive of Baring Brothers & Co., Limited, which is now, in part, available for consultation (with previous permission) at the Guildhall Library of the City of London. Barings, with Rothschilds, were the leading financiers of the age. Their archive is truly astonishing. Preserved in one large, dry, strong-room in a building that survived the Second World War and was only recently demolished, it consists of the accounts of the firm and the 'private' letters of the partners to and from their firm's correspondents at home and (mainly) abroad. Several hundred thousand of these letters still exist, respectably organised and listed by Major T. L. Ingram, Barings' former archivist. The routine correspondence was stored separately and has almost entirely disappeared. I am grateful to the directors of Barings for permission to see and use their papers, and to Dr Christine Nicholls in particular for her help with the Baring side of the research.

Some part of this huge, under-used archive supplies a core for the five country studies in this book. No financial archive of a similar quality exists, although the papers of the London Rothschilds, now in the course of organisation and listing, may ultimately have as much to offer to multilingual scholars. Meanwhile I make no apology for drawing so heavily on Barings. It is these papers that have suggested so many of the revisions advanced. The financial history of the middle decades of the nineteenth century looks very different through the eyes of the partners and their correspondents, and to date only the Baring archive can supply such a level of professional and contemporary understanding. The price to be paid is that this book is limited to countries in which the Barings themselves were interested. It could not have been otherwise if some balance between the quality of evidence in each chapter were to be maintained.

Within this constraint (less formidable than it might be, since Barings' interests were widespread) perhaps half of the evidence in this book is taken not from Barings at all but from the financial columns and notes of newspapers, investors' guides and almanacs, official reports, theses, published articles and books. I am deeply indebted to the libraries from which they were extracted, and especially to the magnificent Bodleian Library at Oxford. Mrs Stowell and her staff at the History Faculty Office have kindly and efficiently typed out my later drafts.

I am grateful, finally, to Sarah Platt who helped me through so many difficulties.

D. C. M. Platt
St Antony's College, Oxford

Chapter 1

Introduction

Foreign finance is traditionally said to have been of singular importance to the economic development of Europe and the Americas. In C. K. Hobson's opinion, for the first half of the nineteenth century, 'British capital and finance were ever ready to lend a helping hand'; British investment in Continental Europe 'attained enormous dimensions during the 'fifties'.[1] Leland Jenks finds that the export of British capital reached its maximum for the nineteenth century in the twenty-five years after the Californian gold strike of 1848.[2] Herbert Feis describes Britain in the early decades of the nineteenth century as 'virtually the only important source of capital for those countries which lay outside the circle of Western Europe'.[3] David Landes talks of the years after 1815 as 'the great age of the Barings and the Rothschilds, . . . of the entry of far-off, exotic countries into the European financial market'.[4] The flow of funds from Britain to the Continent, Landes thinks, reached a high point during the railway boom of the 1840s; most went into the government securities and public works of France.[5] Eric Hobsbawm estimates a rise in British overseas credits from about £160 million in the early 1840s to almost £1 billion by the time of the international financial crisis of 1873.[6] Others have followed the same, exhilarating path – Penelope Hartland,[7] A. R. Hall,[8] Matthew Simon,[9] Philip Cottrell.[10]

Yet there is another, quite separate, tradition. For Albert Imlah, 'the size of British credit balances and the amount of capital exported [for the first part of the nineteenth century] have generally been exaggerated'.[11] S. B. Saul explains that *internal* accumulation accounted for the main supply of capital for economic development.[12] The importance of capital exports in giving rise to growth, John Knapp believes, was much inflated; Western Europe financed itself, and so did Russia and Japan.[13] Sir Alexander Cairncross has indicated that, over the past two centuries, the contribution of foreign capitalists in general has been 'if not negligible, far smaller in amount that the contribution made by domestic savings'. Cairncross agrees with Sir Kenneth Berrill that 'the great bulk of the savings needed for growth and industrialisation were generated inside each country'.[14]

The material gathered in this book, for France, Russia, Austria, Spain and the United States, and the conclusions reached in all the chapters, go far towards supporting and confirming the Imlah/Cairncross position. Furthermore, importance is attached to such evidence as exists of the ability of local capital and enterprise to meet domestic requirements. I have suggested elsewhere that even Cairncross's revised (and reduced) estimates for British capital exports may be too high – that is, that his total of £785 million for the value of foreign securities held in Britain in 1870 might be reduced to about £500 million (which, in turn, is half of the £1 billion usually ascribed to Britain's portfolio investment overseas at this period.)[15] The ground is already covered, and I need not repeat myself; the intention of this book is to strengthen the conclusions of my article in the *Economic History Review*, and to add much besides. The tradition of down-valuation, after all, was established by Leland Jenks himself when he showed that Britain's foreign investment was barely half the conventional estimate.

It is not clear how far the revaluation of capital exports may now be taken. Obviously the estimates for France will have to be looked at again.[16] It is absurd to accept an estimate for French investment abroad in 1870 that closely approaches or even exceeds Britain's. My own re-estimates for Britain may themselves still be too high. But it should be possible to reach more realistic conclusions for the limits within which foreign finance was able to operate.

No doubt the magic of a name, Rothschild or Baring, has contributed to the confusion. While Bertrand Gille has described the activities of the Paris Rothschilds until 1870,[17] nothing comparable exists for Barings (or indeed for the other Rothschilds in London, Frankfurt, Vienna and Naples). The glamour of such great financial houses has encouraged the manufacture of a formidable legend for the power of foreign finance. Money, said the German philosopher Heinrich Heine, 'is the god of our age, and James Rothschild is his prophet'.[18] According to Chaim Bermant, Lionel Rothschild of the London house was the 'Imperial Crown Agent' for Russia for twenty years after 1830, and 'organised a constant flow of British capital to St. Petersburg'.[19] Rothschild was not, and did not. But the myth is overwhelming. Frederick Morton quotes an estimate (a mysterious calculation) for 'the total wealth of the Rothschild family for most of the nineteenth century' of well over £400 million; 'no-one else, from the Fuggers to the Rockefellers, has come even close to that hair-raising figure'.[20] As for the 'hair-raising figure', *se non è vero, è molto ben trovato.* Other estimates are more likely to be reliable. Bertrand Gille calculates that the capital of the Paris Rothschilds in 1824 was some 33 million francs (£1.32 million), which, as he said, was large enough for the day.[21] The London house, at the time, was even more wealthy. Nathan Rothschild himself, by 1825, is described as a millionaire, and Stanley Chapman estimates the Rothschild family capital generally as more than £5 million.[22] These figures fall short of popular mythology, but all the same the resources of the Rothschilds were twice as large, in the 1820s, as those of their closest competitors.

The power of foreign finance is a theme that deserves both scrutiny and revision.[23] Theorisers and ideologues have had their say. The notion that finance capital was the engine of imperialism must depend, after all, on the existence of an adequate stock of finance capital; it is unlikely to be sustained by arguments for the greater importance of domestic finance. Capital requirements have not always been as insistent as they have since become. Peter Mathias explains that while capital shortages derived from inadequate savings may indeed be a profound constraint for the twentieth century (where technology is ample but expensive, and demand for social overhead capital overwhelming), this was not so for Britain in the eighteenth century, when technology was simple, when social overhead capital was expanding at a modest rate, and when requirements for productive investments were slight in relation to the rate of savings already achieved within the British economy.[24]

This was indeed the case for many countries over most of the *nineteenth* century. It was never obvious for all national economies at all times that there was a real and consistent need for foreign finance. The new republics of Spanish America came to Europe in the early 1820s to find finance for their wars of independence; thereafter, for forty or fifty years (sometimes longer), new government borrowing ceased on world capital markets. The republics neither needed foreign finance, nor could they raise it. They returned only when, at home and abroad, sufficient trade was generated to require a system of railways. Railways, which were immensely expensive, turned the balance. But even here, the contribution of domestic finance was greater than is often imagined.

I have argued that the overestimation of foreign capital has arisen from some rather glib and implausible assumptions – that a publicly issued loan was actually taken on the market, that it was bought by the citizens of the country in which that market lay, that 'nominal' and 'real' capital were virtually indistinguishable. The argument is simple, but surely effective. Many examples occur in the text and in the article to which I have already referred. But at this point some random illustrations may have their uses. The huge Egyptian loan of 1873, for a total of £23 million nominal (of which £8 million were intended for the British investor), attracted a total allotment in London of only £912,000.[25] The large Peruvian loan of June 1870 (£11.9 million nominal) appears on Jenks' list of *London* issues, when it was taken almost wholly in *Paris*.[26] Herbert Feis, a guru among students of capital exports second only to Leland Jenks, gives figures in his text that represent *either* 'original actual investment' *or* 'nominal value', as if the two were interchangeable! Yet, for instance, the £66.2 million that Feis calculates for Portugal's state debt in 1870[27] represented a real investment of not much over £30 million (because of the low price at which it was issued).

The intention of the chapters that follow is to explain the function of foreign finance for the middle decades of the nineteenth century. Furthermore, since so many of the sources and authorities (including the Baring archive) are British, and since Britain (even after a substantial down-valuation) was so clearly the major exporter of capital at the time, the aim is to define the areas for which British capital in particular was recruited. Leland Jenks once wrote that 'during the century which culminated in the First World War, Great Britain was the principal source of capital supply for countries that drew upon foreign resources'.[28] Jenks too, like Hobsbawm, thinks that the outstanding total of Britain's overseas investment in 1914 was £4 billion. His figure is wrong (obviously so). But taken in aggregate, Jenks is right to describe Britain as the principal supplier of foreign finance. Much more, however, can now be said of foreign finance in general, of its derivation, its functions, the preferences of financiers, the tastes of investors, and the direction in which the money flowed.

Notes

1 C. K. Hobson, *The export of capital* (London, 1914), pp. 97, 239.
2 Leland H. Jenks, *The migration of British capital to 1875* (London, 1971 edn), p. 162.
3 Herbert Feis, *Europe, the world's banker 1870–1914* (New York, 1965 edn), p. 4.
4 David Landes, 'The old bank and the new: the financial revolution of the nineteenth century', in F. Crouzet *et al.*, eds, *Essays in European economic history, 1789–1914* (London, 1969), pp. 117–18.
5 David Landes, *The unbound Prometheus: technological change and industrial development in Western Europe from 1750 to the present* (Cambridge, 1969), p. 158.
6 E. J. Hobsbawm, *Industry and Empire: the Pelican economic history of Britain*, Vol. 3 (London, 1969), p. 139.
7 Penelope Hartland, 'Private enterprise and international capital', *Canadian Journal of Economic and Political Science*, 19:1 (February 1953), 71.
8 A. R. Hall, *The London capital market and Australia, 1870–1914* (Canberra, 1963), pp. 10, 15.
9 Matthew Simon, 'The enterprise and industrial composition of new British portfolio foreign investment, 1865–1914', *Journal of Development Studies*, 3:3 (April 1967), p. 285.
10 P. L. Cottrell, 'Investment banking in England, 1856–1882' (unpublished Ph.D thesis, University of Hull, 1974); P. L. Cottrell, *British overseas investment in the nineteenth century* (London, 1975).
11 Albert, H. Imlah, *Economic elements in the Pax Britannica: Studies in British foreign trade in the nineteenth century* (Cambridge, Mass., 1958), p. 42.

12 S. B. Saul, *Studies in British overseas trade, 1870–1914* (Liverpool, 1960), p. 66.
13 John Knapp, 'Capital exports and growth', *Economic Journal*, 67 (September 1957), pp. 433–4.
14 A. K. Cairncross, *Factors in economic development* (London, 1962), p. 42.
15 D. C. M. Platt, 'British portfolio investment overseas before 1870: some doubts', *Economic History Review*, 2nd ser., 33:1 (February 1980), pp. 1–16.
16 Harry D. White calculates French investment abroad at the outbreak of the Franco-Prussian war at 11 billion francs (£440 million): *The French international accounts, 1880–1913* (Cambridge, Mass., 1933), p. 95. Rondo Cameron's estimate is £540 million: *France and the economic development of Europe, 1800–1914* (Princeton, NJ, 1961), p. 8.
17 Bertrand Gille, *Histoire de la maison Rothschild, dés origines à 1870* (2 vols, Geneva, 1965, 1967).
18 Quoted by M. E. Ravage, *Five men of Frankfurt: the story of the Rothschilds* (London, 1929), p. 290.
19 Chaim Bermant, *The cousinhood: the Anglo-Jewish gentry* (London, 1971), p. 130.
20 Frederick Morton, *The Rothschilds: a family portrait* (London, 1962), p. 60.
21 Bertrand Gille, *La Banque et le crédit en France de 1815 à 1848* (Paris, 1959), p. 62.
22 S. D. Chapman, 'The international houses: the Continental contribution to British commerce, 1800–1860', *Journal of European Economic History*, 6:1 (Spring 1977), p. 27.
23 I have tried to do something of the kind for Latin America: D. C. M. Platt, ed. and contr., *Business imperialism, 1840–1930: an inquiry based on British experience in Latin America* (Oxford, 1977).
24 Peter Mathias, 'Capital, credit and enterprise in the Industrial Revolution', in his *The transformation of England: essays in the economic and social history of England in the eighteenth century* (New York, 1979), p. 90.
25 Minutes of Evidence, *Report of the Royal Commission on the London Stock Exchange*, Parliamentary Papers, 1878, XIX, QQ.1494, 1497. This particular case was widely publicised at the time, but there were many like it.
26 Jenks, *Migration of British capital*, p. 423; *The Economist*, 11 June 1870, p. 731, and 18 June 1870, p. 763.
27 Feis, *Europe the world's banker*, p. 243.
28 Leland H. Jenks, 'British experience with foreign investments', *Journal of Economic History*, Supplement (December 1944), p. 68.

Chapter 2

France*

Introduction

It is commonly supposed that overall savings in France, after the middle of the nineteenth century, were sufficient for domestic purposes, and that the problem in mobilising French capital resources was not so much insufficiency as allocation.[1] In fact, one might be tempted to go further than this to say that France was self-sufficient in capital resources back to the restoration of peace in 1815. For these earlier years, Bertrand Gille describes France as 'une pays de capitaux abondants', so much so that, before 1830, she was actually an exporter of capital.[2] After 1830, French capital found full employment in the modernisation of France until capital began to go abroad again in and after the 1850s. The Franco-Prussian war (1870–1) imposed great pressure on French finance, and temporarily put a stop to capital exports. But Lionel Cohen, an experienced jobber on the London Stock Exchange, was probably right when he told the Royal Commission of 1877 that there was just as much money in France as there was in the United Kingdom.[3]

France was rich, but her bankers and investors were timid and inexperienced; she 'discovered' her wealth after her neighbours.[4] The function of foreign investment in France, so far as it existed, was to stimulate domestic finance, to supply domestic savings with the confidence and familiarity that capitalists required for new forms of investment. Foreign stimulus was not always necessary. During the Second Empire (1852–70), French financiers and investors showed a zest for investment and speculation that went well beyond the experience of the London market. All the same, solid investment in France, outside the traditional areas of state and railway finance, was not adventurous. In the early 1870s, native capital was still described by a Paris correspondent of *The Times* as 'timid' and 'shy'; it 'reserves itself for the needs of the state, or, at any rate, it waits for the co-operation of foreign capital'.[5]

The characteristic role of foreign finance and financiers in France was to supply the initiative and then to retreat into second place in cooperation with domestic finance. Its principal contribution was to

* 25 francs to £1 sterling may be taken as an average rate of exchange throughout the period.

the restoration of public credit in 1817–18, and to the initiation of the railway boom of the 1840s. In these respects, foreign finance can claim some limited responsibility for what François Crouzet describes as the 'creditable, but not brilliant' performance of the French economy in the nineteenth century.[6]

Foreign Finance and the Reconstruction of Public Credit

French public credit suffered far more than private credit during the collapse of Napoleon's empire. Private finance was relatively abundant for ordinary commercial and financial transactions; money could be borrowed in Paris in 1814 at 4–5 per cent, when it cost over 5 per cent in London; Alexander Baring told the Commons that money could be had in Paris for as little as 3 per cent.[7] French public borrowing, however, was far more expensive. In Paris after the war, the government was paying up to 10 per cent.[8]

In a country with the resources of France, public credit was bound to improve sooner or later. Foreign capital merely accelerated the inevitable. In 1815–17 there was, among domestic bankers, 'partout une gêne extrême, trahissant la mobilisation insuffisamment rapide des fonds et des crédits'.[9] The *haute banque parisienne*, the private bankers on whom the government would have to rely for any large operations, were themselves not individually of great wealth. Perrégaux-Laffitte & Cie, whom Gille describes as certainly the leading house in 1815, had a capital of only some 4 million francs (£160,000), a third of the capital of the leading London houses of the day. Gille explains that such of the *haute banque* as survived the Revolution had been decimated by the crises of 1806 and 1810. Of more importance than their capital, however, was their stability and the personal influence of their senior partners, which gave them 'une prépondérance sans rivale' over the financial market in France.[10] That financial market itself could call on great resources. The Receveurs Généraux, who were both receivers and bankers of public funds, could dispose of as much as 150 million francs (£6 million) in the service of the Treasury. There was money to hand in France if someone took the lead. The point was that it had to be taken. Capefigue is right in his timing when he concludes that the mobilisation of domestic capital and the restoration of the public credit of France occurred on the day that foreign capital converged on Paris in pursuit of *rentes* (government securities).[11]

In 1815–16 the *haute banque* needed reassurance before it undertook large operations in an area so generally distrusted as public credit. P. C. Labouchère, when attempting to select a Paris house in 1801 as a *maison de confiance* for Hope & Co. of Amsterdam, had advised the Hopes to form their own house in Paris; the Paris bankers, he said, seemed to have lost their nerve, and the old houses had tied up much of their capital in good funds rather than risk it further in business.[12] By 1816, more than a decade of renewed warfare, personal and political uncertainties and financial crises had not increased their taste for experiment and adventure: 'Parler à les banquiers de Paris de grands projets financiers,' said the Dutch banker, Isaac Thuret, 'c'est vouloir leur parler arabe.'[13]

The budget for 1816 authorised the sale of 6 million francs of *rentes*. Some doubt exists about its disposal. Capefigue reports that the Paris bankers would not take the *rentes* at any price, since they had little faith in France's future; the *rentes* were finally sold, bit by bit, in Amsterdam at the low price of 57 (100 nominal).[14] If Capefigue is right, the omens were not encouraging for a sale on the domestic market of the 30 millions of *rentes* (300 million francs net, or £12 million) on which the government had decided in its budget for 1817. Laffitte himself, who was later to make large claims for the capacity of the *haute banque* in the management of French government finance, 'se moqua hautement de la pensée d'un emprunt'; he was convinced that a loan of the size required to meet the government's deficit could be realised only by an alliance of the great merchants of Europe.[15]

Count Corvetto, the Minister of Finance, shared Laffitte's opinion. He held a series of discussions with the more important bankers of Paris in November 1816 at which the bankers, Laffitte included, refused to participate in a domestic operation on this scale. The bankers thought that it would be necessary to enlist the guarantee of financiers in Britain, where such large and difficult operations were well understood.[16] Corvetto, who was aware of the unpopularity of an appeal to foreign finance and of the desirability of giving preference to domestic capital, argued that an alliance with the first commercial names of Europe would ultimately attract and enlist the home investor.[17]

What seems true of the funding of heavy government deficits became even more so when France was called on to meet its large indemnity of over 700 million francs (£28 million), payable to the Allies before they would withdraw their army of occupation. It must have seemed inconceivable that such a sum could be raised from Frenchmen alone. But such turned out to be the case, and Rondo Cameron's belief that the Allies' indemnity was borrowed abroad is mistaken.[18] Two factors distinguish the French indemnity loans, negotiated in 1817 and 1818, from other foreign government loans of the first decades of the nineteenth century, and both serve to emphasise the unusual capital resources of France, the sophistication of the *haute banque* and the 'agency' role of a London financial house like

Barings. The first is that Paris bankers were brought in from the beginning; the second is that the larger part of the loans was raised in France, with only a small proportion held for investment in Britain.

Fritz Redlich has emphasised that it was Jacques Laffitte who opened the way to modern French investment banking when, in 1817–18, he became the principal ally and subcontractor of Barings of London and Hope & Co. of Amsterdam.[19] Indeed, under the umbrella of the leading houses of Europe, the *haute banque* took an increasing part in the promotion of French government credit. Although the *haute banque* did not feel powerful enough on its own to undertake the 1817 issues of *rentes*, there was never any question of its exclusion from the contracts. Corvetto insisted that Paris bankers should take a share in the first Baring–Hope contract of 10 February 1817 (for 100 million francs net, 182 million nominal), and Baguenault, Laffitte, Hottinguer and Greffulhe took a quarter of the loan between them together with the responsibility for handling the Paris sales.[20] The contractors had the option of taking the second series, 10 April 1817, on the same terms and the same participation, foreign and Parisian. The success of these two large issues, for a total of 200 million francs net (£8 million), encouraged the Finance Minister to bring out a third issue of 115 million francs net at a new contract price of 61.50 in place of the original 55. The contract of 22 July, again under the direction of the Minister of Finance, gave half the issue to the Paris bankers, Baguenault, Delessert, Greffulhe, Hottinguer and Perrégaux-Laffitte, while Barings and Hope & Co. each took a quarter.[21]

Count Corvetto, defending his decision to bring in the foreign bankers, told the Commission des Finances in 1820 that the Paris bankers, when approached, had refused to take charge of the operation, whereas the result of the 1817 issues had been to lay the foundations of public credit, 'de vaincre la répugnance des capitalistes pour des pareilles opérations'.[22] There could be no question, Jenks says, as to the financiers who would be called upon to manage the indemnity loans – 'not even the Rothschilds occupied the commanding position then held among moneyed men by Baring Brothers and Co.'.[23]

The union of Barings and Hope & Co. with the public credit of France supplied the confidence needed to attract the speculator and investor in France and abroad; by doing so it helped to convince the Paris bankers that public credit was a remunerative business within the scope of their resources. The government's large internal issue of May 1818, for 14.6 millions of *rentes* at 66.50 per cent, was subscribed ten times over, and it was the first time that a public issue of this kind had succeeded. The privately negotiated loan contracts of 1818, although nominally contracted by Barings and Hope & Co. in competition with a group of Paris bankers headed by Périer, were in fact shared equally with their Paris associates of 1817. From this point onwards, and more particularly during the huge increase in *rentes* between 1820 and 1825, speculations in *rentes* became an essential part of the banking business of Paris.[24]

It is clear that the contribution of foreign finance was to mobilise French bankers rather than to replace them. It was also to draw on the capital resources of France rather than to supply French needs from abroad. The idea of borrowing from the Allies the money that they demanded to meet their own indemnity claims had a certain charm, and the heavy drain on French resources – although no larger than the *annual* loan requirement of the British government during the Napoleonic wars – might have been expected to damage French credit and depreciate the international value of the franc if undertaken without an injection of foreign capital. These were among the reasons put forward for asking Barings and Hope & Co. to sell *rentes* in London and Amsterdam, the only two markets of consequence outside Paris itself. But the response in Paris was far beyond expectation, and for the first loan of 1817 the overwhelming proportion of sales were in Paris to French investors. The re-establishment of public credit made *rentes* attractive to foreign investors, while wild speculation in 1818 spread them beyond their traditional markets to Antwerp, Frankfurt, Berlin and Vienna.[25]

Speculation makes it difficult to supply any reliable estimate for the *rentes* actually held for investment in Britain. William Haldimand (a former director of the Bank of England, a loan contractor, and a merchant whose speciality was the exchange business with Paris) calculated in February 1819 that the French issues of *rentes* in 1817 and 1818 totalled £27.7 million. He did not believe that more than £5 million had been paid out by British investors, although the total in Britain was swollen by a further £2 million of profit. On a similar basis of payments and profits, Alexander Baring took the British total to be about £8 million; his partner, Swinton Colthurst Holland, thought that the quantity of *rentes* permanently in Britain, although higher in the past during periods of speculation, could not, by 1819, be more than £3 million. Both Holland and Nathan Rothschild felt that even this remainder would soon leave the country if a real rise took place in French funds. Rothschild reminded the Parliamentary Select Committee, to which they had all been giving evidence, that when French funds had risen from 64 to 80 in 1818, the exchange, which had been low, rose 3–4 per cent in favour of Britain, and the greater part of the stock that Rothschild himself had handled returned to Paris.[26]

The peculiar circumstances of 1817–18, even in a wealthy country like France, brought foreign financial houses forward as a leading element in the reconstruction of French public credit. Barings and Hope & Co. were unlikely to have been allowed to retain this position against domestic competition, nor did they seek to do so, and it is a sufficient indication of the change in their relative standing that when French contractors (Hottinguers, Baguenault and Delessert) bid successfully for the 1821 issue of 12 million of *rentes*, it was Hottinguers' turn to allot 500,000 each to Barings and Hopes.[27] Half a million was as much as the three contractors had kept for themselves. It was not the full extent of foreign interest in the 1821 issue; Alexander Baring asked for a further allotment for his private account, and Haldimand took an interest of 300,000. But the loan was taken by Frenchmen principally for French account, and this was to be the pattern in future. Redlich, in fact, dates the complete autonomy of French public credit from 1821: 'In this year for the first time French investment bankers were able to supply the capital needs of the French government; foreign houses were now expelled for good.'[28]

Thereafter, the part taken by foreign finance in the *public* credit of France was indeed unimportant. Before the overthrow of the July Monarchy in 1848, foreign financial houses served principally as allies to a section of the Parisian *haute banque* in its battle with James Rothschild. But for foreigners the battle was unequal and unattractive. James Rothschild had achieved what Gille calls 'une nette prédominance' in French government loans over the period 1830–48.[29] A foreign banker, like Thomas Baring, could see that while it was of the greatest importance to Rothschild's position in Paris to be successful in the major loan contracts, it was of little consequence to a foreign house; the 1844 French government loan was worth a franc more to Rothschild (in calculating his bid for the contract) than it was to his competitors.[30] In London, sales of the 1844 loan were negligible. Rothschild made a bad estimate, and a year later he was said still to have more than half of the 1844 *rentes* on his hands, for which he was paying out upwards of 5 million francs monthly.[31]

Predictably, London houses did not even enter the competition for the third great loan of the 1840s, the 1847 loan of 250 million francs. Dupont-Ferrier is right in saying that the consolidation loan of 1847 could not have been undertaken by anyone other than James Rothschild.[32] But then, nobody else would touch it. Capefigue called the 1847 loan an excellent affair.[33] In reality the timing proved most unfortunate, and Rothschild, who was alone in the field, took the loan simply as a means of putting some life into a chronically depressed market (in which he himself was over-committed). In the words of Rothschild's historian, the 1847 loan 'allait peser assez lourdement et sur la maison Rothschild et sur les finances publiques'.[34]

Public Credit and the Foreigner, 1848–51

The revolutions and wars of France in the mid-nineteenth century were powerful contributors to an almost unbroken deficit in government finance throughout the period. The government's total income from 1841 to 1850 was 12.8 billion francs; total expenditure was 15.3 billion. Income for the following decade was 15.3 billion and expenditure 19.2 billion.[35] From 1853 to 1866, the boom years of the Second Empire, there was an excess of expenditure over revenue of 3.6 billion francs; the excess would have reached 6.6 billion without the proceeds of 'extraordinary' revenue derived almost entirely from government loans.[36] Government borrowing was extensive, but it was not financed from abroad. The government found its money almost entirely at home, even during the huge loan flotations of the Crimean and Franco-Prussian wars.

The revolution of 1848 and its prolonged aftermath had a catastrophic effect on French public finance. A full recovery was delayed until after Louis Napoleon's successful *coup d'état.* Even before the outbreak of the revolution, the financial crisis of the autumn of 1847, which at first left France relatively unscathed, had spread via Frankfurt to Paris; early in January 1848, the bankers Ganneron and Gouin were said each to have lost half a million francs in the Frankfurt failures, and Marcuard a still larger sum, while Julius Cohen had stopped altogether.[37] Brokers panicked after the Bourse closed on 17 January, and Francis Baring reported the next day that:

> the alleged cause of all this was the King's health, but in reality the country is in a state of disquiet and fever which exceeds anything I have seen since 1830. They are kept in alarm by Italy, where they say the Pope is hard pressed by the liberals, Naples where the King is not safe, and the risk of the Austrian marching into some of the neighbouring States, the greatest risk of all, and [by] the state of Switzerland. If you add to this a King of 75, and an unpopular ministry daily losing ground, and menaced by a Reform cry, you will understand that there is a very abundant cause of uncertainty . . . In short, the Country is in a mess.[38]

The King abdicated on 24 February. Many of the major Paris banking houses failed in the first half of March (including Gouin, Dassier, Ganneron and Laffitte & Co.), there was a severe run on the Bank of France, and on 16 March the Bank suspended cash payments. Rothschild, with a large quantity of unsold 1847 *rentes* on his hands and much of his money locked up in railways and Austrian stock, was severely shaken, and nobody could understand how he survived. Hottinguers' friend, Baron D'Eichthal, suspended business on 25 March; Laffitte, Blount & Co.'s creditors were called together on 1 April; Delessert and Co. were wound up in May.

Francis Baring left Paris during the revolution. When he returned to Paris once more, he reported to his partners that only five or six of the principal houses kept their credit – Hottinguer, Mallet, Thurneyssen, Pillet-Will, and Blanc Colin. He thought they were all safe but every day brought 'mischief to their porte-feuilles', and Hottinguers 'look very low'; 'the Jew [Rothschild], of course, is safe, but this Vienna business won't improve him, and his losses must be enormous.'[39]

For some months Hottinguers and their principal associates among the *haute banque* suspended business altogether, and it was years before they and the Paris Bourse recovered their nerve. Under the impression that Hottinguers might be interested in a commodity safely removed from revolutionary disturbances, Barings invited them in April 1849 to join in a bid for the Spanish government's mercury contract; Hottinguers replied that they had been so shaken by their unfortunate revolution and alarmed by its sequel that they, and all their friends, had parcelled their capital out in small quantities in as many countries as they could, keeping enough in Paris to meet only their day-to-day business.[40] In the summer of 1849 it was known that some £20 million of Continental capital was lodged in London for safety.[41] All the heart and spirit seemed to have gone out of Parisian finance. A few months before the 1851 *coup d'état,* Hottinguers were still 'peu confiante dans l'avenir' and reluctant to accept any long-dated bills, and at the end of the year their resources remained spread 'un peu partout dans la crainte des événements'.[42]

In fact there was plenty of money in France, even if the *haute banque* had sent so much of its capital abroad. Nobody was anxious to tie up money in land, and the value of real estate even in 1851 was absurdly low. The enormous accumulation of idle savings took up every *rente* that came on the market, while less secure and conservative outlets in railways and commercial operations of all kinds were starved of capital. Baron A. D'Eichthal, in a series of letters to Thomas Baring for June and July 1851, lamented the fact that the leading members of the commercial and financial community were standing aside and, by refusing business themselves, making it impossible for the lesser members to undertake it. Writing again only a few weeks before Louis Napoleon's coup, D'Eichthal reported general fatigue, deep disgust with politics and a desire for rest at any price, which would give power to anyone who chose to seize it. A colossal fortune was to be made, he said, in landed property, which was depreciated beyond all reason by what could only be temporary phenomena. With the immense mass of unemployed capital, an enormous rise in all securities could be expected the day that peace and stability were restored.[43]

French finance for the four years 1848–51 was virtually stagnant. When Joshua Bates (a senior partner in Barings) visited Paris in September 1848, he found nothing with which to occupy himself; all seemed to be enveloped in a sort of political fog that no one could penetrate. Bates had pretty well made up his mind that Barings' interests would best be consulted by wasting none of their thoughts or resources on European business and by turning their greatest attention to the United States and to the East; it was impossible that France could get right for many years, and Germany seemed likely to be in hot water.[44]

Barings joined Hottinguers in a bid for the *rentes* contract of 23 December 1850, but they asked for only £100,000, which they intended to dispose of in Paris. The French competed vigorously among themselves for the comparatively small amount on offer. Hottinguers and their friends linked up with Rothschilds, in whose bid their own was eventually incorporated. When the contract was lost to the Receveurs Généraux, Barings were not sorry; their share, reduced to £25,000 within the Rothschild list, was unimportant, the price offered little margin for speculation, and they saw no object in 'swelling the tail of Messrs. Roth[d].'[45]

No English capital could be attracted into French public securities at such a time, and none was required since French capital was unemployed and government *rentes* were the only security still readily saleable to the French investor. In London, by contrast, British investors were unlikely to seek out any Continental government security so long as the condition of France remained unresolved. *Rentes* recovered their place in European markets as French politics improved. In times of peace they became a standard international security – safe, realisable, but expensive. During the frequent periods of revolutionary disturbance and political adventure, they were favourite objects of speculation, subject to great fluctuations but ultimately secure because nobody ever expected the government of such a rich country as France to default. By the end of the century, in 1895, 11 per cent (90 million francs) of the payments to holders of *rentes* were still directed abroad.[46] France herself, however, was and remained the obvious market for French government securities

Foreign and Domestic Contributions to Public Finance from 1851

So intemperate has been the reaction to the personality and political record of Napoleon III that an objective view of imperial borrowing is unattainable. Napoleon's detractors insist that the warm welcome that his loans received on the Paris and provincial markets was purely speculative, deliberately fostered for political reasons on underpriced government securities. There is some truth in what they say, as there is in the argument that the huge loans of the period 1852–70 diverted much French capital away from more productive employment within the economy as a whole.

The nominal capital of the six loans of 1854–68 was 2.75 billion francs. All six were heavily oversubscribed (to a total of nearly 29 billion francs), and they were subscribed almost entirely within France.[47] The last great loan of the Second Empire, the loan of August 1869 for 450 million francs nominal, was oversubscribed thirty-three times, so that the total subscription was larger that the whole of the national debt of France.[48] Again, from 1852 to January 1868, local loans (department, city and commune) amounted to 850 million francs, while City of Paris loans reached 1.2 billion,[49] almost exclusively subscribed in France. Speculation was a large element in French subscriptions, particularly for the national loans. *The Times* described the terms of one national loan as simply the casting of government money to be scrambled for by the mob: 'It may be questioned if among the engines which can tend to corrupt a country, any could be found more potent than this system of offering bribes to the populace from the Bourse.'[50] But as the *Bankers' Magazine* said of the 1868 loan, 'there must have been something more than a desire to obtain 4½ per cent on the speculation to draw out such a large amount of capital at once . . . France is proved to be an enormously wealthy country'.[51]

The 1868 loan was wholly taken in France. Bankers abroad subscribed small sums as a speculation, but they evidently had no intention of holding for investment. The uncertainty of international politics in 1868, and the consequent fluctuation of the price in Paris of *rentes,* made *rentes* unattractive to the foreigner. No English banker, in any circumstances, would 'ever touch' a French loan.[52]

Although the actual capital for government loans under the Second Empire seems to have been supplied almost exclusively within France, foreign financiers were occasionally invited to participate in such loans simply to improve the reputation and sale of a particular issue. Foreign participation in loan promotion may have tended subsequently to mislead; the part taken by London financiers in the management of a loan did not mean that British investors subscribed. Furthermore, the role of the London bankers was participation, not leadership. When London bankers were approached to take charge of new French loans, they answered that they could not engage in a French public loan without the cooperation of Parisian financiers. Their attitude was the same for French railway finance.

The experience, in any case, was that *rentes* always found a home within France, in the domestic market. The French economy, after December 1851, was booming. Subsequently the boom collapsed, and war with Russia in the Crimea had the expected consequences. The first Crimean war loan of March 1854, for 250 million francs, was not an outstanding success in France, although fully subscribed. In London it did not find much favour.[53] Napoleon III and his advisers were still sufficiently uncertain of the outcome of their second Crimean war loan of January 1855 to open a subscription in London; London names would boost applications, and for his political position in France the Emperor needed an outstanding success in the subscriptions. Under pressure from Napoleon himself, Barings were persuaded, against their better judgement, once more to open a list in London. Total applications from everywhere were four and a half times the 500 million francs required. Even allowing for intense speculation, it was, as Baron d'Eichthal said, 'une frappante démonstration de l'énorme richesse de ce pays'.[54] The Baring list (for London) was a disappointing £2½ million, and it was returned to Paris unused.[55]

When the French government re-entered the market in July with a third Crimean loan, this time for 750 million francs (£30 million), it was a 'useless puff' to issue it in London when so much was subscribed in France.[56] British subscribers, disappointed by the refusal of their applications six months before, did not come forward – which was fortunate since the loan was subscribed, almost entirely in France, to the extent of £146 million![57]

Government loans found so easy a domestic market throughout the Second Empire that there was no incentive to make any special effort to place them abroad. War with Prussia shook the confidence of the French investor. A large war loan for 750 million francs in August 1870 was fully subscribed, but this time only by a narrow margin.[58] In October, in the belief that the domestic market was saturated, the provisional government at Tours introduced a 'national defence loan' for 250 million francs (£10 million), in London and Paris. The French subscription was 93.9 million francs (£3.7 million); British subscriptions accounted for the rest (although it was well understood that these included a large portion of French émigré capital).[59]

The national defence loan (the 'Morgan' loan) was the only substantial contribution by British investors to the war finance of France. Although the Morgan loan was small by French standards, the decision to turn to the London market was deeply resented in France, so much so that the loan was not admitted to the official price current of the Paris Bourse until November 1871.

The idea that, subsequently, the great indemnity loans were financed to the extent of 50 per cent from abroad is unrealistic.[60] If evidence of the capacity of France to meet her own needs for government finance is still required, it was amply supplied by the huge success of the indemnity loans in mobilising domestic subscriptions. The defeat of 1871 left France committed to an indemnity of 5 billion francs (£200 million). The cost of the war to France, including the Prussian indemnity, has been estimated as 8–15 billion francs, the higher total (from the *Economiste Français*) including the devastation caused by the Paris Commune and, presumably, the ravages endured in occupied France.[61] Yet *The Times*, describing the enthusiastic response within France herself to the first of the indemnity loans (£80 million), felt that 'there has been nothing like it in our days',[62] while the *Investor's Chronicle* referred to the success of the 1872 loan (for £120 million) as 'the greatest financial event in history'.[63]

Prussia was paid off at an amazing speed, and the last German troops left France in mid-September 1873. A part of the huge subscriptions for both loans, particularly the second, came originally from abroad. About 1 billion francs were subscribed abroad for the 1871 loan, and 3.5 billion in France.[64] Much more foreign capital was subscribed in 1872, when it was estimated that foreigners may have taken more than half of the capital of the second indemnity loan – although allowance must be made for the very large subscriptions in foreign markets by French financial institutions such as the Comptoir d'Escompte and the Crédit Lyonnais.[65] The great majority of the securities soon returned to France. Leon Say was clearly right in his prediction that 'the year 1874 will not pass before it can be said that the five milliards [francs] of the loans are invested within the country [France] and without the aid of the foreigner'.[66] France employed her great capital resources to repatriate her debt and, by 1875, she had succeeded.[67] Lionel Cohen explains that, of the £240 million of French 5 per cents (the indemnity loans) quoted on the London Stock Exchange, probably not more than £5 million were held in the United Kingdom by the later 1870s.[68]

The ability of France to absorb the Prussian indemnity was not suspected by contemporaries in France and abroad. It was generally believed that France would have to borrow abroad. An experienced Paris banker argued, early in 1871, that even 1 billion francs would be too much for the enfeebled, postwar economy.[69] The French government itself was not confident that it could raise the money in France, and called on a syndicate of French, British and German bankers to guarantee £40 million of the first indemnity loan; the guarantee of the foreign bankers was an 'enormous advantage to the French Government . . . because not only it ensured its success, but it ensured its most wonderful success'.[70] Although foreign bankers were again called upon to support the second indemnity loan in 1872, they formed the subordinate part of a syndicate headed by the Paris Rothschilds. The competition in 1872 was between French bankers: the Rothschild group (the *haute banque*) on the one hand, and the domestic commercial banks on the other. Both groups drew on foreign allies (as was always the case with such large operations), but the initiative and the major part of the resources were French. By the mid-1870s, Seyd reported the French government debt as once more 'almost entirely held in France'.[71]

Foreign banks took the lead in re-establishing the public credit of France in 1817–18, after which *rentes* found a sufficient domestic market. The great public loans of the July Monarchy were taken in France under the direction of the Paris Rothschilds, while the bankers of London and Amsterdam merely helped to encourage the 'Christian' element in the *haute banque* in its battle with the Rothschild monopoly. During the Second Empire, even under pressure of war and foreign adventures, French government loans were enthusiastically received by French speculators and investors. Apart from the small 'Morgan' loan, the financing of the Franco-Prussian war (and its indemnities) was managed in France.

Foreigners and the First Generations of French Railways

After 1818, France had no real occasion to seek support for her public credit abroad. Nevertheless, foreign finance may have been important in private investment, notably in railways. In 1840, only 410 kilometres of railway were open in France; by 1850 there were 2,004 kilometres, and, by 1870, 15,544.[72] The capital investment was enormous, and some of it came from abroad.

As the figures indicate, railway development did not begin on a significant scale until the 1840s. The very first railways in France, as in practically every country of importance, were financed at home. The Paris–Rouen railway (initiated by the Laffitte group in 1838–9) was the 'first recorded case of a French rail-road financed with capital obtained partly from England and built chiefly by English engineers and contractors'. Its planned extension to Le Havre had obvious attractions to the directors of the London and Southampton Railway,[73] but its shares, in 1838, were heavily oversubscribed in an excited Paris market, and its London subscribers received only one-fifth of their original application.[74]

British contractors and engineers continued to take a significant part in French railway construction. During the 1840s Thomas Brassey was contractor for Paris–Rouen (1841), Orleans–Bordeaux (1842), Rouen–Le Havre (1843), Amiens–Boulogne (1844), and Rouen–Dieppe (1847). He built six further railways in France, between 1852 and 1860.[75] It does not follow, however, that a contract for the construction of a railway abroad brought British investment, beyond the modest extent of whatever the contractor and his friends could mobilise themselves.

The estimates for British capital in French railways in the 1840s range widely from the implausibly high estimate endorsed by Tom Kemp (namely, that two-thirds of the share capital raised for French railways in the 1840s came from abroad, mainly from Britain[76]), to the more modest figures suggested by Bertrand Gille and Rondo Cameron (200–300 million francs).[77] Total investment in French railways over the 1840s is conventionally estimated at 1 billion francs (£40 million).[78] Cameron argues that the private capital actually invested in 1847 cannot have exceeded 600 million francs.[79] It may well have been considerably less.[80] Yet, whatever the final figure, it is hardly accurate to maintain that 'until 1848 the British furnished almost as much capital for French railways as did French private investors'.[81]

The truth is that if genuine investment were distinguished from speculation, and from arbitrage operations between the security markets of London and Paris (sales to take account of small differences in price between markets), British *investment* in French railways was very much smaller than any of the estimates published to date. The instability of Anglo-French relations, notably during the Spanish Marriages dispute of the autumn of 1846, promoted fluctuations and price differentials between London and Paris, and opened up opportunities for speculation. London financiers took advantage of such fluctuations for arbitrage, so that at any time estimates for the absolute amounts of French railway securities 'held' in each market are open to doubt. But the trend is evident enough, and the trend was for French railway securities to find a permanent home in France.

Foreign financiers still had a role to play, even if they did not represent much genuine investment. Milward and Saul are very positive that the idea that Parisian merchant bankers were too conservative to provide the necessary capital for railway building in France is 'quite false'.[82] They go too far. Foreign capital may not have been considerable in relation to domestic investment, but it is still true that foreign financiers, much as they had done already for the restoration of the public credit of France, were at least partly responsible for a change of attitude among French bankers, speculators and investors. Gille remarks the fact that French savings turned slowly towards home railways, 'entraînees par l'example anglais'.[83] Jenks explains that the vogue of railway finance, like the *rentes* in 1817–18, had to be imported from across the Channel.[84] Few, other than Milward and Saul, would deny, for France in the late 1830s and the 1840s, 'the timid approach of private capital to the whole field of railway construction'.[85]

Contemporaries well understood the problem. The French, said Joshua Bates, 'seem to have no great confidence in themselves or their own operations until they find they are liked in England'.[86] He was exaggerating, but it is correct to say that the fact that French railway securities were actively dealt in on the London market undoubtedly helped their sale in France where investors and speculators were less experienced in the operations of an impersonal capital market.

English financiers were interested in the initial stages of French railway development, from which they occasionally made large profits. They stimulated the *haute banque* and opened the floodgates for domestic speculation and investment. Thereafter their role was much diminished. It may indeed be possible that the decision of James Rothschild, head of the Paris house, to interest himself in railways was, in the end, more of a stimulant to French finance than any interest from abroad. Bouvier points to the 'rôle de catalyseur' that Rothschild played in Parisian finance: 'il suffisait que son nom fût prononcé pour qu'une affaire prenne vie'.[87] And it is obvious that he is right.

Frantic negotiations between rival syndicates (domestic and foreign) may have given an impression that foreign capital was far more deeply engaged in French railways than it actually was. It is true, for example, that a first agreement was reached, in December 1844, by which the syndicates organised by James Rothschild and the Durand/Baring/Hottinguer group should join in the bidding for the Northern railway (the Compagnie du Chemin de Fer du Nord), each syndicate supplying half the capital and sharing whatever sacrifice became necessary to buy off competition. But the blackmail and concessions began almost at once. By the end of August 1845, when the 400,000 shares (of 500 francs) were finally distributed, only 59,000 were left for the Hottinguer/Baring group. These, in turn, were subdivided as follows:

The Duc de Galliéra's company	22,200
Hottinguers	6,000
Barings	8,800
Dennison	8,800
Morris Prevost & Co.	4,400
Sir J. L. Goldsmid	4,400
Morrison Sons and Co.	4,400

Laffite had to be bought off with 87,652 shares, Admiral Rosamel's company with 43,000, the Pepin-Lehalleus company with 30,000, and the Decan company with 41,000. Rothschild came out of it equally badly, although he was allowed an eighth of the total shares for 'Secret Service', presumably to subborn officials, politicians and financial journalists. 'The affair', said Hottinguers, 'has been the most fatiguing and most annoying one we were ever engaged in.'[88]

The negotiations for the Paris–Lyon line (the Compagnie du Chemin de Fer de Paris à Lyon) took much the same course. In the expectation that London would be called upon for a large part of the capital and that Barings would have to open a London subscription, the first agreement of 17 December 1844 was to distribute the shares equally between the Hottinguer group (Hottinguer, Blanc Mathieu, Odier and d'Eichthal) and the Baring syndicate (Baring, Dennison, Morris Prevost, Morrison Sons and Goldsmid). In the course of 1845 it became clear that there was quite enough interest in Paris and among the *haute banque* to dispense with a London subscription and, after the incorporation of a group of Paris bankers, Barings' portion of the 400,000 shares to be adjudicated on 20 December 1845 was reduced to 7/20ths, leaving the remainder for an enlarged Hottinguer group.

The intention of the London group, by this time, was simply to profit from the premium; no real investment of English capital was contemplated. A fusion of the rival groups was finally achieved on 4 December. Further concessions to possible competitors, and hard bargaining immediately before the adjudication, left the Hottinguer group – which now included the Receveurs-Généraux, the Messageries and the Sud-Est and Decan companies, – with 157,500 of the 400,000 shares. In the final partition at the end of 1845, Barings and their London friends had a 7/20ths share of the 43,333 shares remaining with Hottinguers (i.e. 15,166 shares, only 5,200 of which went to Barings themselves). The shares were for 500 francs apiece, 150 francs of which were called initially. The English stake was low, and no English administrators were nominated for the Company. James Rothschild did slightly better within his group, with 10,000 shares, but he did not get the position of banker to the line, which was his main reason, during a period of considerable tightness in his capital resources, for joining the administration of the Paris–Lyon company and taking part in the original group.[89]

Britons and Railway Investment in the 1840s

The interesting question is the share that British capital had actually taken in the financing of the French railway system. The answer lies very much within Britain herself. The mid-1840s were a period of massive overcommitment in British railways. Henry Burgess, the editor of the *Circular to Bankers*, described British railway speculation at the time as 'a bubble as dangerous as Law's Mississippi scheme . . . more absurd than the tulip mania of the Dutch . . . more fraudulent than Pennsylvanian Banks or Louisiana repudiation, more superstitious than touching the Holy Cloak'.[90] The 'gambling saturnalia' (McCulloch's *Commercial Dictionary*) continued until as late as the autumn of 1846. In 1845, 4,346 kilometres of railway were authorised, with a capital of £60 million. In the peak year (1846), 7,303 kilometres were authorised and capital powers granted to the extent of £132.6 million. Even when speculation collapsed, expenditure on railway construction continued, reaching its peak in 1847 at £29.2 million and remaining high until 1851.[91]

In the midst of this immense demand for capital on the domestic market, and of the wild speculation with which it coincided, it is unlikely that much British money remained for investment abroad. The figures for total calls on railway capital in 1847 are indicative: they were calculated at £43 million, of which only £6.7 million were foreign.[92]

The fact was that, for at least four years after the 1846 peak, Britain was 'absolutely committed', by contract and existing works, to an annual expenditure of as much as £15 million.[93] A recent calculation shows that, in the fifteen years after 1843, British railways received no less than £259 million.[94] Britons were entirely unprepared to invest further and massively overseas; in fact, they were selling any foreign security they could to meet their domestic commitments. Even as early as the first months of 1846, large sales were made in Paris for the account of English capitalists, and this applied equally to Northern shares, generally well-held by sound investors.[95] Dutchmen, Belgians and Germans were taking up British holdings of foreign railway securities (principally French) that had been unloaded on their markets by Britons in search of cash.[96]

During the boom in railway securities in France, there was always a tendency for foreign holdings to return to France. Cottrell dates the recall of British capital to as late as 1853–4.[97] Jenks thinks that, while the movement of British capital to France began to 'flag perceptibly' in 1846 and stopped altogether in 1847, the reversal of capital flows between Britain and France did not occur until the beginning of 1848, as a consequence of the Revolution in France.[98] Refugee capital (French in nationality) was certainly a phenomenon of 1848. But it is evident that the major part of British investment had long left France, and well before the financial crises of 1847.[99] It had begun to leave as early as 1845. By 1846 *The Economist* reported 'a gradual and steady absorption of the railway shares held on English account by French capital':

> The almost entire absence of banks of deposit throughout France and other parts of the Continent, causes an enormous amount of capital, in small sums, to be held unemployed, and always ready for investment in anything that once acquires confidence . . . There can be no question [for France and Belgium] that much of

> the English capital embarked at the beginning will be returned to us with a good profit by the investments of the people of the country who have not the enterprise to undertake these works but are quite willing to invest in them when they are undertaken.[100]

Dealings in French railway scrip never ceased altogether on the London market; the Paris Bourse itself remained highly speculative, and British speculation was sometimes extensive until well into 1846. Nonetheless, it was probably true that British *investment* in French railways, by contrast with *speculation*, had ceased by the later months of 1845. Very little disposition was shown in London to invest in foreign schemes. Early in 1845 English holders of French railway securities, tempted by high prices on the French market, had sold out to French speculators.[101] By the autumn, Dutch and Anglo-Belgian railway stock was all neglected in London and impossible to realise, while the shares of the French Northern seemed mostly to be finding their way back to Paris, to which those of the Rouen, Orleans and other railways had already returned.[102] British speculators took large quantities of shares in the Northern and Paris–Lyon railways at the adjudications of September and December 1845, but they unloaded them soon afterwards, alarmed by the slump in domestic railway securities.

During 1846, English investors preferred the bonds of the best British railways. In October 1845 speculation in implausible domestic railways had collapsed – proposals for a capital of £700 million had come before the public during the 'railway mania' of 1844 and 1845. Reed calculates, nevertheless, that paid-up railway share capital in 1850, at £187 million, was £144 million more than it had been in 1843.[103] James Capel, a leading London broker, giving evidence before the Select Committee of the House of Lords on railway accounts a few years later, confirmed that, although the largest amount of business had been done in 1845, 1846 had also seen considerable business; throughout the period, irrespective of speculative excesses, the capital invested in British railways had given rise to 'a great deal of real business, real transactions'.[104]

The fact was that in 1846 English railway securities were in constant supply, and easily realisable on the London market; they gave an interest of 4–5 per cent. Meanwhile, French railways were trying to dispose of more shares than the Paris market could easily digest. By the end of the year, tightness in the money market, bankruptcies among speculators and premonitions of financial crisis both in Britain and France had put an end to further investment. No matter how urgent the need for foreign capital to tide France over until her own capital had caught up with her ambitions, there was virtually none to be obtained.

A first-class line could still attract genuine investors. The Northern railway of France was such a line. But Jenks' view that about one-third of the Northern shares were marketed in the first place in England seems to have been arrived at by adding together the sum of the stakes taken by British financiers.[105] In practice, only a portion of these shares appeared on the British market, and even then they were bought often by brokers to sell back to France. The largest holders, Barings and Dennisons, and in all probability the other members of the British syndicates, disposed of their shares at a handsome premium on the excited Paris market. Once it was clear that fierce competition in Paris had pushed the price of railway securities too high to be attractive for steady investment, English financiers consoled themselves with the knowledge that they could sell out what little was assigned to them. The extravagant premium reached by Northern shares in Paris and London in the autumn of 1845 was, as Thomas Baring told Henri Hottinguer, a misfortune not only for the French government, which could have made a better bargain, but also for everyone concerned, since it checked bona fide investment in England by pricing French lines too high in competition with sound railway investment at home. All 30 million francs of shares sold on the London market up to mid-October 1845 had been for the French market; the rage, among Britons, for British railway projects continued, 'and we do not yet see when it will end'.[106]

Domestic Investment in Railways during the 1840s

British *financiers* were attracted to French railway development in the 1840s, but the same was not true of British *investors*. Real investment, by contrast with premium-hunting and speculation, was comparatively slight and soon withdrawn. The contribution of London finance was not so much British capital as the creation of an atmosphere of confidence in which both the *haute banque* and the ordinary French investors felt able to put their considerable resources at the disposal of the French railway companies.

No doubt the mass of the French subscriptions to railway issues were speculative, although the shares became favourite investments, in small parcels, among all ranks of society. The conventional belief is that France could not have raised her railway capital without outside assistance, and it was a belief shared by many Frenchmen up to the 1845 boom. The failure of Rothschild's *rente* contracts of 1844 and 1847 suggests that they were right, at any rate for single operations. But the £40 million estimated as invested in French railways up to 1848, when paid up gradually over years of railway construction, was not an impossible sum for the French investor. The barrier was not the sum required, nor a shortage of capital in France; it was the conservatism of the ordinary investor, and the timidity, at least in the early years, of the *haute banque*.

Up to the end of 1844 French bankers were encouraged to believe that the British market would help them with the two major enterprises under discussion, the Northern and the Paris–Lyon. It was only the experience of mounting French interest in railway investment (and even more in speculation) during the first half of 1845 that convinced the *haute banque* that they could do without a London subscription. The state of the exchanges for the early months of 1845 indicated that no great mass of English capital had found its way to Paris, while in Paris itself there was a growing fever for railroads.

It was 'really madness'; the shares of the Orleans, Rouen, Bordeaux and Boulogne railways were bought up in Paris immediately they arrived from foreign markets.[107] The provinces, Francis Baring reported from Paris in April 1845, had been emptying themselves of money to secure shares, and in Paris there was hardly a house where the servants were not holders to some extent.[108] To his evident embarrassment, Jameson (partner in Hottinguers) had to explain that so much of the 200 million francs of the proposed Northern stock was promised away to first-rate Paris bankers that there was only a very small amount to be distributed to the *agents de change* and to such people of the Paris Bourse as it was impossible to leave out; 'we can do nothing therefore for foreign subscribers'.[109]

Without the knowledge that Barings were behind them, it seems unlikely that Hottinguers would have come forward in December 1844 as the leader of what was probably the most powerful syndicate in competition with the Rothschild group for the great railway contracts of 1845. No doubt the railways would still have been contracted, certainly on terms even less favourable to the French government, if Barings and Hottinguers had stood aside; the market was too excited to let such opportunities slip, and sooner or later Paris financiers would have taken advantage of the general disposition to speculate and invest. What Barings were able to do was to give the *haute banque* confidence in railway finance, just as Robert Stephenson and Thomas Brassey gave France and the British capitalist confidence in French railway design and construction.

Furthermore, the Baring/Hottinguer combination did much to break what promised to be a dangerous monopoly for the railway finance and public credit of France. Thomas Baring was always aware of this, and he opposed Hottinguers' wish, in the pusillanimous tradition of the *haute banque*, to take shares under Rothschild. It would be better, he argued, to come forward openly in the administration of the Northern railway; to shelter behind James Rothschild would be to destroy all future chance of competition and to increase and establish his complete ascendancy – which was 'much more a Paris than a London question but it would seem rather inconsistent and infra dig to figure on his list after having pretended to equal terms in the Loan and Railroad business'.[110]

James Rothschild's position in Parisian finance during the last years of the Orleanist monarchy owed as much to the legend (which he himself was the first to promote) as it did to real means. It is true that he had a powerful psychological hold over his contemporaries. Bankers and clients were driven to distraction by his circumlocutions, and by the infinitely complex and protracted process by which he made up his mind. But they all, to some extent, came under his spell. Alexander Herzen described him in 1849, when in reality he was under severe financial pressure, as sitting calmly at his table surrounded by rank and file capitalists, members of the National Assembly and aristocratic riffraff 'looking through papers and writing something on them, probably millions, or at least hundreds of thousands . . . Every minute a small door opened and one Bourse agent after another came in, uttering a number in a loud voice; Rothschild, going on reading, muttered without raising his eyes: "Yes – no – good – perhaps – enough –" and the number walked out.'[111] Herzen was himself a suitor and more likely to be impressed. But much the same was implied by Joshua Bates, the least impressionable of men. Writing to Thomas Baring from Paris in August 1840, he reported that he had just seen James Rothschild:

> I complimented him on his reported gains. Oh, he replied, I have only made 10 millions. A mere bagatelle, said I, for you. By the by, he remarked, I have not been well since I met you at dinner at Mr. Jaudon's [agent of the Bank of the United States], I got so sweated by sitting my back to the fire. Young Rothschild remarked you sweated him pretty well before so you are about even. There will be no war [between France and England] rest assured, the old one replied, but don't tell Hottinguer what I say. Turning to a broker, le demi à 25, et le demi à 20 j'achette pour Mr. Bates qui ne m'autorise a payé plus haut n'est ce pas. I answered oui and he bo't some Stock of some sorts after begging me to dine with him which I declined. I left him as wise as I entered.[112]

The legend was always more powerful than the facts. James Rothschild's wealth has been much inflated. Morton believes that in the 1830s he was worth over 600 million francs, which was '150 million francs more than all other French financiers put together'.[113] It is true that James Rothschild was richer individually than any single member of the *haute banque*, but his disposable wealth was likely to have been tens of millions of francs, rather than hundreds.[114] And

Paris, in any case, was not a market for individuals; financial operations were shared among members of the *haute banque* by the 'système des fusions' that preceded each of the major railway contracts in the 1840s. Gille points out that Rothschild's own subscription to the railways in which he was interested averaged only 10 per cent.[115] And even here Gille may be overstating the case. For the Northern railway, the largest of Rothschild's railway interests and the one that swells Gille's list, the share that eventually came to Rothschild's inner circle was no larger than that of Henri Hottinguer and his London friends. When the shares in the Lyon railway were allotted some months later, the Rothschild share may even have been smaller than Hottinguer's.

Without subscribing to the legend, it is still possible to say that James Rothschild's role in French railway finance was, like that of the foreign financiers, decisive in creating the climate for entrepreneurship, investment and speculation. Neither Rothschild nor foreign finance was irreplaceable; railways were too large and promising a business to be ignored for long. But both helped by speeding and promoting a tendency that might otherwise have been further delayed. The tendency derived above all from the offer of generous state support for railway construction, supplied by that most fundamental instrument of railway expansion in France, the Railway Law of 11 June 1842.

Railway Finance, 1848–51

The troubles of 1848 had a severely depressing effect, on private finance as on public credit. Foreign capital was not quite as reluctant to touch French railways as French government bonds; the security of a solid railway line, even in the midst of political chaos and uncertainty, might always be expected to exercise some attraction for the nineteenth-century investor. But French railway shares, even in France itself, were 'mere trash' in the autumn of 1848; the shares of the Marseilles and Avignon railway, which had once risen as high as 1,200 francs, were now worth scarcely 155–160.[116] In England, on the other hand, unemployed capital was abundant, and financiers were interested once more in railway promotion abroad. The problem was to persuade French bankers to come forward.

Although many attempts were made between 1849 and 1851 to find further capital for the Lyon railway, hostility to the Paris financiers in the Chamber and the anxiety of the *haute banque* to keep out of the public eye put a stop to business. In the summer of 1849 Hottinguers were asking whether British capital could be interested in a new initiative on behalf of the Lyon railway. Thomas Baring and his partners found the business very tempting, though they doubted whether

English money would go much into the scheme, at least for the moment (and their opinion was supported in *The Economist* where it was reported that 'few English capitalists are ready to take an interest in the affair'[117]). If English investors and other foreigners showed confidence, however, the French would recover theirs, French capital would manifest itself, and it would be found that English capital, after pointing the way, would not be much required. As for Barings, they would act only if Hottinguers 'ostensibly and actively engaged and interfered in it', and Hottinguers' last letter put that out of the question.[118]

This became something of a refrain in the correspondence up to the *coup d'état* of December 1851. The Minister of Finance, Achille Fould, wanted to sell the Lyon railway, and asked Thomas Baring and Henri Hottinguer to meet him in December 1849 to discuss the operation. Thomas Baring, in Paris, did not think that much could be done either on the spot or in London for French railways; English capital should be kept for American railway bonds where enough would be wanted. As for French railway securities, the time was not ripe and, when it was, Paris was the place for them.[119] But as Joshua Bates pointed out from London, the English investor was in a sort of maze about what he should do with his money: he was afraid of land, consols were too high and, while American stocks were likely to attract his attention, a respectably sponsored and directed Lyon railway with a 99-year lease 'would probably take even here'.[120] Hottinguer, Blanc, Odier and Pillet Will were interested but unwilling to bring their names before the public, and on this occasion and in two other cases where the government made the same approach (in 1850 and 1851) Henri Hottinguer and his Paris allies lost heart and refused to go ahead.

Hottinguer had said, during one of the attempts to raise 140 million francs for the Lyon railway, that if England 'nous donne son appui moral par des bonnes souscriptions, on suivra l'exemple ici',[121] and the evidence is that London houses were interested. But London's interest, in turn, depended on Paris. It was pointless to expect London financiers to be interested when the *haute banque* held back. By 1851, while many speculators, including Britons, were attracted to cheap French rail securities, there was not much real investment. In France, Hottinguer and his friends argued that the newly announced railway concessions would find difficulty in attracting general investors ('amateurs'); the election of 1852, when Louis Napoleon was due to stand down, was too close for them to wish to expose their capital in affairs of this kind.[122]

James Rothschild was temporarily out of the running. His capital was locked up and he was intensely unpopular in the Chambers. The *haute banque* held the initiative, and no action could be expected from the more traditional houses until the political stability of Paris could be guaranteed. Barings were perfectly clear that whatever they themselves might feel about the merits of particular railway operations in France, it would not suit them, as foreigners, to put themselves forward while Hottinguers and the Paris banking interest in general were determined to keep in the background. Barings were not prepared to lose the active cooperation of the *haute banque*, nor could they carry with them the British investing public unless they had the stamp of approval of well-known Paris houses.[123] This, then, was the complete block to further progress in railway finance before the December coup.

Louis Napoleon's *coup d'état* took place early in the morning of 2 December 1851. The leading legislators were arrested, a ten-year presidential term was decreed and the powers of the Chambers were sharply reduced. The barricades went up the following day, several hundreds died, and many thousands were arrested. Henri Hottinguer had an uncomfortable few days. Thanking Francis Baring for sending some game from Baring's Norfolk estate, he said that his plans to make a party of it were interrupted by the *coup d'état*; he had had the satisfaction, however, of eating his present *en famille* before he could be obliged to share it with the socialists who had chosen his part of town for their operations. Not a pane of glass had survived in one of the neighbouring banks in the Rue Bergère, two banking houses had been hit by cannon balls, and the fabric of another was so shaken that it had had to be propped against collapse. He and 'les gens sages' knew very well that only the military could save them and their country from 'le fanatisme socialiste'.[124]

Francis Baring passed the letter to Thomas Baring, with the comment that Hottinguer was evidently 'not so low as usual', and it was true that the recovery of the *haute banque* and of the French investors was immediate. The coup was what they had all been waiting for; it promised a stable government backed by force, and all the pent-up capital and energy of the previous four years were thrown back on the market. It was, said Louis Girard, a new Peru, with quicker profits. Every railway seemed destined to offer the success of the Northern and Paris–Lyon. The boom ended in 1856, but "le pas était franchi; le pays avait atteint le palier supérieur'.[125] Even before the plebiscite of 20 December, which was expected to confirm Louis Napoleon's new authority, many of the great banking houses were bringing their capital back from abroad and, once Paris financiers were back in circulation, London's services were much less in demand.

The new position became immediately obvious in the contract for the Lyon railway, for which the Finance Minister began negotiations with Henry Hottinguer less than a fortnight after the coup.

Hottinguer's first instinct, even for the 80 million francs then thought to be necessary, was to call in Barings' assistance. Money was abundant in Paris, but some action had to be taken to banish distrust: 'Il n'y aura que votre exemple qui pourra avoir cette influence; si une fois on vient a rompre la glace, tout sera facile'.[126] By 23 December the amount required had risen to 120 million francs in 500-franc shares and there were twelve bankers in the syndicate, all from Paris except Barings, with Rothschild brought in to pre-empt his opposition. At this point Barings were still expecting to have to open a subscription in London, where there was plenty of interest in French railways. As it turned out, London was not called upon to take a share. Paris went wild, and Hottinguer reported at the end of December that the demand had been so considerable that the whole 240,000 shares could be placed easily among the friends of the contracting houses, without any appeal to the public. In the final distribution, now between fourteen houses, Barings were given just under 12,000 shares in place of the 50,000 for which they had asked; 35,000 were set aside for the agents on the Paris Bourse, and the London Stock Exchange got nothing since the English groups (Barings, Locke and Devaux) either unloaded their small allotments in Paris at 100 francs premium on each 500-franc share, or kept back some fraction for the investment account of each partner.[127]

Railway Finance after 1851

British financiers, then, played a modest part in the revival of French interest in domestic railway development after 1851. More decisive, however, was the recovery of confidence among French financiers and investors, which owed much to the re-establishment of firm government in France and little to foreign finance. The overwhelming success of railway shares in the Paris market after the coup indicated the anxiety, when circumstances were right, to invest. Henri Hottinguer was clearly correct in reminding Joshua Bates (some years later, when the affairs of the Crédit Mobilier were in full flood) that railway shares and bonds during the previous decade had tended a good deal to give the masses the notion of investing their hoarded money in securities – that they did so, Bates added, was 'equivalent to the discovery of mines of Gold'.[128]

Blanchard finds 'no possible argument about the Second Empire being the vital period as far as [French] railways are concerned'. At the beginning of 1852, 3,000 kilometres of line were in use, 'discontinuous sections, incoherent, divided among many companies'; by the end of the Empire, there were nearly 20,000 kilometres of line, 'grouped in a few [six] coherent units'.[129] Almost without exception, this vast expansion was financed in France. After the *coup d'état*, French refugee capital returned from London to Paris; Paris was not so secure as London, but French investments offered a far better return. In the early months of 1852, French investors were reported as buying up their own railway shares and buying into their own funds; they were selling low-yield English and other securities in the London market.[130] France experienced a recurrence of the kind of 'mania' that had attacked the Paris market for railway shares in 1845–6. Violent speculation took charge of the Bourse for years, and there was an enormous increase in the number of joint stock companies. Napoleon himself took a 'strong personal interest' in the formation of railways, and clearly hoped to buy political support through railway grants in the provinces. Money was abundant in France for both speculation and investment. The return on the best French railways was attractive once political stability was re-established: the Northern railway paid an average dividend on its securities of 6.14 per cent for 1850–9, and 6.85 per cent for the following decade.[131] Bank finance replaced the sale of securities to a substantial extent from the late 1850s, as it did for many other countries at the time. But the origin of this finance continued to be French, not foreign.

Some of the French railways became solid investments, and naturally they continued to be quoted on the London Stock Exchange. Britons, however, were still deeply engaged in the financing of domestic railway development; when they invested abroad, they chose the railways of India and the United States. The Board of Trade calculated that, by the end of 1870, just under £530 million had been spent on British railways,[132] and 21,558 kilometres of line were open in 1871.[133] The capital was British, and the boom in domestic railway finance in 1851–3 was a sufficient distraction from the opportunities now reopened in France. During that 'great advance' in the railway market, which was reported for London in December 1852, fancy prices were 'confined to English descriptions; French were comparatively neglected'.[134] British speculators were interesting themselves in Australian banks and in Australian and Californian gold mines. French railway securities never, in practice, left the London market altogether. Foreign *speculation* in French rails, like speculation in *rentes*, found handsome margins in the upsets of home politics and the lunacies of Napoleon III's foreign policy. Foreign *investment* was a different matter.

The part taken by British financiers in arranging the financing of French railways was sometimes considerable, but it does not follow that they found their money in Britain. Calls on railway capital in London were large. For July 1852 a total of £1.8 million was due to be called, £1.2 million of which was on the shares of the Paris–Lyon company, 'of which, in consequence of long-continued sales in this market [London sales to France], probably not a twelfth part will have to be supplied from Britain'.[135] The drift continued. A year later, in November 1853, 'not a twentieth part' of the shares in the Paris–Strasbourg line were reported as held in England.[136] Abundant capital in Britain in 1853 brought money to France, although even more so, at the time, to the United States. Jenks remarks of the 1850s that the meetings of the French railway companies were rarely reported in the British railway press; residents of France were supplying 'an increasing proportion of the actual capital cost'.[137] The *Railway Monitor* published a weekly account, in the 1850s, of advertised railway calls on the London market. It added, as a standard footnote to each statement, that foreign calls included heavy payments on the guaranteed Indian lines 'and also on some French and other continental lines, which are held only to a moderate extent in this country'.[138] Subsequently, nothing emerged to change this position, and although foreign contractors and suppliers of railway material remained interested in French railways, it was obvious that railways in France found their basic capital resources on the domestic market.

Conclusion

The effect of foreign finance on France was minimal during the period described in this book. France, as Thomas Baring once said, was a country of abundant capital and limited enterprise – the reverse of the United States. For the restoration of public credit and the first stages in railway development, foreign financiers were called upon to show the way for the Parisian banker and the domestic investor, rather than to open the door to foreign capital.

The financial market in Paris in the late 1850s and throughout the 1860s was volatile and unpredictable. Napoleon III was a nightmare to businessmen. No one could tell what he would do next. His wild adventures in foreign policy seriously damaged financial operations all over the Continent. Hottinguer congratulated himself, during a brief interval in the summer of 1862, that Napoleon had at last left Paris; they would all be left in peace until he took up his winter quarters again, unless he were compelled by Garibaldi or others to interrupt both his rest and their own.[139] The Italian troubles in the late 1850s and early 1860s, French relations with Russia during the Polish revolution, the Mexican expedition, the ambiguities of French policy towards Denmark and Austria during the Prusso-Danish and Austro-Prussian wars, contributed to a state of political uncertainty that from time to time brought all business completely to a standstill.

Political anxiety had much to do with the shape that French finance took during the Second Empire. It acted as a constant check on the

Paris bankers, who in any case remained conservative, cautious and timid by temperament and inclination. Political anxiety accounted in part for the *haute banque*'s interest in Russian railways, since Russia was regarded as a haven from revolutionary disturbance; in part, it determined general French investment, which tended to hedge its bets in large institutions like the Crédit Mobilier, to put money into France's expanding railway system (which was regarded as a kind of gilt-edged security), or to place it abroad for safety. 'Ce pays ci', said Henri Hottinguer, 'n'a pas de sécurité politique, et tous les 20 ans nous perdons en masse ce que nous avons gagné en détail . . . la prudence exige qu'on ne se lance pas dans des affairs de longue haleine . . .'[140]

Stocks of the best French railways were the highest class on offer on the Paris Bourse during the 1860s , while *rentes* provided a secure base, although their price fluctuated wildly with political developments. In other stocks, the Paris market was highly speculative, and Italian, Iberian, Turkish and Egyptian securities were largely in the hands of speculators. An event like the Austro-Prussian war brought total prostration. French speculators had invested heavily in the Austrian loan of 1866, which had been issued by a Franco-Austrian institution (the Crédit Foncier d'Autriche), and the Paris bankers were under large advances to the Austrian government. Austria was soon and crushingly defeated. Rodolphe Hottinguer (Henri's son, and in 1866 his successor) felt that it would be a long time before the French public again threw itself into foreign adventures. They had been the ruin of everyone; among French investors good French *rentes* and railway bonds were, and continued to be, in great demand.[141]

The fall of the Crédit Mobilier in 1867, which had individually contributed so much to the spread of French investment outside France, merely echoed what was happening on the Paris market, and suggested the real aversion felt by so many French investors to foreign commitments. The Crédit Mobilier's activities may have given an impression of French enthusiasm for foreign investment that, with most investors, had never existed. On the face of it, the existing estimates for France's foreign investment in 1870 (£540 million, in Cameron's view[142]) are implausible, and ought much to be reduced.[143]

For the whole period of the Second Empire, the enlarged capacity of the Paris market and the activity and resources of the Paris bankers and of the new credit institutions, left little for the foreign financier. Abroad, the occasions for Paris and London to work together declined as French financiers found themselves fully able to undertake large operations on their own with French and native capital, without calling for foreign alliances or assistance. *Rentes* and French railways were by now a French preserve, held for investment in France at rates unattractive to the foreign investor. The speculative character of most of the remaining securities actively dealt in on the Paris Bourse held foreign interest at bay. Furthermore, French investors did not share British tastes, and the securities sold by London financiers were not suited to the French market. Frenchmen were not interested in Russian stock except during times of political disturbance in France, nor did they like the securities of the individual North American states. Under certain circumstances they could become engaged in Italy and in central and southern Europe generally, especially in railways, where British investors were decidedly cool. But the conclusion can only be that, at home and abroad, French finance profited from guidance and direction but remained itself always autonomous.

Notes

1 Charles P. Kindleberger, *Economic growth in France and Britain 1851–1950* (Cambridge, Mass., 1964), pp. 39–40.
2 Bertrand Gille, *La Banque et le crédit en France de 1815 à 1848* (Paris, 1959), p. 234.
3 Minutes of Evidence, *Report of the Royal Commission on the London Stock Exchange*, Parliamentary Papers, (hereafter P.P.), 1878, XIX, Q. 3076.
4 Robert Bigo, *Les Banques françaises au cours du XIXe siècle* (Paris, 1947), p. 5.
5 *The Times*, 21 February 1872, p. 4d.
6 François Crouzet, 'French economic growth in the nineteenth century reconsidered', *History*, 59:196 (June 1974), p. 172.
7 Sidney Homer, *A history of interest rates* (New Brunswick, 1963), p. 230; *Hansard* (Commons), 8 November 1814, 73.
8 Homer, *History of interest rates*, p. 222.
9 León Cahen, 'L'Enrichissement de la France sous la Restauration', *Revue d'Histoire Moderne*, 27 (May/June 1930), p. 197.
10 Gille, *La Banque et le crédit*, pp. 52–3.
11 J. B. H. R. Capefigue, *Histoire des grandes opérations financières*, Vol. III, (Paris, 1858), p. 82.
12 P. C. Labouchère to Robert Voute, 5 December 1801, Archives of Baring Brothers and Co. Ltd, Guildhall Library, London (hereafter 'Baring'), Northbrook papers, A. 13.
13 Gille, *La Banque et le crédit*, p. 163.
14 Capefigue, *Grandes opérations financières*, III, 73.
15 G. Labouchère, 'Un Financier diplomate au siècle dernier: Pierre-César Labouchère (1772–1839)', *Revue d'Histoire Diplomatique*, 28 (1914), pp. 77, 81. Laffitte's position is confirmed in Fritz Redlich's article 'Jacques Laffitte and the beginnings of investment banking in France', *Bulletin of the Business Historical Society*, 22:4 (December 1948), p. 143.
16 Chancelier Pasquier, cited by Paul Mallez, *La Restauration des finances françaises après 1814* (Paris, thesis, 1927), pp. 158–9.
17 Gonzalve de Nervo, *Les Finances françaises sous la Restauration 1814–1830*, Vol. 1 (Paris, 1865), pp. 245, 247.

18 Rondo E. Cameron, *France and the economic development of Europe 1800–1914: Conquests of peace and seeds of war* (Princeton, NJ, 1961), p. 76.
19 Redlich, 'Jacques Laffitte', pp. 137–61 *passim*.
20 *The Times*, 7 March 1817, p. 3a; Gille, *La Banque et le crédit*, p. 164; Maurice Lévy-Leboyer puts the French share at a third: *Les Banques europeénes et l'industrialisation internationale dans la première moitié du XIXe siècle* (Paris, 1964), p. 441, fn. 96.
21 Text of the agreement for the third loan of 1817, and the subsequent division of the *rentes*: Alexander Baring's papers, Northampton archive, Castle Ashby.
22 Gille, *La Banque et le crédit*, p. 166.
23 Leland H. Jenks, *The migration of British capital to 1875* (London, 1971 edn), p. 33.
24 Gille, *La Banque et le crédit*, pp. 166–7.
25 Alexander Baring to Count Décazes, 24 June 1818: Alexander Baring's papers, Northampton archive, Castle Ashby.
26 Minutes of Evidence, *Report of the Select Committee on the Expediency of the Bank resuming cash payments;* P.P., 1819, III, *passim*.
27 Alexander Baring's stock book, Baring, and the correspondence between Hottinguers and Barings, August–November 1821, in Baring, HC 7.1.
28 Redlich, 'Jacques Laffitte', p. 148.
29 Gille, *La Banque et le crédit*, p. 169.
30 Thomas Baring to Barings, Paris, 7 December 1844: Baring, HC 1.20.4. As it turned out, Rothschild overbid the Baring/Hottinguer/Durand syndicate by just under 1 franc, and he bid too high. Three months later Francis Baring (the sleeping partner in Paris) was making 'a burnt offering in thanks for being out of the loan; Roth[d] is enormously loaded with it': Francis Baring to Barings, Paris, 25 March 1845: Baring, HC 7.17.
31 Hottinguers (Farquhar Jameson) to Barings, 26 November 1845: Baring, HC 7.17.
32 Pierre Dupont-Ferrier, *Le Marché financier de Paris sous le second Empire* (Paris, 1925), p. 77.
33 Capefigue, *Grandes opérations financières*, Vol. III, 230.
34 Bertrand Gille, *Histoire de la maison Rothschild, des origines à 1848* (Geneva, 1965), p. 310.
35 Report by Mr Grey, HM's Secretary of Embassy, on the Finances, etc., of France, dated Paris, 31 January 1862: P.P., 1862, LVIII, 203.
36 Report by Mr Sackville West, HM's Secretary of Embassy, on the Finance, Railroads, Trade, Education etc. of France, dated Paris, 1 February 1870: P.P., 1871, LXVII, 282.
37 Charles Agie to Joshua Bates, Antwerp, 11 January 1848: Baring, HC 13.2.
38 Francis Baring to Barings, 18 January 1848: Baring, HC 1.20.5.
39 Francis Baring to Barings, 22/23 March 1848: Baring, HC 1.20.5.
40 Hottinguers to Barings, 23 April 1849: Baring, HC 7.1.
41 Joshua Bates to a nephew (unnamed), 26 July 1849: Baring, PLB 1849.
42 Hottinguers to Barings, 18 July 1851, and Henri Hottinguer to Barings, 21 December 1851: Baring, HC 7.1.
43 The letters are in Baring, HC 7.27.
44 Joshua Bates to C. B. Young, 23 September 1848: Baring, HC 1.20.8.
45 Barings to Hottinguers, 2 January 1851: Baring, PLB 1851.
46 Harry D. White, *The French international accounts, 1880–1913* (Cambridge, Mass., 1933), p. 101.
47 Frederick Martin (ed.), *The statesman's yearbook for 1870* (London, 1870), p. 70.
48 *Fenn on the funds* (12th edn, London, 1874), p. 315.
49 *La Finance* (Brussels), quoted in the 'Commercial History and Review of 1867',

p. 38 (attached to *The Economist*, 14 March 1868).

50 *The Times*, 22 July 1861, p. 7b.

51 *Bankers' Magazine*, 28 (September 1868), p. 915.

52 *The Economist*, 15 August 1868, p. 925.

53 *The Economist* (Bankers' Gazette), 18 March 1854, p. 292.

54 D'Eichthal represented the Crédit Mobilier. He was writing to Thomas Baring, 12 January 1855: Baring, HC 7.27.

55 The correspondence between the London issuer, Barings, and A. d'Eichthal (Paris) is in Baring, HC 7.27 and PLB 1855.

56 Thomas Baring to A. d'Eichthal, 31 July 1855: Baring, PLB 1855.

57 Thomas Tooke, *A history of prices*, Vol. VI (London, 1857), pp. 662-3.

58 *The Times*, 26 August 1870, p. 10b.

59 *The Times*, 27 October 1870, p. 9d; *The Economist*, 29 October 1870, p. 1321, and 19 November 1870, p. 1400.

60 This is the position taken by C. K. Hobson, *The export of capital* (London, 1914), *passim*. Curiously (since it is obviously untrue), it has been endorsed recently by Maurice Lévy-Leboyer, 'La capacité financière de la France au début du XXe siècle', in Lévy-Leboyer, ed., *La position internationale de la France: Aspects économiques et financièrs XIXe–XXe siècles* (Paris, 1977), pp. 10–11. It was assumed to be the case in Harvey H. Segal and Matthew Simon, 'British foreign capital issues, 1865–94', *Journal of Economic History*, 21:4 (December 1961), pp. 569–70.

61 Quoted in *The Economist*, 12 March 1881, p. 46.

62 *The Times*, 1 July 1871, p. 9f.

63 Quoted in the *Investor's Monthly Manual*, 31 August 1872, p. 254.

64 *The Economist*, 1 July 1871, p. 778.

65 Roger Catin, *Le Portefeuille étranger de la France entre 1870 et 1914* (Paris, thesis, 1927), pp. 23–4; Jean Bouvier, *Le Crédit Lyonnais de 1863 à 1882* (Paris, 1961), pp. 416–17.

66 Quoted by Charles A. Conant, 'Securities as means of payment', *Annals of the American Academy of Political and Social Science*, 14:2 (September 1899), p. 40.

67 Catin, *Le Portefeuille étranger*, p. 24.

68 Contribution to the discussion following Hyde Clarke's paper, reprinted as *Sovereign and quasi-sovereign states: their debts to foreign countries* (London, 1878), p. 45.

69 Emil Brandeis writing to Bleichröder on 17 February 1871: Fritz Stern, *Gold and iron: Bismarck, Bleichröder, and the building of the German empire* (London, 1977), p. 152.

70 H. R. Price, member of the Committee of the London Stock Exchange: Minutes of Evidence, *Report of the Royal Commission on the Stock Exchange*: P.P., 1878, XIX, Q. 1559.

71 Ernest Seyd, 'The fall in the price of silver, its consequences and their possible avoidance', *Journal of the Society of Arts*, 24 (10 March 1876), p. 309.

72 B. R. Mitchell, *European historical statistics, 1750–1970* (London, 1975), pp. 581–4.

73 A. L. Dunham, 'How the first French railways were planned', *Journal of Economic History*, 1:1 (May 1941), p. 16. Blount suggested that he himself had raised half of the initial capital for the Paris–Rouen line in London (i.e. £600,000), while the other half was subscribed in France. The French government guaranteed a third £600,000: Stuart J. Reid (ed.), *Memoirs of Sir Edward Blount* (London, 1902), pp. 52–3.

74 Barings received 500,000 francs out of their total subscription of 2.6 millions: Hottinguers to Barings and vice versa, Baring, HC 7.1 and PLB 1838.

75 Arthur Helps, *Life and labours of Mr. Brassey, 1805–1870* (London, 1872), pp. 161–6.

76 Tom Kemp, *Economic forces in French history* (London, 1971), p. 127.

77 Gille, *La Banque et le crédit*, p. 238, and Cameron, *France and the economic development of Europe*, p. 77.

78 Gordon Wright accepts 1 billion francs as the total, of which (he says) 600 million came from abroad, mainly from Britain: *France in modern times, 1760 to the present* (London, 1962), p. 204. Leland Jenks calculates paid-up British capital in French railways at rather over 300 million francs: *Migration of British capital*, pp. 148–9. Jean Bouvier talks of 'massive British investment in the railway companies in the reign of Louis Philippe': 'The banking mechanism in France in the late nineteenth century', in Rondo Cameron, ed., *Essays in French economic history* (Homewood, Ill., 1970), p. 344. A. L. Dunham thinks that about half of the capital invested in French railways between 1840 and 1848 was British: *La Révolution Industrielle en France (1815–1848)* (Paris, 1953 edn), p. 68, in which he is joined by Philip Cottrell, 'La Coopération financière Franco-Anglaise, 1850–1880' in Lévy-Leboyer, ed., *La Position internationale de la France*, p. 178. C. K. Hobson reports that the proportion of French railway shares held in Britain at the beginning of 1848 was 'said to be extremely large': *Export of capital*, p. 119.

79 Cameron, *France and the economic development of Europe*, p. 77.

80 François Caron calculates the initial capital (to 1847) of the main railway, the Compagnie du Nord, as only 160 million francs: *An Economic History of Modern France* (New York, 1979), p. 72.

81 Cameron, *France and the economic development of Europe*, p. 213.

82 Alan Milward and S. B. Saul, *The economic development of Continental Europe 1780–1870* (London, 1973), p. 346.

83 Gille, *La Banque et le crédit*, p. 238.

84 Jenks, *Migration of British capital*, p. 139.

85 L. Girard, 'Transport', in H. J. Habakkuk and M. Postan, eds, *Cambridge economic history of Europe*, Vol. VI (Cambridge, 1965), p. 239.

86 Joshua Bates to Francis Baring (in Paris), 24 March 1844: Baring, PLB 1844.

87 Jean Bouvier, *Les Rothschilds* (Paris, 1967 edn), p. 129.

88 The correspondence (December 1844 – September 1845) is in Baring, HC 7.1, HC 7.17 and PLB 1845. A slightly different version is given by François Caron, *Histoire de l'exploitation d'un grand réseau: La Compagnie du Chemin de Fer du Nord 1846–1937* (Paris, 1973), pp. 49–50.

89 The correspondence for the Paris–Lyon line (December 1844 and July/December 1845) is in Baring, HC 7.17 and PLB 1845.

90 Burgess was a particularly violent opponent of the railway 'mania', against which he frequently and vociferously warned his country bank subscribers: *Circular to Bankers*, 24 October 1845, p. 121.

91 A. G. Kenwood, 'Railway investment in Britain, 1825–1875', *Economica*, new ser. 32 (August 1965), p. 317.

92 Wyndham Harding, 'Facts bearing on the progress of the railway system', *Journal of the Statistical Society*, 11:4 (November 1848), p. 339. Since many of the foreign shares *issued* in London had since returned to their own domestic investors, the proportion represented by £6.7 million is an absolute maximum; actual holdings of foreign railway securities by *British* investors were very much less (as is indicated in the estimates of share ownership for the Paris–Lyon and Paris–Strasbourg lines in 1852 and 1853 respectively).

93 *The Economist*, 28 March 1846, p. 403.

94 Seymour Broadbridge, *Studies in railway expansion and the capital market in England, 1825–1873* (London, 1970), p. 173.

95 *The Economist*, 11 April 1846, p. 491.

96 *Circular to Bankers*, 24 April 1846, p. 342.

97 Philip L. Cottrell, 'Anglo-French financial cooperation, 1850–1880', *Journal of European Economic History*, 3:1 (Spring 1974), p. 58.

98 Jenks, *Migration of British capital*, p. 153.

99 This is the point chosen by Roger Price, *The economic modernisation of France* (London, 1975), p. 21.

100 *The Economist*, 18 October 1846, p. 1009.
101 *The Economist*, 29 March 1845, p. 295.
102 Barings (Thomas Baring) to Baron Stieglitz, 14 October 1845: Baring, PLB 1845.
103 M. C. Reed, *A history of James Capel & Co.* (London, 1975), p. 38.
104 ibid., p. 39.
105 Jenks, *Migration of British capital*, p. 379.
106 Barings (Thomas Baring) to Hottinguers, 10 October 1845: Baring, PLB 1845.
107 *The Economist*, 8 March 1845, p. 226 (report from Paris).
108 Francis Baring to Barings, 15 April 1845: Baring, HC 7.17.
109 Hottinguers (Jameson) to Barings, 9 August 1845: Baring, HC 7.17.
110 Barings (Thomas Baring) to Hottinguers, 16 June 1845: Baring, PLB 1845.
111 Dwight Macdonald, ed., *My past and thoughts: the memoirs of Alexander Herzen* (London, 1974), p. 403.
112 Joshua Bates to Thomas Baring, 11 August 1840: Baring, HC 1.20.8.
113 Frederick Morton, *The Rothschilds: a family portrait* (London, 1962), p. 73.
114 Gille's estimate seems more reliable. He calculates the capital of the Paris Rothschilds in 1824 at 33 million francs (£1.3 million): *La Banque et le crédit*, p. 62.
115 Gille, *Maison Rothschild*, Vol. I, pp. 374–5.
116 *The Economist*, 4 November 1848, p. 1251.
117 *The Economist*, 1 September 1849, p. 970.
118 Barings to Hottinguers, 1 August 1849: Baring, PLB 1849.
119 Thomas Baring to Barings, 25 and 26 December 1849: Baring, HC 1.20.4.
120 Joshua Bates to Thomas Baring, 26 December 1849: Baring, HC 1.20.4.
121 Hottinguers to Barings, 23 July 1850: Baring, HC 7.1.
122 Hottinguers to Barings, 18 July 1851: Baring, HC 7.1.
123 Barings to Hottinguers, 24 May 1851: Baring, PLB 1851.
124 Henri Hottinguer to Francis Baring, 9 December 1851: Baring, HC 7.1.
125 Louis Girard, *La Politique des travaux publics du second Empire* (Paris, 1952), pp. 396–7.
126 Hottinguers to Barings, 14 and 18 December 1851: Baring, HC 7.1.
127 The correspondence is in Baring, HC 7.1 and PLB 1851 and 1852.
128 Joshua Bates to Thomas Baring, 3 August 1855: Baring Papers, Public Archive of Canada, Ottawa, frame no. 916–17.
129 M. Blanchard, 'The railway policy of the Second Empire', in François Crouzet *et al.*, eds, *Essays in European economic history, 1789–1914* (London, 1969), p. 100.
130 *The Economist* (Bankers' Gazette), 17 January 1852, p. 71; 27 March 1852, p. 350.
131 Maurice Lévy-Leboyer, 'Capital investment and economic growth in France, 1820–1930', in Peter Mathias and M. M. Postan, eds. *The Cambridge economic history of Europe*, Vol. VII, pt 1 (Cambridge, 1978), p. 257.
132 Reported in *The Times*, 1 January 1872, p. 9d.
133 Mitchell, *European historical statistics*, pp. 581–4.
134 *The Economist*, 4 December 1852, p. 1364.
135 *The Economist* (Railway monitor), 3 July 1852, p. 743.
136 *The Economist*, 19 November 1853, p. 1314.
137 Jenks, *Migration of British capital*, pp. 165–6.
138 *The Economist* (Railway Monitor), 13 January 1855, p. 49 and *passim*.
139 Henri Hottinguer to Thomas Baring, 20 August 1862: Baring, HC 7.1.
140 Henri Hottinguer to Thomas Baring, 27 February 1860: Baring, HC 7.1.
141 Rodolphe Hottinguer to Thomas Baring, 26 July 1866: Baring, HC 7.1.
142 Cameron, *France and the economic development of Europe*, p. 80.
143 I have suggested some reasons for believing this to be the case in a recent article: D. C. M. Platt, 'British portfolio investment overseas before 1870: some doubts', *Economic History Review*, 2nd ser. 33:1 (February 1980), p. 14.

Chapter 3

Russia*

Introduction

Before the 1860s foreign finance was of only slight importance to the development of the Russian economy. Foreign *commercial* finance – the financing of international trade – was of more value to Russia than direct investment in government loans and railways. Nebolsin was probably mistaken in his calculation, for 1847, that purely Russian firms handled a mere 3 million rubles out of total exports worth 13 million rubles.† Russian merchants, he thought, were active only in the commerce with China, from which foreigners were excluded by law.[1] The Crimean war provided the occasion for a more accurate assessment. *The Economist* reported that before the war the whole of British trade in Russia, even the purchase of raw produce in the interior, was carried on by means of British finance – which was not to say, of course, that it was handled by British nationals. At the time that the war broke out, it was computed that about £7 million of British finance was employed actually *in* Russia, in British trade.[2] Nebolsin describes the export trade of the southern ports as almost exclusively in the hands of Greeks and Italians, by whom, presumably, it was financed. The immigration of foreigners (in and after the new tariff barriers of 1823) to establish manufacturing plants inside Russia herself meant that 'the great majority of the superior manufactories, throughout the Empire, are either owned or conducted by foreigners'.[3]

Before the railway age, Russia had no considerable requirement for the more conventional forms of foreign investment: government bonds and private securities. Foreigners provided a valuable resource for the funding of deficits; they helped to pay for wars, for the suppression of rebellions, and for an adventurous foreign policy; they stimulated hopes and plans for the re-establishment of a sound

* Where necessary, the dates in this chapter (in both text and notes) have been converted to the Gregorian style. The Julian calendar was observed in Russia until 1918.

† The ruble exchange was very variable. The silver ruble was pegged at 3s 1d sterling in 1822, although in 1870–1 it was valued at approximately 2s 10d (i.e. about 7 rubles to £1). The paper ruble, which depreciated sharply during the Crimean war, reached its lowest level at 2s 1¾d in 1866; by 1870–1 it was discounted at 10–20 per cent below its par value.

currency. But the volume of foreign lending was inconsiderable. Count Egor Kankrin, who was Minister of Finance from 1823 to 1844, had a 'wholesome dislike for piling up the national debt, especially foreign debt'.[4] His economic policy, Westwood says, was 'characterised by a quiet determination to do nothing'.[5] In the late 1830s, when the construction of railways was first discussed seriously in Russia, there was a general belief that foreign capital should not be enlisted and that whatever could not be raised on the domestic market should be provided, through additional taxation, by the state. Kankrin himself argued that, in view of the scarcity of both private and public capital, domestic resources were better employed on the 'productive forces' of Russia, principally in agriculture.[6]

Certainly, foreign borrowing was slow to assume the importance that it was later to acquire within the Russian economy. The 'extensive foreign borrowing' that, in Cameron's view, became essential at an early date[7] takes shape more realistically in Gille's estimates for the proportion of foreign capital in the total capital invested in Russia. Gille's figures are implausibly precise, but the proportions may be more or less right, and they are at least indicative. Foreign capital formed less than 13.5 per cent of total capital invested in Russia in 1861, rising to nearly 25 per cent in 1889, 28.18 per cent in 1900, and nearly 33 per cent by 1914.[8]

Gille, in defiance of his own figures, speaks of the 'véritable colonisation de la Russie par le capital étranger'.[9] By the 1860s and early 1870s, this was far from the case. Gille's belief may derive from an underestimation of domestic Russian participation in the subscriptions to the lottery loans of the 1860s, but more influential, perhaps, was his illusion (which is rather central to the argument) that the St Petersburg financier, Baron Alexander Stieglitz, was a Berliner![10] In reality, it is only from the 1890s and 1900s that it becomes more plausible to argue that 'the modernisation of the Russian economy was not feasible without considerable cooperation by groups of foreign capitalists'.[11]

National Resources

In the meantime, the domestic resources of Russia deserve greater recognition. Falkus has already pointed to the need for additional research on such topics as the mobilisation of indigenous capital, although he pre-empts argument by remarking on the extreme scarcity of domestic sources of capital investment in 'such a backward country as Russia' as late as the 1870s and 1880s.[12] But where was this scarcity most felt? Where and why did domestic capital require foreign assistance? How much was required, and whence was it derived?

Russia's domestic resources are customarily undervalued.

Gerschenkron describes the Russia of before the First World War as 'still a relatively backward country by any quantitative criterion'. Of course he is right in many respects, and the burden of his argument is that, in 1914, Russia was nonetheless well on her way towards a 'westernisation' of her industrial growth.[13] But the proportion of domestic to foreign finance in Russia's economic growth is interesting. In the early years, Russia's domestic capital was tied up unproductively in the financing of government deficits, and little remained for investment elsewhere. But equally there was little occasion for investment. Later in the nineteenth century, when opportunities for investment *did* arise, the volume of domestic capital was substantial.

Russia in the 1840s was neither overburdened with public debt nor particularly short of domestic capital. Her total funded debt on 1 January 1848, less sinking fund, was £41.6 million (at a time when the British government owed as much as £776.5 million). Deposits in loan banks, commercial banks and savings banks of one kind or another amounted to £97.7 million and a further £43.4 million were outstanding in exchequer bills and silver notes. Frederich Scheer, who was reporting these figures to a London bank, remarked that the fact that deposits to the amount of £97 million should have been entrusted to the Russian government was 'at once a singular proof of confidence and of the power of Saving of a nation'.[14] It was not as simple as that. In Scheer's own period (the 1840s), Russian savings, through the banks, had been absorbed into current government expenditure, with the residue almost entirely locked up in long-term mortgages and unavailable for new engagements.

After the inevitable collapse in Russian banking that such a policy entailed, and the creation of the State Bank in 1860, a new banking system was more successful in mobilising domestic finance. At the end of 1869, 180 million rubles were deposited on call at the State Bank.[15] Banks, after railways, became the favourite investment, so that between 1861 and 1873, 226.9 million rubles had been invested in seventy-three newly created banks.[16] *The Times* in 1877 reported that the deposits and capital together of the joint stock deposit banks in Russia, added to those of the State Bank, constituted a fund of about £90 million – 'so large a fund implies . . . that there is probably a constantly accruing surplus available for new investment'. Other credit institutions were not so important, but the *crédit mobilier* companies employed about £13.5 millions of deposits, the urban commercial banks held the same, and the *crédit foncier* banks (deriving much of their money from abroad) had made advances of about £13 million in the year 1873/4. The savings banks, with total deposits of only about £600,000 at the end of 1874, were insignificant.[17] In 1875 there were twenty-five banks in St Petersburg and five in Moscow, and the assets of the five major banks amounted to 247 million rubles.[18] In the circumstances, it is hardly realistic to maintain that 'only a rudimentary commercial banking structure existed prior to the 1880s'.[19]

The activities of the Petersburg Bourse suggest the scale achieved by Russian domestic finance in the decades following the Crimean war. In 1856 the Bourse was open on only two days a week, and its dealings were confined to exchange business, to three public loans and to sixteen private companies. From 1872, the Bourse opened on six days a week, while Horne reports for a single day, 30 December 1878, Bourse dealings in:

> four issues of five per cent bank bills; sixteen classes of public securities, including guaranteed railroad bonds; fifty-nine series of mortgage bonds (issued by cities and provinces); the shares of twenty-five commercial and ten foncier banks; the shares of about twenty manufacturing and fifteen insurance companies; the stock of twenty-one and the bonds of five navigation companies; the shares of thirty-six railroads and the bonds of twenty-four.[20]

Nor can it be said that foreigners, for the period under discussion, financed the large part of Russia's privately owned railways. Crihan claims that, in the late 1860s and early 1870s, Russian railway loans were placed almost exclusively abroad.[21] This was not the case. It is true that much foreign capital was absorbed by Russian railways in the first stages of the railway boom, in 1867 and 1868. By the last months of 1868, however, money markets in Britain and on the Continent were saturated with Russian railway securities, and unwilling to take more. At the same time, Russia herself was experiencing much the same kind of railway mania as had existed in Britain and France during the 1840s, – a 'mad carnival of speculation', which was still unchecked by the summer of 1869.[22] Telegrams from St Petersburg reported continued enthusiasm in the autumn of 1870 (although diminished in scale); the new railway loan of £1.5 million received applications in Russia herself for five times the sum to be allotted.[23]

Of course, such 'carnivals' are no guide to the resources genuinely available for investment. Russian banks were fuelling speculation by advancing money on railway stock at up to 90 per cent of the day's quotation. The National Bank, which had advanced 4.5 million rubles on bills, had lent 8.25 million on stock. The Moscow Commercial Bank (with a capital of 1.25 million rubles and deposits of 10.5 million) had made loans of 6 million rubles on the security of stock, reserving only 4.6 million rubles for the 'regular and less venturesome business of the bill discounter'.[24]

The Russian journal *Golos* called attention to the illusion, fostered by railway speculation, that there was abundant unemployed capital in the land, and that soon Russia would be independent of the London and Berlin money markets and able to dispense with them altogether.[25] All the same, there *was* an 'abundance of money in the market',[26] and even if it might well have been more productively employed elsewhere, there can be no doubt that the great extension of the Russian railway system from the late 1860s into the 1870s (8,603 kilometres in the four years 1868–71, by contrast with only 5,038 kilometres in operation in 1867)[27] was financed to a large extent by domestic capital. Indeed, the experience of this railway boom throws doubt on the large estimates now current for foreign capital in the private railways of Russia. Berend and Ránki report that foreign capital in private railways, only twenty years after the boom, accounted for as much as 85 per cent of total investment, rising to 93 per cent by the end of the first decade of the twentieth century; they conclude that 'the modernisation of the Russian economy was not feasible without considerable cooperation by groups of foreign capitalists'.[28] That conclusion is not quite so self-evident as it might seem.

If the Russians themselves contributed so much to the financing of their railway system, the contribution of the Russian State should not, in turn, be underrated. George Garvy recently explained that, for almost the whole of the nineteenth century, 'the State, through the agency of official banks, and later by controlling the activities of commercial banks, provided equity funds, credit, and markets for important segments of the manufacturing industry and mining, and strong support for the railroad and utility industries'.[29] In the first four years of the Russian railway boom (1866–69), the state devoted 115 million rubles of its funds to railway building.[30] *The Times* calculated that at the end of 1874 the Russian government, between what it paid in guarantees and its advances from the general funds of the Treasury and from loans, had a sum of over £50 million 'out' in railways.[31].

Lyaschenko estimates the entire capital of Russian railways at the turn of the century at 4.7 billion rubles, of which approximately 3.5 billion belonged to the government. Foreign investment, he adds, covered about 341 million rubles of the 4.7 billion total: 'the bulk of the capital was raised within the country, chiefly through the general budgetary government resources'.[32] It has been separately estimated that by January 1909, state railways had cost 5 billion rubles, very much more than the capital of all private railways together.[33] Some 2 billion came from state budgets and 3 billion from loans, a part of which was raised abroad; but the larger share of the loans for state railways was absorbed by the domestic market. The first lottery loan of 1864, taken up almost entirely within Russia, provided for two years of railway expansion. Over 76 million rubles of the second lottery loan of 1866, principally domestic, were devoted to railway building.[34] The total of guarantees and interest standing to the debit of the Grande Société des Chemins de Fer Russes in the government's account on 1 January 1870 was no less than 92.7 million rubles.[35]

Domestic Capital

It may be that the ability of Russia to mobilise domestic capital has been consistently underrated. Neither the Empire nor its inhabitants were totally impoverished. A Reuter telegram from St Petersburg in August 1868 reported a return from the Customs Department according to which Russian exports across the European frontiers had doubled within the previous eleven years.[36] Over the longer period 1860–1913, exports (in total) were 6.5 billion rubles higher than imports; in only twelve years out of fifty-three had there been a negative balance of trade.[37]

Understandably, the investible funds of the bourgeoisie (traders, manufacturers, civil servants, small landowners, bankers and the professional classes – over a wide Empire) were not inconsiderable. The experience of the Russian lottery loans of 1864 and 1866 suggests as much. The first lottery loan was for 100 million rubles, and Gille is mistaken when he describes it as a failure on the domestic market:[38] 80 million rubles were taken up without difficulty within Russia herself from accumulated savings. The second lottery loan, by contrast, which followed only two years after the first, *was* a failure, and the 100 million rubles took a couple of years to place. By the end of the 1860s, however, both lottery loans were well held in Russia and consequently were too highly priced for other European markets. Treasury bills, bearing 4⅓ per cent interest and readily marketable within Russia, were also a favourite form of investment in all classes of society and 216 million rubles were in circulation at the end of 1869, together with 56 million in 4 per cent *billets de banque,* equally realisable. A further 180 million rubles were deposited on call at the State Bank.[39]

Furthermore, Russia was a country of many great fortunes. Compensation paid by the government to the landowners between 1863 and 1872 for the emancipation of the serfs is estimated to have reached 850 million rubles nominal in redemption bonds, while a further 165 million were received for sales of land. From this must be deducted the 425 million owed by the proprietors to government credit institutions, as debts on their mortgaged estates,[40] and much of the surplus was used unproductively. But some remained for investment and speculation. St Petersburg merchants, like George Wyneken and E. M. Meyer, acted as agents and brokers for a large clientèle of grand dukes and noblemen, often with very considerable sums to invest. Wyneken gave some examples in a letter to Thomas Baring in 1868. He had bought 1.5 million rubles of Russian stock the previous winter for the Queen of Greece, daughter of the Grand Duke Constantine Nikolaevitch. He was daily buying all kinds of stock for her father. Prince Volkonsky had just told him to subscribe for £150,000 in shares of the Yaroslav railway, and noblemen were constantly coming to him with business.[41] As a hedge against the threatened collapse of the ruble, wealthy Russian families acquired $3 million of United States stock between July 1866 and April 1867. It was said, probably inaccurately, that the personal fortune of Alexander II, invested abroad in 1880, was 30 million rubles.[43]

In fact, most of the genuinely productive investment opportunities in the Russian capital market were eagerly taken by the domestic investor. When Émile Mercet was sent to Russia by the Crédit Lyonnais in the summer of 1874 to see whether there was any scope for railway investment or short term city loans, he reported that circumstances were no more favourable for good, foreign investment at advantageous rates in 1874 than they had been in the boom of 1868. It was an echo of the experience of foreign finance in France. The Russian market was characterised by an abundance of capital:

> Cet argent, qui est en dépôt dans les banques, est timide. Il ne se porte, ni vers les fonds publics, ni vers l'industrie. Il attend de sûres occasions de placement. Quand les affaires se présentent, nos capitaux ne sont alors pas nécéssaires.[44]

Domestic interest in private, joint stock companies was always preponderant. In 1861 there were seventy-eight joint stock companies in Russia, with a combined capital of 72 million rubles, only 9.7 million of which had come from abroad. By 1889 the number had risen to 504, representing a capital of 911.8 million rubles, of which still only less than a quarter was foreign.[45]

René Girault has made a special study of the relative position of domestic and foreign capital in the Russian economy. He argues that until the late 1880s (when very large quantities of French capital began to flow towards Russia) 'le capital russe reste encore prédominant dans l'économie russe'.[46] He points out that France may have held as much as 35 per cent of the 571 million francs of *foreign* capital estimated as invested in Russian joint stock companies in 1891, but that this, in turn, was only a little over 8 per cent of joint stock capital in Russia as a whole.[47]

Girault's views are rather closer to the truth than those of an earlier generation of scholars. Ernest Seyd, for example, was confident that the 'greater portions' of the Russian state debt in 1876 (£275 million) were held abroad.[48] Crihan believed that foreign capital markets played 'un rôle préponderant' before and after the first large Paris loan in 1888.[49] Huge investments were made in Russia over the next decades. Pasvolsky and Moulton calculate that the foreign component of the total state debt rose from 30 per cent in 1895 to 48 per cent in 1914.[50] Even if this were true of investment in the public debt (which is unlikely), it does not apply to foreign investment in Russia in general. McKay points to a particular period, the late 1890s, when foreign capital reached its most influential stage: 'foreign investment accounts for a huge 55 per cent of the new capital formation of industrial enterprises operating in Russia in the years from 1893 to 1900'. But he adds that thereafter, while there was no liquidation of foreign holdings, the foreign portion of the total common stock of all corporations operating in Russia (three-eighths in 1900) increased only slightly to the First World War.[51] Sontag's conclusions, taken over a much wider area of investment, are an interesting extension of the argument. He admits that Russian economic development would have been greatly retarded without foreign loans. But the growth of the domestic money market and the large export surpluses of the 1900s were supplying the means to repay old debts and avoid new debts. It would appear, he says, that after 1906 Russia might no longer have been dependent on foreign capital.[52]

Foreign Finance and the Railways: to the 1860s

Foreign finance was less important to Russia than it has often seemed, but there were clearly conditions under which it became important to look for assistance abroad.

The first major railway line in Russia, the Nicholas railway (Moscow–St Petersburg), was financed principally by foreigners. The line proved immensely expensive – about 121 million rubles for a line of 604 versts (649 kilometres) at 200,000 rubles per verst. The predictable result was that money had to be found outside the domestic market. During the construction period, 1842–50 (the line was opened to traffic in 1851), no less than five loans were contracted abroad, bringing in a total of 70 million rubles to the Russian exchequer.[53] Given that a proportion of the capital had to be raised abroad – and there can be no doubt of that – the question of its origin is worth pursuing. Mosse, who confuses engineers with contractors and contractors with investors, is confident that the line was constructed with *American* capital.[54] Cameron, characteristically, gives credit to the *French*, in particular for their contribution to the loan of 1850.[55] In reality, such capital as was raised abroad was largely Dutch and German.

Baron Ludwig Stieglitz, German by birth but a St Petersburg

banker since 1803, handled the financing of the line. His first loan – for only 8 million rubles, priced rather too high for either London or Amsterdam – was offered in portions of 1 million by Hope & Co. of Amsterdam, 2 million each by Mendelssohn in Berlin and Rothschilds in Frankfurt, and the remainder in St Petersburg. William Borski, the Amsterdam broker, reported that at the price of 89 'on compte beaucoup sur l'Allemagne car ici il n'y aura pas de souscription'.[56] The 28 million rubles in stock, issued by the end of 1846, were taken in Germany and Russia.[57]

In 1850, the Russian government made a very positive approach to the London market, and applications of all kinds, British and foreign, reached nearly £19 million for a loan of £5.5 million of 4½ per cents at 93; £3.5 million were distributed to solid British investors and, after allotments to St Petersburg, little was left for other markets.[58] But the time was not ripe as yet for any permanent commitment of British investment in Russia. Russian 4½ per cents of the 1850 loan were reported to have 'very much passed to the Continent' by the early summer of 1852.[59] France was selling out her limited holdings, and the foreign market for Russian securities returned to its traditional home in Holland, Belgium and Germany.

Railway construction, the most costly element in modernisation, continued to draw on foreign investors, although not, perhaps, to the degree that is often supposed. After the Moscow–St Petersburg line, the next major railway system to be financed and constructed was that of the Grande Société des Chemins de Fer Russes, for which it was proposed to finance a network of lines likely to cost, from 1856, some £40 million spread over the next eight to ten years. For all its faults and frictions, the Grande Société was a considerable technical achievement. Under the supervision of the French engineer Charles Collignon, a former inspector-general of Ponts et Chaussées, 1,720 kilometres of track were built in five years, as much at the time as the four great railways of France together, and twice the rate of construction of railways in British India.[60]

French engineers and equipment were largely responsible, but it would not be correct to say that the finance for the Grande Société was primarily French (a view taken almost unanimously to date).[61] The core of foreign finance for the Grande Société was the private resources of the international financiers who had undertaken the issue, in combination with the steady power of absorption of Dutch investors through Amsterdam. Applications for the first issue of Grande Société stock, 300 million francs (£12 million) in 600,000 shares of 500 francs each, opened in St Petersburg, London, Paris, Amsterdam and Berlin at the end of April 1857. The bankers, after much horse-trading, agreed to distribute the shares in fixed proportions between the competing markets. The Russian government insisted on a large allocation for its own investors, and this, together with Stieglitz's portion, brought the St Petersburg quota to 220,000 shares; Paris was to receive 170,000, London 140,000, Amsterdam 60,000 and Berlin 10,000.[62]

The London issue was a total failure. The great Russian railway scheme was 'received with indifference by the public'.[63] Barings, who handled the London issue, contracted to take 40,000 shares for themselves. Other British applications amounted to only 18,631 shares, and most even of the 8,826 actually allotted were for speculation rather than investment. The reason was clear. The Russian government insisted, against Barings' advice, on bringing out a 5 per cent railway stock at a time when 6½ to 8 per cent could already be obtained by Britons on excellent security. Consequently there was little money on offer either for investment or for speculation, and the small amount that might have been attracted to a good Russian railway was diverted by an exceptionally violent campaign in the press against putting money into Russia's 'military' railways. The fact that no English engineer had been asked to report on the line and that no Englishmen were to be employed as contractors or engineers, might also have been expected to count against the success of the London issue if there were not already such strong reasons for keeping out of the stock.

Paris was overladen with companies, shares and stocks, and sales of Grande Société stock fell far short of the French quota. The Dutch portion was fully subscribed, for investment rather than speculation. The German subscription was negligible: the bankers Mendelssohn in Berlin and Merck in Hamburg unloaded their shares at the expense of their colleagues in the Paris syndicate, who were trying, by mutual agreement, to maintain the stock at a premium.

The great surprise was Russia. Experience of the 1850 loan suggested that Russian applications would be for speculation, to be unloaded at a premium at the first opportunity. As it turned out, Stieglitz reported from St Petersburg on the fourth day of subscription that 227,830 shares had already been sold to 1,514 subscribers. The majority were held for investment, with the larger portions securely in the hands of banks and charitable institutions confident in government credit and attracted by a government guarantee of 5 per cent interest on the stock.

It is an oversimplification, however, to claim that Russian capital built the line. Westwood's conclusion, in his history of Russian railways, that most of the capital in the Grande Société at this time and later was Russian, and that 'the expected and much needed inflow of "hard" currency from abroad did not materialise', is incorrect.[64] The first instalment of £6 on each £20 share was expected to keep the company going until the middle of 1858. Barings undertook to supply the £6 instalment on the full amount of 140,000 shares allotted to London, sold and unsold, and the more responsible of the Continental bankers agreed to do the same, so that between one half and two-thirds of the first operations were financed from abroad. The Crédit Mobilier paid the coupons on 170,000 shares in Paris in the first part of 1858, and most of these, although not fully paid up, were believed to be held in France.[65] The unexpected bonus (for which one explanation may be the Russian government's decision in 1857 to lower interest on domestic bank deposits in order to encourage investment in railway stock) was that by the beginning of 1858 a large sum of money had been paid in at St Petersburg by the acquittal of Russian shares in full, and a year later 106,000 Russian-owned shares were fully paid up.[66]

Popular notions of the distribution and employment of capital in the nineteenth century can be very misleading. Money moved freely between the markets and, as shares depreciated in St Petersburg or Paris, they became, with a Russian government 5 per cent guarantee, more attractive for permanent investment in Holland. Speculation in the late 1860s pushed up prices to a point where it made sense for Dutch investors to sell up and reinvest in a stock that offered a higher return. The contribution of foreign bankers and investors to the finances of the Grande Société at any one point could be determined only if day-by-day records were available (which they are not) of the distribution of the Société's income from the sales of fully paid and part-paid stock. What is clear is that without the cash supplied by payments on the stock administered and owned by Barings, the Crédit Mobilier, Hope & Co. and Stieglitz, the railway could not even have started, let alone been completed and in operation by 1863.

Foreign Finance and the Railways: the 1860s

Although so much of the Russian railway system was financed internally, inevitably there were occasions when local resources were supplemented by funds from abroad. This had been the case with the £40 million estimated as required for the Grande Société's lines. It was to be true again in the late 1860s, when annual average railway construction rose from 443 kilometres in 1861–5 to 1,378 kilometres in 1866–7.[67] Given sufficient time, the money could doubtless have been raised within Russia herself. But the need was for rapid construction, both for military purposes (as demonstrated during the Crimean war, and put to effect by the Grande Société against the rebellious Poles in 1863), and for the all-important development of the Empire as an exporter, the opening of international markets for grain from the south, and the reversal of an endemic deficit in the balance of trade. These were powerful factors in inducing the Russian government to apply for the assistance of foreign finance.

In 1863 Count Reutern, the new Finance Minister, attempted unsuccessfully to encourage foreign interest in Russian railways. In London at any rate, and probably also in Paris, the prejudice against Russia and Russian investment was too strong, and it was reinforced to the extent of the total exclusion of Russian securities from the London market after the harsh suppression of the Polish Insurrection. Thomas Baring believed that there had been little disposition in London since the Crimean war to go into Russian securities; Russian stock gradually found its way to Holland, and it was better to keep clear of it.[68]

In the justifiable hope that capital, native and foreign, would be attracted by a system of state and local guarantees (a state-guaranteed rate of interest on capital invested in Russian railways), the state in 1864 initiated a system of guarantees with the help of which a number of important lines were completed in the period 1864–6:

> Foreign capitalists, at first German, next Dutch, and finally but more warily, English, then native corporations and private individuals, were successively drawn into advancing money on such undeniable security as that of the Imperial Exchequer, and at such tempting rates of interest as those offered . . .[69]

The official policy, however, was as far as possible to construct Russian railways with native capital, and the government itself was making progress with the important lines to the south, intended to open the fertile provinces of central and southern Russia to the Black Sea. The success of the first lottery loan on the domestic market in 1864 seemed to suggest that, over time, the money could indeed be raised at home. But the minister, Count Reutern, was under heavy pressure from the Emperor and from the provincial nobility to speed up railway construction, both to release Russian commodities for export and to compensate for the losses anticipated by landowners from the emancipation of the serfs in 1861. The relative failure of the second lottery loan (1866) showed that Russia was not accumulating savings at a rate that could cope with a heavy programme of railway development. This was entirely clear to the government, and it was the reason why the Minister of Finance was considering, early in 1867, the possibility of selling the Moscow–St Petersburg line to foreign capitalists to finance further railway construction in the south. Baron Alexander Stieglitz, who approached Barings on the subject in a letter of 22 March 1867, explained that the great railway lines towards and in the south of Russia, which were being undertaken for government account, would require 30–35 million rubles in each of the next three years, and there was 'no possibility of further exploiting interior loans'.[70]

The Russian government had a choice between floating its own loans abroad while itself continuing the construction of railways, or handing over the task to private entrepreneurs assisted by a government guarantee. Barings and Hope & Co. would have preferred the former. It would have kept the business, in all probability, in their own hands and under their control as the favourite financial agents of Russia abroad; the government could borrow more cheaply than a private company, while a flood of private railway issues, insufficiently regulated and controlled, would injure Russia's credit and diminish the government's chances of raising money for itself at fair prices abroad.

Against advice, the market was thrown open to private finance, and the expected happened. In the autumn of 1867, the average issue price for fully guaranteed Russian 5 per cent railway stock was 75, when the government, until then, had been able to borrow at 85–86. The government's reasons for choosing to support private railway construction are not fully explained, and they may well have included an element of *laissez-faire*, which had characterised so many of Count Reutern's proposals. Reutern had also expressed, back in 1863, the suspicion that private railway construction was cheaper than government construction. Experience had borne him out. The Odessa–Balta section of the Odessa–Elisabethgrad line, which was said officially to have cost 52,718 rubles per verst, was known really to have cost about 100,000 rubles, while the working expenses of the new state lines amounted to 10 per cent more than those of the lines belonging to private companies.[71]

The Anglo-Dutch loan of 1866 provided for the government's general needs for the next couple of years. At the same time, however, it showed that there were definite limits to the amount that the government could expect to raise entirely on its own from conventional sources in Amsterdam and London. Domestic capital was inadequate, and a more rapid railway building programme would depend on the skill and persuasive powers of Russian and foreign entrepreneurs in European capital markets – Germany and France included.

The solid asset at the disposal of the Russian government was the Nicholas railroad (the Moscow–St Petersburg line). In a confidential letter to Barings of 22 March 1867, Stieglitz argued that the Nicholas railroad, properly managed and free of the expenses 'unavoidable with a bureaucratic Administration', was potentially profitable. It should find ready buyers at a price that would furnish the government with the money necessary to finish its other railways, 'establishing the principle of a rolling capital for continuing the construction by selling the ready lines'. The Minister of Finance (Reutern) estimated that the government would want not more than 20–25 million rubles for railway construction during 1867, which amount, Stieglitz said, must however be procured.[72] Thomas Baring replied that the moment was not right for such an operation. The politics of Europe were disturbed and investors deeply distrustful of permanent investments after the 'insane' operations of the last two years. Russian credit was undoubtedly good, and foreigners seemed more disposed to invest their money in Russian securities than the inhabitants of Russia themselves. But credit was a tender plant that might suddenly and irretrievably be blighted by exposure to unfriendly comment. Russia's foreign borrowings had been raised to £31.5 million since November 1866. The public would inevitably want to know whether Russia was borrowing at a high cost because she anticipated a war; if so, the same motive that made the government an anxious borrower would make capitalists very unwilling investors.[73]

However unfavourable the moment, the government had to have its money if it were to fulfil its railway obligations at home. An attempt was made to sell the Moscow–St Petersburg line to the Grande Société, but the price was too high and the money could never have been raised on the Sociéte's credit alone. Nobody else wanted, or was able, to buy a line that was in a poor state and notoriously badly administered. The loan that was finally negotiated with Barings, Hope & Co. and a Paris syndicate (which included Hottinguers and the Comptoir d'Escompte) was, as Thomas Baring said, 'cooked to suit the French taste'; he did not anticipate any great success for it in London. It was for 300 million francs (£12 million) of 4 per cent stock, issued in Paris, London and Amsterdam on 7 August 1867 at just over 60. Known misleadingly as the Nicholas railroad loan, the purpose of the loan, as explained in the Imperial *ukase*, was to ease the path for the sale of the railway and to create a special reserve for the construction of other lines. The security was the Nicholas railroad itself. Since nobody could be found to buy the line, a loan on its security was the only way to finance Stieglitz's 'rolling' programme for government railway development.[74]

Speculation during the 'railway mania' of 1868–9, which helped to sell the Nicholas bonds, reached absurd proportions over the next eighteen months. Concessions and government guarantees were given freely, and Russian railway loans, often for quite small amounts, were floated in every market of Europe. Barings and Hopes deeply disapproved of the variety of small loans, and feared for the damage that they must do to Russian credit, Thomas Baring was convinced that the only sensible policy for the Russian government was to consolidate all Russian railway borrowing. At the end of

1868, 6,157 kilometres of railway were open to traffic in Russia, with a further 7,753 kilometres under construction. The nominal capital, at an estimated average of £15,000 per verst (1.1 kilometres), was £158 million, the annual interest on which, including the sinking fund, was more than £8 million. Charles Jutting (writing at the peak of the boom, before foreign speculators began to unload railway securities on St Petersburg) thought that at least two-thirds were owned by foreigners; with another 2,000–3,000 versts applied for, requiring a nominal capital in 5 per cent shares of £30–45 million, it was difficult (he said) to see how any of the schemes could be carried into effect unless the stock could find buyers abroad.[75]

The Russian government saw the virtue of a single, large operation – a second issue of Nicholas bonds that would finance the continued construction of government lines and provide the necessary advances for other new railway undertakings. Private applications to the market could then be postponed until after the time required for the digestion of the Nicholas bonds. The Minister was determined to gather money as fast as he could while the enthusiasm for Russian railways lasted, and he was probably right to ignore Thomas Baring's opinion that the market had changed and that the eagerness to buy Russian railway bonds was rapidly diminishing. The second series of Nicholas bonds, £11.1 million nominal with interest at 4 per cent, was offered to the public at 63 on 16 April 1869. The prospectus contained the promise, on which Thomas Baring had insisted and to which he subsequently ascribed much of the success of the loan, that there would be a nine-month halt in the issue of further railway loans with Russian government guarantees.[76]

The second issue of Nicholas bonds reinforced the lesson of the first, that Russia could now draw on strong capital markets outside London and Amsterdam. In 1867, once it became clear that local resources were inadequate for rapid and extensive railway development, the Russian government decided to appeal for capital abroad. Subsequently, when the Nicholas loans of 1867 and 1869 had shown the limit of British and Dutch support, the Russian Government turned to Paris, Berlin and Frankfurt. By 31 December 1870, 10,770 kilometres of railway were completed and a further 10,282 were under construction, conceded or approved (but not yet conceded) by the Railway Committee of the Empire.[77] By the end of 1871 it was calculated that the total cost of the 12,627 versts of line open to traffic was 1,130 million rubles (£149 million), an average of £11,000 per kilometre.[78]

For a capital as large as this, raised in so short a time, there can really be no argument that Russia was in need of foreign assistance. Nobody had any doubt about it at the time, either in the government or among those professionally concerned with Russian finance. The problem was not whether foreign assistance was needed, but from where and in what quantity it was to be obtained.

Foreign Finance and the National Budget

Within limits, then, foreign finance was required for railway construction in Russia. It was also a necessary element in ironing out problems in the balance of payments (i.e. the funding of recurrent overspending abroad), and in matching the budgetary deficits that plagued imperial finance.

Although Russian statistical services were to gain a high reputation, especially after the publication of the *Annuaire des Finances Russes* from the early 1870s, they were rudimentary into the 1860s. Gille remarks that most of the official information on Russian finance even for the second half of the nineteenth century was 'plus ou moins falsifiées'.[79] No account of the revenue or expenditure of the Empire was published before the 1860s, and the credit of Russia was sustained simply by her determination to pay the dividends on her foreign debt. In 1854, Leon Faucher described the Russian government as 'without the rules and traditions of political economy'.[80] The first budget was published only in 1862, and even then it 'did not furnish a full account of the situation; it did not even include all of the national receipts and expenditures'.[81] Before 1862, the annual confidential summaries of revenue and expenditure prepared by the ministers of finance were 'grievously incomplete and often misleading'; after 1862 the budgets and reports 'had a strong tendency towards over-optimism'.[82] Charles Jutting, a keen observer of Russian finance, had come to the conclusion by 1866 that Russian budgets were 'entirely fictitious'. The government admitted to an excess of expenditure over income of 188 million rubles for the previous four years; Jutting himself would not have been surprised to find an accumulated deficit of 250 million.[83] The average government deficit from 1832 to 1861 was about £7 million a year.[84] Between 1861 and 1866, the Russian government borrowed £75 million, although the rising revenue of the period, in all some 25 per cent, was a ray of hope to the investor.[85] The 1872 budget was the first to show a surplus in the forty years for which any calculation can be made.[86]

Russian deficits had to be met somewhere, and a portion was derived from abroad (although the advance of 42 million silver rubles from 'l'allemand Stieglitz' may not have been as foreign as it looked, and the £5.5 million supposedly contributed to deficit finance by 'l'anglais Baring' in 1848/9 must surely refer to the railway loan of 1850).[87] Fortunately, Consul Michell compiled a breakdown of the total of the financial expedients resorted to by the government between 1832 and 1861.[88] The average proceeds over the entire period were £7 million per annum, a total of 1,375 million rubles (£216 million). The total can be broken down as follows:

	Rubles	*£ sterling*
Foreign loans	228 m.	36 m.
Loans from Russian banks	557 m.	88 m.
Loans from the Commission for the Extinction of the Debt	90 m.	14 m.
Issue of bank notes	407 m.	64 m.
Issue of Treasury bills	93 m.	14 m.

The conclusion must be that the greater part of Russian deficits to 1861 were met by borrowing from state-owned banks and by the printing press; only some 15 per cent was supplied from foreign loans.

The Baring correspondence gives some indication of the government's own administrative needs (as distinct from its support of railway finance) for foreign borrowing during the 1860s. To get the proportions right it might be remembered that actual revenue raised within Russia in the 1860s rose from £49 million in 1863 to £68.7 million in 1870.[89] Nonetheless, Jutting's view was that unless the government could open a railway from Moscow to the Black Sea, and unless some effective reform could be introduced into the Customs (where smuggling reduced the duties by perhaps a half), government revenues would never be sufficient to cover expenditure, while Russia's foreign earnings could never match her payments, abroad.[90]

In reply to an enquiry from Baron Alexander Stieglitz in November 1865 about the possibility of a second Anglo-Dutch loan, this time for £8 million nominal, Thomas Baring asked a number of pertinent questions. Why did Russia require a foreign loan, larger or smaller but always for a considerable sum, every two years, with an intermediate internal loan (the first lottery loan of 1864)? Was it intended that annual deficiencies should always be filled by foreign loans, 'because this would be a chronic malady which must end by exhausting the means of the country'? Did the government intend to put right the mass of paper money, since its depreciated and varying value had the most unfavourable effect on the commercial relations of Russia and upon her internal improvement?[91]

Stieglitz's reply, which he concerted with the minister, was misleading on several points of detail, but it did lay down the main structure of Russia's external finance. He began by saying that Barings knew best how the last Anglo-Dutch loan had been employed economically for purposes calculated to uphold the basis of Russia's credit, by which he meant the punctual fulfilment of Russian obligations abroad:

> For this purpose we shall still be obliged to have recourse from time to time to the medium of a foreign loan, in order to avoid too strong a

> pressure on our exchanges, which as you are aware of, cannot always support the heavy burden of the large remittances required . . . As to the internal loan, it was employed partly to repay the debt of the Government to the former bank-establishments, partly for the construction of railways. So the employment of the proceeds of the different loans has two distinct aims – to provide for our wants abroad and thus to uphold the value of our paper money, and to furnish the required funds for internal useful and productive undertakings. If you consider at the same time that Russia is just now in a period of very important reforms, such as the emancipation of the peasantry, the change of the judicial process, and the construction of important lines of railway traffic, you will agree that the usual resources cannot suffice in this time of transition.

The currency, Stieglitz thought, could be left to look after itself. Cautious management and strict fulfilment of Russian liabilities, connected now and then with a foreign loan of not too large an extent, with railways and the development of Russia's vast productive resources, and with the diminution of unproductive expenditure in the Department of War and the Ministry of the Marine, would bring the ruble gradually back to its normal level.[92]

Stieglitz gave no statistics, and Jutting regarded the official account of the disposal of the 100 million lottery loan, 'translated from official Russ into plain English', merely as a way of disguising a much larger budgetary deficit than the one admitted by the Finance Minister. Jutting himself had compiled, from papers printed for circulation among the members of the government (a copy of which had been passed in his direction), a more or less comprehensive estimate of the amount that Russia must pay in gold or abroad in the course of 1865. This totalled about £10.25 million, made up as follows:[93]

Interest and sinking fund on the foreign debt	Ru 34.2
Interest and sinking fund on the 4 per cent *métalliques* payable in gold	3.0
Annuity due to Denmark for sound dues	0.6
Railroad securities guaranteed by the government	6.5
Amount spent abroad by the imperial navy	5.0
Russian families travelling or permanently residing abroad	15.0
Total payable in gold or abroad	Ru 64.3

Estimates for the government's annual requirements for foreign borrowing in the 1860s are diverse. Baron Stieglitz thought, at the beginning of 1862, that the government needed about £3 million a year to cover all government expenditure abroad.[94] At the end of the

1860s, over 50 million rubles were payable annually abroad for interest and sinking fund and, so long as the resources of the Empire proved insufficient to remit any considerable part of that amount in bills, gold or produce, the balance could be met only by borrowing abroad at the rate of about 40 million rubles (approximately £5 million) per annum. During the eleven years 1860–70 the government raised (for its own use and for railways) £51.5 million abroad, by contrast with the £25 million in lottery loans borrowed at home; and the requirements of exchange were sufficient reason to persuade officials of the virtue of foreign borrowing irrespective of whether or not the government could have obtained its money locally. In practice, with interest and sinking fund for 1870 amounting to 44.5 million rubles on the internal debt, and an 'admitted' budgetary deficit (probably far short of the real deficit) running at 47.5 million rubles during the 1860s, the 40 million rubles borrowed annually abroad became, for the Minister of Finance, rather more than an exercise for the adjustment of the balance of payments.[95]

The problem was indeed larger than payments of interest and sinking fund on government borrowing abroad. Soon after his arrival as Barings' agent for the Grande Société in St Petersburg early in 1864, Charles Jutting sent home an estimate of 42–44 million rubles (nearly £6 million) payable abroad as the interest and sinking fund on Russia's debt. Thomas Baring was surprised at the figure. Jutting explained that the funded foreign debt on 1 January 1863 amounted to 661 million rubles (£102 million); the annual interest on this debt and on the 4 per cent *billets de banque*, together with the interest payable abroad on railroad securities guaranteed by the Russian government, amounted to 31 million rubles. The real total, with a loss on the exchange, was larger; it would not, Jutting thought, be overstated at 42 million rubles. A further 1.5 million rubles were remitted annually for Russian embassies, legations and consulates, and large sums were paid abroad by the Navy and War Offices for the purchase of iron-clads, rifled guns and general armaments. Russia produced about £13.3 million of gold in government and private mines,[96] against which Russian families, in travel or permanent residence abroad, spent some £3 million annually (which was not counterbalanced by money brought to Russia by foreigners since Russia was hardly ever visited except on business).[97]

So long as the balance of trade was against Russia, which it was for 1863 and again for the late 1860s when imports were vastly increased to meet the demands of railway construction, the only way to match these annual commitments and to right the exchanges was to borrow abroad. Understandably, foreign loans that were originally intended to meet inevitable expenditure abroad, to balance the import/export trade and to prevent the drift of gold out of Russia (and hence further depreciation of the currency) became diverted to less respectable employment – notoriously the funding of deficits. Attempts to stabilise the ruble were abandoned. Alexander Stieglitz, in search of another foreign loan in the autumn of 1866, told Barings and Hope & Co. that such a loan would be 'employed, as you are well aware of, merely to supply us with the funds requisite abroad'. His loan materialised as the Anglo-Dutch loan of November 1866,[98] from which the extraordinary resources required to make up the deficit on the 1867 budget, amounting to 15 million rubles (£2 million), were intended to be derived.[99]

There can be no doubt of the need for the support of foreign finance, although it would be too much to say that new foreign borrowing 'became essential' to the Russian Empire and continued in 'a vicious upward spiral until national bankruptcy resulted'.[100] In Russia, like France, foreign financiers (supported by relatively small amounts of foreign capital) performed an entrepreneurial function that was of real importance to the development of the Russian economy. As Westwood says, 'foreign industry and foreign money filled the gap left by the lack of domestic enterprise'.[101] The nature, extent and direction of foreign support and the power of domestic capital have formed the subject of this chapter. The question that remains to be answered is one of nationality. Where did the finance come from, and why?

French Investment

The finance did not come from France. The importance later to be assumed by French investors in Russia has undoubtedly misled historians for earlier periods. In 1914, according to Herbert Feis, 80 per cent of the Russian public debt owned abroad was held in France, while about one-third of foreign capital invested in private enterprise was also French.[102] Feis' figures would not now stand up to examination; they are far too high. But as Olga Crisp explains, by the end of the nineteenth century Russian loans had in fact 'become "placements du père de famille", enjoying in the heart and "portefeuille" of the French investor a place almost equal to that of the French state rente'.[103]

The point is that massive French investment in Russia was a late development. Cameron thinks that French investors took part in the £5.5 million railway loan issued in Paris and London in 1850.[104] But the loan was deliberately manufactured for the London market. Although French investors would have liked a larger share (to get their money into a politically safe autocracy at a time of extreme uncertainty in France), the loan was 'gobbled up greedily' by the

British investor and, once allotments had been made to Hope & Co. of Amsterdam and Baron Stieglitz in St Petersburg, little was left for the French investor.[105] Catin also believes that French investors were active in the 1850 loan, when Russia first came 's'adresser à nos épargnants'; he adds that between 1862 and 1870, four Russian loans with a total nominal value of over 1 billion francs (£40 million) were issued in Paris.[106] In Catin's view, the French were very heavy investors in Russia during the 1860s, and Cameron thought the same.[107]

It is now possible to be rather more precise. In Henry Labouchère's opinion, 'never anything profitable has arisen as yet [1861] for the Finances of Russia' from France.[108] Some years later, in 1866, Hope & Co. told Baron Stieglitz that the Paris Bourse 'n'a jamais montré des dispositions favorables pour les fonds Russes'.[109]

It was the Nicholas loan of 1867 that genuinely marked the beginning of a long (although subsequently much interrupted) and intimate connection between French investors and Russian public finance. British investors did not take to the Nicholas loan, and only 4.6 million francs were subscribed towards the 300 million requested. Dutch appetites were more than satisfied by the recent abundance of Russian loans; the Amsterdam subscription reached the slightly more respectable figure of 32.6 million francs, mainly for investment. The Paris applications, at 145.6 million francs, were larger than Thomas Baring expected. Although less than two-thirds of the bonds were applied for, the loan was not taken to be a disaster and, after some hesitation, the unsold bonds were disposed of in the three markets by May 1868.[110] What is more, they seem to have found their way into good hands. They were at a premium of 5 per cent by the autumn, well and solidly placed, so much so that they were being bought for investment even by *Spanish* capitalists![111] The saving grace was undoubtedly the low price at which the loan was issued. This damaged Russian credit in London, and displeased subscribers to previous loans, and the London financial press was unfavourable to the new issue. In Paris, the reaction was quite different and, although the loan was too large to be absorbed at once without the assistance of other markets, the Paris subscriptions were well held and Paris continued to be the leading market until the securities were finally disposed of.

In the natural course of events, Paris would now have become the first resort for Russian foreign borrowing. Russian securities were suddenly sought after; they were favoured by speculators, but they were also taken, at all levels of society, for solid investment. 'Pour le moment', said the director of the Crédit Lyonnais to his representative at St Petersburg (22 July 1868) 'nous n'avons qu'un cri de ralliement: Russie! Russie!'[112] The second Nicholas railway loan (1869) again experienced its greatest success in the Paris market. London subscribed less than £2 million to the £11.1 million offered, about half of which was supplied by Barings themselves and much of the remainder by the friends who had come to their assistance. In Amsterdam, the subscription was £2.8 million. In Paris, the loan caught the market at the crest of the wave. It was 'puffed' on traditional Parisian lines by the issuing house, the Comptoir d'Escompte, which plastered the walls of the city with posters and paid out 230,000 francs in bribes to the financial press. Paris subscriptions closed at £13.9 million.[113]

To the Russian government, the experience of the two Nicholas loans seemed to indicate that Paris alone could be depended upon for large and successful operations. In the very short run, this was exactly right. The Rothschild loan of 1870, issued on 20 January simultaneously in Paris, London, Frankfurt, Amsterdam and Berlin at the low price of 80, was for £12 million nominal in 5 per cents to cover the consolidated requirement for railway construction in Russia. It was an immediate success. The London Stock Exchange was allotted only 10 per cent of its subscription, 6 million were subscribed in Frankfurt, and the allotment in Amsterdam was 1 per cent;[114] St Petersburg subscribers asked for more than the full amount of the loan; Parisians besieged Rothschild with applications,[115] and the loan was declared to be a 'brilliant success'.[116] *The Times* reported that the total subscription in the five places of issue came to about £40 million.[117]

However, the disastrous defeat of France in the Franco-Prussian War and the drain of French capital into the Prussian indemnity loans, took French investors out of international markets. France's recovery was remarkably swift, but in the meantime German finance had established a very firm position in Russian securities. It was only when the Germans left the Russian market at the end of the 1880s that France returned, with great vigour and huge resources. The first great financial operation on Russia's behalf to take place in Paris alone was at the end of 1888; a couple of years previously, French finance had felt no urge to take part.[118] Girault calculates that Russian public securities placed in France in 1888 amounted to 1,240 million francs (£49.6 million), with only 219.8 million francs in direct private investment; in 1914, by contrast, French investment was 10,123 million francs in public securities and 2,245.2 million in private.[119]

British Investment

France's decision to abstain from Russian investment for the greater part of the nineteenth century was perfectly understandable, and in important respects it was shared by British investors. The Paris correspondent of *The Economist* expressed a commonly held view (in the context of the Grande Société) when he said that nobody in France believed that Russian railways would ever pay a reasonable dividend; the interest of 5 per cent guaranteed by the Russian government was no more than could be procured by judicious investment at home. France's own railways were estimated as requiring about £60 million within the next few years (the late 1850s and early 1860s), and further millions were engaged for enterprises at home and abroad. Engagements were greater than capacity and it would be a 'grievous mistake' to think that France could find the capital needed for Russian railways 'or the greater part of it, or any considerable portion of it'.[120] A couple of weeks later, the same correspondent referred to 'the small favour with which the [Russian] railways are regarded in England'.[121] The sentiment was familiar. Although Russian securities found favour intermittently on the London market, Britons remained reluctant investors in Russia throughout the nineteenth century.

There is clearly a tendency to see France and Germany as having replaced Britain as the principal foreign investor in Russia from the 1860s.[122] It may simply be a misunderstanding. Bouvier, for example, believes that Barings and Hambros were the traditional bankers for the Russian government before the late 1860s, when by Hambros (of London) he means Hope and Co. (of Amsterdam)![123] It makes a difference. But the illusion is widespread: Gille thinks that between 1860 and 1885 almost all Russian loans were placed on the London market,[124] and Herbert Feis describes Russian bonds as 'widely held' in Britain by 1870.[125]

The result, it seems, is a very considerable overestimation of British investment in Russia at the end of the 1860s. Douglass North, basing his estimate on *Fenn on the Funds*, calculates British investment in Russian *government* bonds alone, in 1870, at £50 million.[126] Cairncross takes British investment (again in the *government* bonds of 'Russia, Italy, etc.') at £78.5 million at the end of 1870.[127] George Medley produces the oddest figure of all: for 1 January 1878 he calculates the amount of Russian state debts issued and taken in London at £114.8 million![128] These estimates are excessive, as the experience of British lending to Russia in the nineteenth century suggests. Michell was inclined to play down the effect of political factors in dissuading the British investor from putting his money in Russia – to suppose that political antipathy had any influence 'would argue complete ignorance of the laws by which the movement of capital is regulated'.[129] But Michell, although one of the best of contemporary observers, was a member of a long-established British mercantile family at St Petersburg, and his familiarity with mercantile opinion led him to underestimate the passionate feeling that the Tsar's policies evoked outside Russia.

It is clear from other quarters that political considerations *were* of high importance. Hope & Co. of Amsterdam gave Barings an interest in the 20 million silver ruble loans of 1831 and 1833. The 1831 loan was not the failure described by Pierre Petit[130] – it was absorbed gradually by the Dutch market; but both the 1831 loan and the 1833 loan failed to attract investment in London. It was widely believed (no doubt correctly) that the proceeds of the 1831 loan were intended for the suppression of the Polish insurrection, and both for this loan and for the loan of 1833 London financiers were careful to keep out of the limelight. The loans were financed on the Continent, principally in Holland.[131]

In July 1849, when negotiations were in progress for a Russian loan, Richard Cobden summoned a public meeting at the London Tavern to express sympathy with 'that noble, maligned and betrayed people, the Hungarians'. In a powerful speech, he pointed out that Russia had always asked Holland for money to support extended campaigns beyond her frontiers, whether in the form of war loans for the Turkish campaign in 1829 or the 'Pole-murdering' loan of 1831. Now an attempt was to be made to raise money in Amsterdam and London for the 'vile, unchristian and barbarous purpose . . . of cutting the throats of the innocent people of Hungary', and Cobden dared any house in the City to come before the citizens of a free country with this blood-stained project.[132] Barings, writing to Stieglitz after the cancellation of the 1849 loan, assured the Russians that such threats would not have deterred them or the discriminating portion of the public on whose support they might have reckoned. But it must have been obvious that a loan at that moment, even with money in London so abundant that it commanded only 1½ per cent on short-term loans, would have failed.

By the end of 1849 the position had changed. There was an over-supply of money in London, the Russians had defeated the main Hungarian army on 1 August, and the loan that Barings brought before the British public in January 1850 was ostensibly for the completion of the Moscow–St Petersburg railway. Cobden denounced it as an 'unholy and infamous transaction', blood money for the devastation of Hungary,[133] but there was enough doubt, and enough anxiety to find a good home for unemployed capital, to keep conscience at bay. No hint is to be found in the private correspondence between the Russian Minister of Finance (Baron Stieglitz) and Barings that the money was needed for any purpose other than the railway, and the government declared subsequently that the Hungarian campaigns were financed by special issues of Treasury bills, 12 million rubles of which were sold on the domestic market by the end of 1849. It would, nonetheless, be beyond anybody's power, now or at the time, to establish what money was actually used for which.[134] Few contemporaries were genuinely in doubt. The editor of the *Banker's Magazine* reported that, although the ostensible object of the loan was to complete the railway between St Petersburg and Moscow, it was 'generally understood' that the money was required to pay the cost of the recent war against the Hungarians. His journal was 'strongly against' the negotiation of any kind of foreign loans on the British market.[135]

The 1850 loan did not, as it happened, mark any permanent shift of interest among British investors towards Russian government securities. Britain was blockading the Greek coast (the 'Don Pacifico' affair) while applications were still being received. The news reached London early in February, when Russian and French protests brought a collapse of confidence in Russian securities that sent much of the speculative holding to the Continent. The storm blew over and Russian stocks were still well liked in London in 1851, on their own merits as investment and because they were saleable on the Continent.

Barings would have liked to bring out another Russian loan in London in 1851 if the government had wished to borrow again, but the 1850 loan proved to be the last government issue abroad before the Crimean war. In the meantime, steadily deteriorating Anglo-Russian relations in the Near East made British holders predisposed to sell even if they had not themselves formed so strong an attachment to the better British railways and (by 1852) to sound United States stock. France, for similar reasons, was selling out, and the market for Russian securities returned to its traditional home in Holland, Belgium and Germany. 'Russian railways', said Laurence Oliphant in the early 1850s, 'seem to be meant for Russian soldiers. . . .' Barbaric hordes had once overrun civilised Europe from the East, and 'it would, indeed, be a singular testimony to the spirit of the age, if the next invaders made their descent by means of railroads'.[136]

Political hostility reached its peak during the Crimean war, 1854–6. There is no truth whatever in Jenks' story of a Russian loan floated and cheerfully marketed by Barings during the war:[137] Barings 'were not hanged for treasonable intercourse with the enemy', not because of the *laissez-faire* of the age but because they did nothing of the kind.

Russia floated two war loans abroad in 1854 and 1855, each for 50 million rubles (£8 million). No transactions took place in either of these loans on the London and Paris markets,[138] although Russian securities were welcomed in Amsterdam and, of course, in St Petersburg itself.[139]

Thomas Baring knew of no single individual in the United Kingdom who had taken an interest in the 1854 loan.[140] As a matter of courtesy Stieglitz wrote to Barings in June 1854 to inform them of the loan, although Stieglitz himself saw no chance of Barings' 'kind and mighty co-operation . . . in the present unlucky state of war between England and Russia'; Barings replied promptly that the war 'must necessarily and legally forbid any co-operation on our part'.[141] Here the correspondence broke off. For the rest of the war there was no business between Barings and the Russian government, or between Barings and their correspondents in Russia. When Barings first wrote privately to Stieglitz after the peace, they expressed their delight at being allowed to consider old and valued friends no longer as national enemies, 'for one of the most painful results of the war for the last two years has been the interruption of our full and confidential correspondence'.[142]

After the war, British investors were slow to discard their suspicions. They had disliked Russian treatment of the Poles in 1831, of the Hungarians in 1849, and of the Turks in 1854. They abhorred Russian attitudes towards the Poles in 1863, the Khanate of Khiva in 1872–3, and Turkey in 1877–8. H. M. Hyndman, in 1874, 'had yet to learn that [Russia's] lines of railways were not constructed rather for strategical than for commercial purposes'.[143] Political distrust was not confined to Russia's foreign policy. British investors had little faith in the stability of the Tsar at home. In 1869 *The Economist* thought that the main reason why investors refused to trust Russia was the internal state of the Empire. The Tsar's administration was not a 'stable Government in the investors' sense of the phrase':

> It is passing through a revolution [after the emancipation of the serfs in 1861] – becoming a democracy instead of a mass of serfs governed by a bureaucracy; and what the upshot will be or what disasters will take place in the process no man can tell.[144]

The Economist was persistently anti-Russian, and its views were not unrepresentative of the investing public. There was a short boom on the London market in Russian railway securities in 1868, although *The Economist* overestimated by as much as 100 per cent when it calculated that £30 million had been borrowed (chiefly in London) for Russian railways between 1866 and 1868.[145] It was a 'singular fact' that, as late as the mid-1860s, Russian financial enterprises had found 'no favour whatever in the London market'.[146] The same was true at the end of the nineteenth century. In 1900 the *Investor's Chronicle* described Russian investments as 'still an unknown land to our moneyed classes', the causes of which lay 'mainly in political prejudice'.[147]

British attitudes were to change very dramatically during the decade before the First World War, and Sontag may be right in saying that, if the war had not intervened, 'Great Britain would probably have become Russia's primary industrial creditor'.[148] But British interest in Russian securities, as the *Financial Times* said in 1913, was 'a feature of the investment markets [only] in the last few years'.[149] The reasons were largely political – distrust of Russian expansionist policies abroad and instability at home – but they were also economic. Russia borrowed too frequently abroad in the late 1860s (during the railway boom) to sustain confidence among investors. Russia's economic position was little known to the British market, and British investors could still find outlets in more familiar areas. The writer of the article on 'Russian investment' in the *Investor's Chronicle* was correct in his opinion that 'the scarcity of good 4 per cent investments will simply drive our capitalists to the one great country which still offers them in abundance',[150] but in March 1900, that time was still to come.

German Investment

In one estimate, Germany appears second only to France as a home for Russian public and private investment in 1914 (£200 million, by contrast with just over £600 million from France and £119 million from Britain).[151] This has been challenged by Anton Crihan, but it is not clear that Crihan's figures are strictly comparable; at any rate, Crihan's estimate for British investment in Russia is implausibly large.[152]

Whatever the position in 1914, it is clear that during the 1870s and 1880s Germany was the principal supplier of capital to Russia. Germans had always been interested in Russia: the Empires were neighbours; immigrants from Germany were prominent in Russian finance, commerce and industry; commercial contact across frontiers was easy and natural. It is probable that a proportion of the capital raised for Russia on the Amsterdam market in the 1820s and 1830s was in fact German, and it seems that the financing of the Moscow–St Petersburg railway was undertaken by investors in Germany and Russia even before it reached Amsterdam (in 1847) or London (in 1850).[153] Pollard reports German capital as flowing outward to Russia, mostly into railway building, in the 1850s and 1860s.[154] Domestic railway securities were expensive in Germany, and, once the Russian government undertook in the 1860s to guarantee the interest on railway securities, foreign markets opened and 'very large sums were supplied by Germany'.[155] When in 1868 the Russian Mutual Crédit Foncier looked for buyers of 100,000 shares (at 100 rubles nominal), it appeared that French subscriptions were not greatly required; the prospectus was drawn up exclusively in German.[156]

It is not clear, however, that German interest in Russian securities was as yet more than speculative. Berlin had a bad reputation in the late 1860s for intemperate speculation. Contemporaries felt this to be the case. Nobody knew the international capital market better than William Borski. Berlin, he said, was much more important for gambling and speculation in lotteries and shares of all kinds than it was for cash investment.[157] Baron Stieglitz, always a firm believer in the German market, tried to insist that Berlin should be included in the second Nicholas loan of 1869; he argued that the first real movement in the 1867 loan began the very day that an official quotation was granted in Berlin.[158] Thomas Baring replied that he was not aware that Berlin had been of much assistance with the loan of 1867; it held very few of the 4 per cent bonds, and what had been taken or subsequently bought for Berlin had found its way to Amsterdam and London. His own opinion was that a great portion of the Russian railway bonds of all subsequent issues negotiated in Berlin was taken not for investment but as a speculation with the aid of advances from banks in Berlin, St Petersburg and elsewhere, and would be thrown back on the market if economic conditions changed.[159] Baring was proved right by the 1869 bonds, which came back from Germany for sale in Amsterdam.

By 1870, however, as a result of the Nicholas and Rothschild loans, Oppenheim & Co. of Cologne were undoubtedly correct in supposing that there was a large market in Germany for Russian loans, of which very important sums were already in the hands of private investors.[160] German interest in Russian railway issues was stimulated by the discovery that much of the capital was subsequently returned to Germany in the form of employment for German engineers and orders for German industry.

Gille suggests that German investors took a share of Russian imports of capital only after British investors abandoned the market in 1885.[161] But French investors, when they retired from Russian loans after the Franco-Prussian war, were swiftly replaced by Germans, who were already deeply committed to Russian securities. Girault quotes an estimated three-fifths of Russian securities marketed abroad between 1870 and 1886 taken in Germany, and he points to the many trade and industrial connections between the two countries that made this plausible.[162] Berlin and Frankfurt were the prime markets for Russian securities at this time. Russian loans were immensely popular in Germany: a 300 million mark loan floated by Bleichröder in Berlin in 1884 was oversubscribed twenty times.[163] By the end of 1886 the leading position of German investment in Russia was still unchallenged: in January 1887 the 2 billion marks' worth of Russian securities in German hands 'constituted well over half of Russia's total indebtedness abroad'.[164] It is almost certain that it was Bismarck's intervention in the market after mid-1887 that shifted the priority from German to French investment in Russia. By the autumn, Bismarck's 'systematic campaign against Russian finances' had turned the balance decisively in favour of the French investor.

Dutch Investment

If Germans were the main investors in Russia between the early 1870s and the end of the 1880s (when French investors took the lead). Who was it, then, who supplied what were, indeed, the limited requirements of the Empire for foreign finance before the late 1860s? The surprising conclusion is that the money was Dutch.

Holland had financed Catherine the Great. Hope & Co. of Amsterdam, the leader in Russian finance (and much else besides), brought out their first Russian loan (to finance the Russo-Turkish war) in February 1788. They had issued no less than eighteen small loans for a total of 53.5 million guilders (£4.5 million) by the time that the French occupation of Amsterdam, in January 1795, put a stop to further business.[165] The loans were exclusively Dutch.

James Riley's careful study of the Amsterdam capital market between 1740 and 1815 ends with the implication that by 1815 the Dutch investor and the financial houses of Amsterdam had withdrawn in large part from international finance: 'there were not sufficient resources [after the Napoleonic Wars] to restore the role in commercial finance and lending to governments that Amsterdam had played in the previous century.'[166] This may have been true of commercial finance, where London was now taking so important a role, but it was not true for government lending.

Russia suspended payment on her foreign debt during the French attack of 1812. She funded the suspended dividends and resumed full payment of interest and principal at the beginning of 1817. Dutch investors were favourably impressed, and the great mass of their foreign investment over the following years was Russian, with some interest in Prussia and Austria and rather less in France. The two Russian loans of 1817 and 1818, issued in St Petersburg for a total of 95 million paper rubles (£4.5 million), offered a 6 per cent return. This was tempting to British investors, and Leland Jenks thinks that about half of the 1818 loan was subscribed in England.[167] Alexander Baring, on the other hand, whose house had taken charge of the sale of the Russian bonds in London, reported that the Dutch had taken probably three-quarters of the whole amount.[168]

Thereafter, the arrangement between Alexander Baring and Hieronymous Sillem, the senior partner of Hope & Co. (Amsterdam), was that Sillem took charge of the management of Russian loan business, with an uncontrolled right to use his own judgement for the common interest 'as related to advances, engagements, and ultimate responsibility'.[169] The loan of 1820, for 40 million silver rubles net (£6.2 million), was managed on this basis, with Sillem periodically sending over parcels of Russian stock for sale in London. It was the first Russian loan in which Barings had come forward openly to the Russian government as associates of Hope & Co. Its success won the compliments of the Russian Minister of Finance. Yet the next Russian loan, a London loan for 43 million silver rubles nominal (£6.5 million), was brought out in 1822 by N. M. Rothschild. Sillem believed that the contract had been obtained, by the intrigues of the Prince de Lieven, Russian Ambasssador in London, in defiance of his instructions from the Minister of Finance (Count Gurev) to make the first approaches to Hope & Co. and Barings.[170] The London experiment failed: English investors did not take to it and only 23 million rubles were raised.[171] Rothschild was left with much on his hands, a proportion of which ultimately and inevitably found its way to Holland.

Dutch investors remained loyal to Russian stock throughout the 1820s, whereas the crisis of 1825–6 gave British investors and speculators their fill of foreign stocks. When General Kankrin, Gurev's successor as Minister of Finance, wrote to Hope & Co. in April 1828 to ask them to undertake an 18 million guilder loan, he explained that he was doing so 'reconnaissant la justesse de vos observations et de celles de Mr Baring sur l'avantage d'un emprunt en Hollande à l'instar de l'ancien'.[172] The loan was successfully disposed of in three instalments over the next year. Barings received a share of the commission, but the management of the loan and the greater part of the sales took place in Amsterdam.[173] The Rothschild loan of 1822 was subsequently 'dealt in to some extent on the London Stock Exchange', but the Russian loans of 1817 and 1818, and the 'Metallics' of 1820 and 1832–3, were 'little known' in London and 'not usually dealt in on the London Stock Exchange'.[174]

To 1850 and even beyond, Russia was only occasionally in need of foreign loans. The outstanding government debt abroad, much of which dated from the Dutch loans of the Napoleonic wars, averaged only 227 million silver rubles over the twenty years 1830–49.[175] New loans were intended to meet extraordinary demands on government resources – the reform of the currency, the Polish troubles of the early 1830s, the construction of the Moscow–St Petersburg railway during the 1840s – for which the capital could be raised in Holland and Germany without recourse to London.

Hope & Co. gave Barings an interest in each of the three Russian government loans of this period – the 20 million silver ruble loans of 1831 and 1833 and the 25 million silver ruble loan of 1840. But the share taken by Barings and by British investors was insignificant.

Estimates of Dutch external investment at the beginning of the 1830s, which range from 640 million guilders (£53.3 million) to 1.6 billion guilders (£133.3 million),[176] are too diverse to be of much use. But Crihan, quoting Hobson, calculates Dutch investment abroad in 1860 at 760 million florins (£60 million), which may have been about right and which, as he says, indicates how much the Amsterdam market was surpassed by London and Paris.[177] Although large loans could not be placed at once in Amsterdam, the point was the reliability of Dutch investment – the ability to take up and hold foreign loans. Dutch investors and re-investors, unable (as in Britain and France) to find a sufficient home for their money in a large domestic market, were on the look-out for suitable openings abroad. Steady sales of parcels of stock at a firm price were well suited to a community of *rentiers*. The interest earned on previous investment gave Dutchmen large sums to re-invest, provided that demand could be spread over a sufficiently long period. For example, Dutchmen initially subscribed 5.5 million rubles for Russia's 20 million ruble loan of 1831, including the 3.5 million taken firm in the government contract by the issuing houses (Hope & Co., Barings and their friends). Yet the remainder, sold in parcels to meet a regular demand, was all disposed of by the summer of 1832.

Sir Robert Giffen, an eminent authority, believed that Russia, like Austria and the South American states, was 'largely "developed" by English capital'.[178] This was certainly the conventional wisdom, but he was wrong for all three. London could not be interested in Russian loans. Continental investors, who looked on Russia as a safe haven for investment, were less bothered by her politics. Hope & Co. closed their subscription lists for the first half of the 1833 loan a few days after it was announced. Money was abundant in Amsterdam, 'and the demands of our correspondents all over Germany and even in France are so considerable that we have already been compelled to shorten the sums which they were willing to participate'. Barings' share, 4 million rubles out of the 40 million for both loans, seems mostly to have been disposed of in Holland.[179]

Dutch investors again took the bulk of the 1840 loan, brought forward by Hope & Co. in two parts. General Hamilton, who was trying to raise a loan in Amsterdam for the new state of Texas, reported sourly that 'the autocrat who wants this Money to throw into the Black Sea or for purpose of present violence or future destruction has had the Lists filled for the Loan in 3 Days when not one of the States of the American Confederacy could have effected a similar negotiation in 3 months or within 10 per cent of the rate at which the subscription was opened'.[180] Hope and Co., working in association with their Amsterdam brokers the Borskis, were perfect masters of the Dutch market. Their hold over the Dutch investor was such that they were able to bring the loan out in Amsterdam at a price well above what the market would bear in London. English investors could take their pick of a variety of good securities for permanent investment that offered a better interest than Russian 4 per cents at 90, and the political uncertainties of the Continent and the Near East made them suspicious of European investment. Barings found themselves unable to dispose of their allotment of 1.1 million rubles from the first issue of 17 million, and they refused an offer of a similar share in the remaining 8 million brought out by Hope & Co. in July 1841.[181]

Whatever the reservations in the employment and recruitment of foreign investors, the scale of Russian resources in comparison with the size of her debt made Russia an interesting arena for financial operations. Hope & Co. were aware of the efforts of the Rothschilds to get a foot in the door. During the negotiations for the 1840 loan, Rothschilds applied to the Russian Minister of Finance; they told him that through their influence they could easily place the loan with British and other capitalists. The threat was sufficiently worrying for Hope & Co. to press anxiously for the opening of the British market to Russian stock. Barings assured them that Rothschilds' attempt to find a home in London for their 5 per cent Belgian loan at 97–98 had been a complete failure; in the current state of the London money market and the uncertainty of politics, Rothschilds would never have succeeded in placing any large amount of a Russian 4 per cent stock at 90 – 'indeed the price you fixed always appeared to us a tour de force and another proof of the influence you possessed in Holland and the predilection of the Dutch for Russian stock'.[182]

Price was a major determinant. If money became abundant in London and less so in Holland, a Russian sterling loan at a cheaper price could well become a favourite among British investors, and this was precisely what happened at the end of the 1840s. The first, informal approaches for a 20 million ruble loan reached Hope & Co. in January 1849. Russian government 5 per cent stock was still a favourite with home and Dutch investors, and the amount held abroad, almost entirely in Holland, had been reduced to 97 million guilders. Holland was overstocked with money, but 20 million rubles was a large request when European politics and finance were still disarranged by the 1848 revolutions, and Hope & Co. thought that a new issue would have to be sold at 1 per cent below the current par price.

The Russian government seemed prepared to wait for its money, but Alexander Stieglitz arrived in London at the end of March 1849 with confidential instructions from the Emperor and the Minister of Finance. Russia needed to raise £4 million before the end of the year to meet the expense, already anticipated, of sending an army to Austria's assistance in Hungary. The understanding was that this was too big a sum to be raised in a few months in Holland, which was no longer sufficiently large a market for Russian needs and where guilders, as Borski used to say, were as pounds sterling in London. Hope & Co., understandably put out by the Emperor's insistence on a joint operation in London and Amsterdam, prevaricated to such an extent that the Emperor, who could already scent victory in his Hungarian campaigns, cancelled the proposals early in July.[183]

The Russian government had now shown itself anxious to break into the London market. It was understandable that when, in December 1849, the Minister of Finance (F. P. Vronchenko) examined Stieglitz's proposals for the latest, largest and supposedly last of the loans to complete the Moscow–St Petersburg railway, he agreed that England, where capital was abundant and unemployed and the political position uniquely stable, would be the best place to raise the money. Barings, who had been so willing to help out earlier in the year, should have the preference; it was a 'moment favorable pour développer dans ce centre du monde commercial et financier la circulation de nos fonds'. Hope & Co. of Amsterdam were not even approached. To try the English market, Stieglitz explained later, was the favourite idea to which all consideration of Hope & Co.'s previous services were sacrificed. Barings were aware that the political motive for interesting British investors in Russian stock probably counted for as much as the cash, since the Russian government was not noticeably short of money at the time.

On this occasion the experiment was successful, although it gave advance notice of attitudes that were to block many subsequent attempts to raise money for Russia on the London market. For reasons already suggested, the 1850 loan (which was the first occasion on which Barings of London took full responsibility for a Russian government issue independently of Hope & Co.) did not mark a permanent transfer of Russian foreign funding from Amsterdam to London. For many years thereafter British investors did not touch Russian stocks. They had other priorities, and as late as the early 1860s they were preoccupied with Indian and colonial securities. Berlin and Hamburg, although a good market for Stieglitz's Moscow railway and Crimean loans of the 1840s and 1850s, had not taken an interest in recent Russian loans, and it was only in the autumn of 1861 that Berlin, by absorbing some of Stieglitz's new 4 per cent *billets de banque*, showed some sign of revival.

Most of the Russian stocks sold since the Crimean War had ultimately found their way to Amsterdam, and the Dutch were almost alone in buying Russian government securities for investment. The Baring and Hope loan of 1860–1 was held exclusively in Holland. But the Dutch could not take much over £100,000 in Russian stock a month, and 'à la longue', said Henry Labouchère (senior partner of Hope & Co.), 'the dwarf cannot uphold the giant'.

Russia had to look further afield. Even the friends of Barings and

Hope & Co. at St Petersburg – Count Nesselrode,[184] Baron Meyendorff,[185] General de Brock,[186] and Baron Stieglitz[187] – felt that the needs of Russia had outgrown the capacity of both houses and of the Amsterdam market. Russia, Stieglitz argued, was passing through a crisis when the value of the ruble must be upheld by every means; this was the great object, and foreign loans were necessary to attain it. The government wanted money, which Barings and Hope & Co. could supply. The two houses had done a great deal for Russia in 1860, and they had now taken a further £800,000 of the £1 million 4 per cents nominally placed in Amsterdam in June 1861. Berlin and Paris had to be brought in; 'it is necessary that you should enlarge the circle'.[188]

The poor reception given to subsequent attempts to interest the London, Berlin and Paris markets, however, showed that Russia was still ultimately dependent for foreign finance on the absorptive capacity of Amsterdam. Baron Stieglitz, in want of funds for the current business of the state (let alone the expansion of the railway system), visited Paris in January 1864. He wanted to negotiate another loan through James Rothschild. Rothschild, who complained that he had lost a great deal of money by the Russian loan of 1862, was dragging his heels; he never liked to see a good business escape him, and he was anxious to maintain the position that he had so recently won for himself in Russian finance. The rumour, much exaggerated, was that he was in advance to the Russian government to the extent of 60–70 million francs, and he kept Stieglitz hanging on in Paris, 'le bec dans l'eau', as long as he could. But James Rothschild was an old man, the zest had gone out of his house, and his associates were not prepared to take the risk of failure on another large Russian loan. His sons, Hottinguer reported from Paris, 'n'ont pas la même energie que lui, et il est toujours malade, et ils aurent voulu gagner du temps, et Stieglitz est parti . . .'.[189]

While negotiating with Rothschild, Stieglitz had already made discreet enquiries in London and Amsterdam, and it was to Barings and Hope & Co. that the Russian government now returned. Stieglitz explained to Edward Baring that the financial position of Russia was not at all as gloomy as some ill-intentioned people had made it out to be. Her wants were not great now that she had abandoned the bold idea towards which she had long been manoeuvring (with foreign support) of paying her notes in gold. At the same time, the Polish revolution was 'extinguishing', and Russia had no intention of intervening in the Prusso-Danish dispute, which was currently preoccupying the politicians of Europe: 'In such times, in former years, Russian stock used to be more sought after, especially in Holland; with another 50 millions of guilders [about £4.5 million] towards the autumn all would be set right again.'[190] Stieglitz was more specific a few days later; Russia's wants to cover pending drafts, dividends, etc. were £5 million, spread over the months April–December. He accepted Thomas Baring's warning that, although Amsterdam was a sponge for Russian stocks that passed into good and firm hands, it would work only gradually and sometimes slowly, 'but then our wants are only gradual, and besides, loans of such moderate amounts were made, even at Amsterdam, at once in former years'.[191]

The Dutch market retained its leadership in Russian finance into the late 1860s. It had the capacity to do so up to the railway boom that at length brought foreign borrowing to a volume no longer to be matched in Amsterdam, although it would be premature to dismiss the Dutch market altogether. Holland was not large enough independently to finance the Russian railways, but she continued to take a good share, and Dutch investment accounted for much of what was nominally placed in Germany. Amsterdam was not immune from speculation. Capefigue called the Dutch speculator 'le joueur le plus déterminé du monde, par calcul, par caractère'.[192] When Charles Crews, a broker on the London Stock Exchange, gave evidence to the Royal Commissions in 1878, he reported that he had very numerous transactions between London and Holland: 'we deal at least ten times a day in Russian stocks between here and Holland'.[193]

The international nature of money markets at the time makes it nearly impossible to tell the precise origins of capital. Dutch investors bought Russian securities in Berlin, Frankfurt, Paris, London and St Petersburg. For this reason, amongst others, it seems unlikely that Dutch investment in the public debt of Russia, on the eve of the 1917 Revolution, was, as Crihan said, only an eighth of the size of Belgian, a third of North American, and marginally more than Swiss.[194] It is clear nonetheless that the leading position of Dutch investors in Russian securities, which they had occupied up to the late 1860s, had long vanished.

Conclusion

Russia's needs for foreign finance were relatively slight before the railway boom of the late 1860s. Commercial credit may, in fact, have occupied a more important role than a conventionally recognisable investment by foreigners in Russian railways or Imperial loans. For both railways and government loans, domestic finance played the major part, as it did in the growth of Russia's banking and industrial activity. Foreign finance was a strong element in Russia's *external* trade; it was less important for the larger, internal traffic of the Empire. Foreigners were called upon to supply a share of the money for the first major railway in Russia (Moscow–St Petersburg), and financiers from abroad provided the cash for the first years of the Grande Société. Foreign finance was recruited during the abortive attempts, in the mid-century, to re-establish the silver ruble. Public loans were regularly issued abroad (and taken in Amsterdam) for the purpose of funding government deficits, preventing the drain of Russian gold, and meeting a recurrent imbalance of receipts and expenditure in Russia's international accounts.

The dramatic expansion of the Russian railway system in the 1860s, and the commitment of the Russian government itself to the financing of new railways, forced foreign borrowing to assume a new, much higher level. Entrepreneurial abilities were required from abroad for the first phases in the financing of the railway boom. The will of the domestic market to take railway securities, although much more powerful than most contemporaries expected, needed reinforcement. At length, Russia began to borrow heavily abroad.

So long as Russia's need for *foreign* finance was regular and relatively light, she found her money in Amsterdam, with only occasional assistance from London, Frankfurt and Berlin. Towards the end of the 1860s the railway boom brought a new generation of foreign investment, principally German, Dutch, British and French. For a short time, Paris, with its larger resources, seemed to have taken over from Amsterdam the role of the market of first resort for Russian securities. The disaster of the Franco-Prussian war (1870–1) gave the lead to German investors, and it was only after the late 1880s that France resumed the place at the head of Russia's external finance that she was to hold until 1914. Certainly to 1870, and probably throughout the nineteenth century, domestic resources formed the backbone of Russian finance.

Notes

1 G. P. Nebolsin's survey of Russian foreign commerce was published in 1850. It is quoted in Michael T. Florinskii, *Russia: A history and an interpretation* Vol. II, (New York, 1953), p. 790.
2 *The Economist,* 7 June 1856, p. 614. Eighteen months before, the same journal had calculated 'the usual advances of British capital to Russian merchants' at 'about ten millions of money'; 20 January 1855, p. 55.
3 From T. Michell, 'Memorandum on the trade between Great Britain and Russia', dated 4 December 1865, and printed in Parliamentary Papers (hereafter P.P.), 1866, LXXII, p. 586.
4 Florinskii, *Russia: A history*, p. 787.
5 J. N. Westwood, *Endurance and endeavour: Russian history 1812–1971* (Oxford, 1973), p. 83.
6 Richard M. Haywood, *The beginnings of railway development in Russia in the reign of Nicholas I, 1835–1842* (Durham, NC, 1969), pp. 186–7.
7 Rondo E. Cameron, *France and the economic development of Europe, 1800–1914* (Princeton, NJ, 1961), p. 414.

8 Bertrand Gille, *Histoire économique et sociale de la Russie du moyen âge au XXe siècle* (Paris, 1949), p. 187.
9 ibid., p. 181.
10 ibid., pp. 139, 159.
11 Iván T. Berend and György Ránki, *Economic development in East–Central Europe in the nineteenth and twentieth centuries* (trans. New York, 1974), p. 104.
12 M. E. Falkus, *The industrialisation of Russia, 1700–1914* (London, 1972), pp. 16 and 60.
13 Alexander Gerschenkron, *Economic backwardness in historical perspective: essays* (Cambridge, Mass., 1962), pp. 138, 142.
14 Scheer to Joshua Bates, 16 January 1848: archive of Baring Brothers & Co. Ltd., Guildhall Library, London (hereafter 'Baring'), HC 3.8.1. Five years later, on 1 January 1853, the internal and foreign debts (£63 million in total) and the notes of the *caisse de crédit* (£50 million) were together 'barely three times the revenue of the state', although the floating debt was estimated at £200 million, 'exceeding by twice that of all the other European States added together': *Fortune's Epitome of the stocks and public funds, English, foreign and American* (17th edn, London, 1856), p. 209.
15 Charles Jutting's report on the floating debt of the Empire, 30 December 1869: Baring, HC 10.28.
16 Yves Barel, *Le Développement économique de la Russie tsariste* (Paris, 1968), p. 197.
17 *The Times*, 22 August 1877, p. 4c.
18 M. C. Kaser, 'Russian entrepreneurship', in Peter Mathias and M. M. Postan, eds, *Cambridge Economic History of Europe*, Vol. VII, pt 2 (Cambridge, 1978), p. 465.
19 M. E. Falkus, 'Aspects of foreign investment in Tsarist Russia', *Journal of European Economic History*, 8:1 (Spring 1979), p. 9.
20 Antoine Horne, 'Banking in the Russian Empire', in Journal of Commerce, *A history of banking in all the leading nations*, Vol. II (New York, 1896), pp. 411–12.
21 Anton Crihan, *Le Capital étranger en Russie* (Paris, thesis, 1934), p. 70.
22 Report by Mr Rumbold, H.M.'s Secretary of Embassy, on the Russian Railways, dated St Petersburg, 15 August 1869: P.P., 1870, LXV, p. 496.
23 *The Economist*, 19 November 1870, p. 1403.
24 This is derived from the third of a series of valuable articles on Russian railways, contributed by *The Times*' Berlin correspondent: *The Times*, 15 February 1869, p. 4b.
25 Quoted in ibid., p. 4a.
26 Rumbold, (first) Report on Russian Railways, p. 494.
27 Falkus, *Industrialisation of Russia*, p. 53.
28 Berend and Ránki, *Economic development in East–Central Europe*, p. 104.
29 George Garvy, 'Banking under the Tsars and the Soviets', *Journal of Economic History*, 32:4 (December 1972), p. 874.
30 Rumbold, (first) Report on Russian Railways, p. 505.
31 *The Times*, 22 August 1877, p. 4b.
32 Peter I. Lyaschenko, *History of the national economy of Russia to the 1917 revolution* (trans. New York, 1949), p. 534.
33 Crihan, *Capital étranger en Russie*, p. 69.
34 Rumbold, (second) Report on Russian Railways, dated St Petersburg, 30 April 1870: P.P., 1871, LXVII, pp. 348–9.
35 Charles Jutting's letters to Barings from St Petersburg in and after 1863 give the annual results of the Grande Société's lines, together with a great deal of other detail on its operations. Jutting had been sent by Barings to Russia precisely to superintend their interest in the Grande Société: Baring, HC 10.28.
36 *The Times*, 24 August 1868, p. 5a.
37 Alexander Baykov, 'The economic development of Russia', in Barry E. Supple,

ed., *The experience of economic growth: case studies in economic history* (New York, 1963), p. 420.

38 Gille, *Histoire économique et Sociale de la Russie*, p. 167. The actual distribution of the lottery loans is described in Jutting's letters from St Petersburg: Baring, HC 10.28.

39 Jutting's report on the floating debt of the Empire, 30 December 1869: Baring, HC 10.28.

40 Hugh Seton-Watson, *The Russian Empire 1801–1917* (Oxford, 1967), p. 404, and Olga Crisp, *Studies in the Russian economy before 1914* (London, 1976), pp. 21–2.

41 George Wyneken to Thomas Baring, 20 September 1868: Baring, HC 10.23.

42 Jutting to Barings, 4 April 1867: Baring, HC. 10.28.

43 Fritz Stern, *Gold and iron, Bismarck, Bleichröder and the building of the German empire* (London, 1977), p. 346.

44 Jean Bouvier, *Le Crédit Lyonnais de 1863 à 1882*, Vol. II (Paris, 1961), pp. 742–3.

45 Crihan, *Capital étranger en Russie*, p. 241.

46 René Girault, *Emprunts russes et investissements français en Russie, 1887–1914* (Paris, 1973), p. 89.

47 René Girault, *Les relations économiques et financières entre la France et la Russie de 1887 à 1919* (Paris, thesis, 1971; edn Lille, 1972), Vol. I, p. 132.

48 Ernest Seyd, 'The fall in the price of silver, its consequences and their possible avoidance', *Journal of the Society of Arts*, 24 (10 March 1876), p. 313.

49 Crihan, *Capital étranger en Russie*, p. 63.

50 Leo Pasvolsky and Harold G. Moulton, *Russian debts and Russian reconstruction* (New York, 1924), p. 17.

51 John P. McKay, *Pioneers for profit: foreign entrepreneurship and Russian industrialisation, 1885–1913* (Chicago, 1970), pp. 25–9.

52 John P. Sontag, 'Tsarist debts and tsarist foreign policy', *Slavic Review*, 27:4 (December 1968), p. 540.

53 Horace Rumbold, (first) Report on Russian railways, p. 477. There is no certainty about these figures, or, for that matter, about any Russian figures of this generation. But Petit's estimate of 222,000 rubles per kilometre ('un chiffre très élevé) comes close enough: Pierre Petit, *La Dette publique de la Russie* (Poitiers, thesis, 1912), p. 51 n. 1.

54 W. E. Mosse, *Alexander II and the modernisation of Russia* (London, 1958), pp. 11–12. Mosse observes that the engineers (by which he means contractors) were American, and that they were working with American capital. The contractor, Major George Washington Whistler, was certainly American; the engineers, on the whole, were Russian; the capital was *not* American!

55 Rondo Cameron, 'The Crédit Mobilier and the economic development of France', *Journal of Political Economy*, 61:6 (December 1953), p. 476, and *France and the economic development of Europe*, p. 84.

56 W. Borski to Thomas Baring, 9 June 1843. Baring, HC 8.8.

57 The Baring correspondence for the Moscow–St Petersburg railway loans, 1842–7 (when an attempt was made to raise a further 15 million rubles in Holland) is in Baring, HC 1.20.4, HC 7.1, HC 8.12, HC 10.1, PLB 1842 and 1847, and Baring Papers, Public Archive of Canada, Ottawa, frame nos 61510–1, 62349–50.

58 The correspondence, December 1849 – January 1850, is in Baring, HC 8.1, HC 10.1, HC 10.14, HC 10.15, and PLB 1850.

59 Barings to Hottinguers, 22 May 1852: Baring, PLB 1852.

60 *Bradshaw's shareholders' guide, railway manual and directory for 1862* (London, 1862), p. 338.

61 For instance: Lyashenko, *History of the national economy of Russia*, p. 491; Cameron, *France and the economic development of Europe*, pp. 279 and 422;

Alexandre Michelson, *L'essor économique de la Russie avant la guerre de 1914* (Paris, 1965), p. 16; Gille, *Histoire économique et sociale de la Russie*, p. 169; P. L. Cottrell, 'Investment banking in England, 1856–82: case study of the International Financial Society' (unpublished Ph.D. thesis, University of Hull, 1974), p. 371.

62 The Baring correspondence for the origins and early development of the Grande Société des Chemins de Fer Russes (April 1856 – December 1857), which is very extensive, is to be found principally in Baring, HC 7.1, HC 7.27, HC 8.1, HC 10.1, PLB 1856 and 1857 (particularly the letters to Baron Stieglitz), and Joshua Bates' Diary, Vol. VI: Baring, uncatalogued.

63 *The Economist*, 20 April 1867, p. 450.

64 J. N. Westwood, *A history of Russian railways* (London, 1964), p. 41.

65 Joshua Bates to Thomas Baring, 29 July 1858, writing from Paris where he had just attended a meeting of the Committee of the Grande Société: Baring, HC 1.20.8.

66 Henri Hottinguer to Thomas Baring, 29 March 1859: Baring, HC 7.1.

67 Falkus, *Industrialisation of Russia*, p. 53.

68 Barings (Thomas Baring) to Jutting, 23 June 1863: Baring, PLB 1863.

69 Rumbold, (first) Report on Russian Railways, p. 482.

70 Stieglitz to Barings, 22 March 1867: Baring, HC 10.1.

71 Rumbold, (first) Report on Russian Railways, p. 490.

72 Baron Stieglitz to Barings, 22 March 1867: Baring, HC 10.3.

73 Thomas Baring to Stieglitz, 15 April 1867: Baring, PLB 1867.

74 The disposal of the Nicholas loan is discussed in Baring, HC 8.1 and PLB 1867 and 1868.

75 Jutting to Barings, 7 December 1868: Baring, HC 10.28.

76 The second issue of the Nicholas bonds is discussed, October 1868 – April 1869, in Baring, HC 7.1, HC 8.1, HC 10.1, HC 10.28, HC 10.37 and PLB 1868 and 1869.

77 Russian official railway statistics, enclosed in Jutting's letter to Barings of 12 May 1871: Baring, HC 10.28.

78 Jutting to Barings, 22 December 1871: Baring, HC 10.28.

79 Gille, *Histoire économique et sociale de la Russie*, p. 163.

80 Léon Faucher, 'The finances of Russia', *Bankers' Magazine*, 14 (December 1854), p. 738.

81 Horne, 'Banking in the Russian Empire', p. 374.

82 Florinskii, *Russia: a history*, Vol. II p. 942.

83 Jutting to Barings, 3 March 1866: Baring, HC 10.28.

84 *The Economist,* 31 August 1867, p. 983.

85 ibid., p. 984.

86 *Investor's Monthly Manual,* 28 December 1872, p. 415.

87 Gille, *Histoire économique et sociale de la Russie*, p. 136.

88 Report by Mr Consul T. Michell on the Finances of the Russian Empire, dated St Petersburg, June 1867: P.P., 1867, LXVIII, pp. 229–30.

89 *Fenn on the Funds* (12th edn, London, 1874), p. 413.

90 Jutting to Barings, 10 March 1866: Baring, HC 10.28.

91 Thomas Baring to Stieglitz, 8 December 1865: Baring, PLB 1865.

92 Stieglitz to Thomas Baring, 20 December 1865: Baring, HC 10.1.

93 Jutting to Barings, 31 March 1865: Baring, HC 10.8.

94 Stieglitz to Barings, 5 January 1862: Baring, HC 10.1.

95 Jutting reported on Russian government finance, budgets and deficits in a long and important letter to Barings, 17 February 1869: Baring, HC 10.28.

96 Jutting to Barings, 2 and 18 March 1864: Baring, HC 10.28.

97 Jutting to Barings, 1 June and 12 October 1864: Baring, HC 10.28. A few years earlier G. J. Goschen had said as much in *The theory of foreign exchanges*

(London, 1861), p. 20. The sums were later enormously increased. Paul Gregory reports an annual average of 33.6 million rubles for 1886 – 90, and no less than 222.2 million rubles for 1909 – 13: 'The Russian balance of payments, the gold standard, and monetary policy: a historical example of foreign capital movements', *Journal of Economic History*, 39:2 (June 1979), pp. 382–3.

98 The correspondence for the Anglo-Dutch loan of 1866 is in Baring, HC 8.1, HC 10.1 and PLB 1866.

99 Report by Mr W. Stuart HM's Secretary of Embassy, on the Russian Budget for 1867, dated St Petersburg, 7 June 1867: P.P., 1867, LXX, p. 346.

100 Cameron, *France and the economic development of Europe*, p. 414.

101 Westwood, *History of Russian railways*, p. 8.

102 Herbert Feis, *Europe: the world's banker, 1870–1914* (New York, 1965 edn; originally published in 1930), p. 211.

103 Olga Crisp, 'Russian financial policy and the gold standard at the end of the nineteenth century', *Economic History Review*, 2nd ser. 6:2 (1953), p. 171.

104 Cameron, 'The Crédit Mobilier', p. 476 fn. 59, and Cameron, *France and the economic development of Europe*, p. 422.

105 The Baring correspondence for the 1850 loan is in Baring, HC 8.1, HC 10.1, HC 10.14, HC 10.15 and PLB 1850.

106 Roger Catin, *Le Portefeuille étranger de la France entre 1870 et 1914* (Paris, thesis, 1927), p. 15.

107 ibid., p. 18, and Rondo Cameron, 'L'Exportation des capitaux français, 1850–1880', *Revue d'histoire économique et sociale*, 33:3 (1955), p. 349.

108 Labouchère to Barings, St Petersburg, 22 July 1861: Baring, HC 8.1.

109 Hope & Co. to Stieglitz, 23 January 1866: Baring, HC 8.1.

110 The disposal of the Nicholas loan, for which Barings and Hope & Co. were the London and Amsterdam issue houses, is discussed in Baring, HC 8.1 and PLB 1867 and 1868.

111 Stieglitz to Thomas Baring, 30 October 1868: Baring, HC 10.1.

112 Jean Bouvier, *Les Rothschild* (Paris, 1967 edn), p. 269.

113 The distribution of this loan is described in Baring, HC 8.1, HC 10.1, HC 10.28, HC 10.37 and PLB 1868 and 1869.

114 Barings to Hope & Co., 8 February 1870, and Hope & Co. to Barings, 12 February 1870: Baring, PLB 1870 and HC 8.1 respectively. The Frankfurt subscription was reported in *The Times*, 1 February 1870, p. 10a.

115 Bertrand Gille, *Histoire de la maison Rothschild, 1848–1870* (Geneva, 1967), p. 495.

116 *The Economist*, 12 February 1870, p. 196.

117 *The Times*, 1 February 1870 (the day after subscriptions closed), p. 5a.

118 Girault, *Emprunts russes*, pp. 84–5.

119 Girault, *Relations économiques et financières*, p. 276.

120 *The Economist*, 8 November 1856, p. 1237.

121 *The Economist*, 22 November 1856, p. 1294.

122 For instance, Crihan, *Capital étranger en Russie*, p. 63 (although he ignores France's brief interest in Russia in 1867–70).

123 Bouvier, *Les Rothschild*, pp. 269–70.

124 Gille, *Histoire économique et sociale de la Russie*, p. 167.

125 Feis, *Europe: the world's banker*, p. 4.

126 Douglass North, 'International capital movements in historical perspective', in Raymond F. Mikesell, ed., *United States private and government investment abroad* (Eugene, Oreg., 1962), p. 19.

127 A. K. Cairncross, *Home and foreign investment 1870–1913: studies in capital accumulation* (Cambridge, 1953), Table 41, p. 183. Britons were not interested in Italy, so presumably this was largely Russian.

128 George Webb Medley's memorandum, 'Loans to Foreign States', printed as

Appendix 4 to the *Report of the Royal Commission on the London Stock Exchange*, P.P., 1878, XIX, pp. 671–2.

129 T. Michell (Attaché to HM's Embassy at St Petersburg), *Memorandum on the Trade between Great Britain and Russia*, P.P., 1866, LXXII, p. 558.

130 Pierre Petit, *La Dette publique* p. 25.

131 The disposal of these loans is documented in Baring, HC 8.1, HC 8.3 and PLB 1831/3.

132 The speech was reported in *The Times*, 24 July 1849, p. 8a–b.

133 Letter printed in *The Times*, 16 January 1850, p. 5b.

134 Correspondence on the 1850 loan has already been cited above (n. 105).

135 *Bankers' Magazine*, 10 (February 1850), p. 79.

136 Laurence Oliphant, *The Russian shores of the Black Sea in the autumn of 1852* (Edinburgh, 1853), pp. 8–9.

137 Jenks, *Migration of Capital*, p. 285. An opposite view to Jenks has been expressed convincingly by Olive Anderson, 'The Russian loan of 1855: an example of economic liberalism?' *Economica*, new ser. 27 (November 1960), pp. 368–71, and Frank W. Fetter, 'The Russian loan of 1855: a postscript', *Economica*, new ser. 28 (November 1961), pp. 421–6.

138 *Fortune's Epitome of the Stocks and Public Funds* (17th edn, London, 1856), p. 404; Henry Ayres, *Ayres's financial register of British and foreign funds* (London, 1857), pp. 360–1; Faucher, 'The finances of Russia', p. 734.

139 *Bankers' Magazine*, 14 (July 1854), p. 364.

140 *House of Commons Debates*, 26 July 1854, p. 779.

141 Stieglitz to Barings, 10 June 1854, and Barings to Stieglitz, 20 June 1854: Baring, HC 10.1 and PLB 1854 respectively.

142 Barings to Stieglitz, 1 April 1856: Baring, PLB 1856.

143 Discussion on Dudley Baxter's paper, *Journal of the Statistical Society*, 37:1 (March 1874), pp. 18–19.

144 *The Economist*, 17 April 1869, p. 439. The same sentiments were expressed in a leading article of 1 August 1868, p. 870.

145 *The Economist*, 5 September 1868, p. 1022. I have suggested the reasons for such a substantial downward revision in my article 'British portfolio investment overseas before 1870: some doubts', *Economic History Review*, 2nd ser. 33:1 (February 1980), p.7.

146 Michell's memorandum of 4 December 1865, p. 558.

147 *Investor's Chronicle*, 6 (March 1900), p. 197. This was the first of a series of articles 'puffing' investment in Russian securities, published during the first half of 1900.

148 Sontag, 'Tsarist debts', p. 532.

149 *Financial Times' Investor's Guide* (London, 1913), p. 74.

150 *Investor's Chronicle*, 6 (March 1900), p. 197.

151 Harvey E. Fisk, *The inter-ally debts* (New York, 1924), p. 302.

152 Crihan, *Capital étranger en Russie*, pp. 75, 250.

153 The Baring correspondence for the Moscow–St Petersburg railway loans, 1842–7, is referred to above (n. 57), as is the correspondence for the London loan of 1850 (n. 58).

154 Sidney Pollard, *European economic integration, 1815–1970* (London, 1974), p. 63.

155 *The Times* (Berlin correspondent), article on Russian railways, dated 14 January 1869: published on 18 January 1869, p. 10c. (The fact that such articles were sent in by the *Berlin* correspondent is evidence in itself of where the investment interest now lay.)

156 *The Economist*, 1 February 1868, p. 63.

157 Borski to Barings, Amsterdam, 4 March 1867: Baring, HC 8.8.

158 Stieglitz to Thomas Baring, 23 March 1869: Baring, HC 8.8.

159 Barings to Stieglitz (in reply to a telegram to the same effect as Stieglitz's letter), also on 23 March 1869 Baring, HC 10.37.

160 Sal. Oppenheim & Co. to Barings, 2 November 1870: Baring, HC 9.17.

161 Gille, *Histoire économique et sociale de la Russie*, p. 167.

162 Girault, *Relations économiques et financières*, Vol. I, pp. 203–18.

163 Stern, *Gold and iron*, p. 348.

164 ibid., p. 440.

165 Marten G. Buist, *At spes non fracta: Hope & Co. 1770–1815. Merchant bankers and diplomats at work* (The Hague, 1974), Appendix D, p. 497.

166 James C. Riley, *International government finance and the Amsterdam capital market, 1740–1815* (Cambridge, 1980), pp. 248–9.

167 Jenks, *Migration of British capital*, p. 350.

168 Alexander Baring's evidence, 11 March 1819: Minutes of Evidence, *Report of the Secret Committee on the expediency of the Bank resuming cash payments*, P.P., 1819, III, p. 188.

169 Reported subsequently in P. C. Labouchère to Thomas Baring, 1 January 1833: Baring, HC 8.2.

170 H. Sillem to Alexander Baring, 25 June 1822: Baring, HC 8.3.

171 *The Times*, 5 August 1823, p. 2c.

172 Kankrin to H. Sillem, 7 May 1828: Baring, HC 8.9.

173 The correspondence between Barings and Hope & Co. is in Baring, HC 8.1, HC 8.2 and HC 8.9.

174 *Fortune's epitome of the stocks and public funds* (16th edn, London, 1851), pp. 142–5. This was confirmed in another publication of the same kind: Gresham Omnium, *A handy guide to safe investments* (London, 1858), p. 63.

175 W. M. Pintner, *Russian economic policy under Nicholas I* (Ithaca, NY, 1967), Table I, p. 32.

176 Buist, *At spes non fracta*, p. 554.

177 Crihan, *Capital étranger en Russie*, p. 19.

178 Robert Giffen, *Essays in finance* (London, 1880), p. 112.

179 The Baring/Hope correspondence for these two loans is in Baring, HC 8.2, HC 8.3 and PLB 1831/3.

180 Hamilton to Barings, Amsterdam, 15 December 1840: Baring, HC 17.132.

181 The correspondence is in Baring, HC 8.1 and PLB 1840/41.

182 Hope & Co. to Barings, 15 January 1841, and Barings to Hope & Co., 22 January 1841: Baring, HC 8.1 and PLB 1841 respectively.

183 The correspondence, covering the period January – July 1849, is in Baring, HC 8.1, HC 8.5, HC 10.1, HC 10.14 and PLB 1849.

184 Charles Robert Nesselrode (1780–1862), Minister of Foreign Affairs, 1822–1856, and Chancellor of the Empire until his death in 1862.

185 Peter Meyendorff (1796–1863), diplomat and member of the Council of the Empire; president of the Grande Société des Chemins de Fer Russes, and head of cabinet for Alexander II.

186 Peter de Brock (1805–1875), Minister of Finance from 1852 to 1858.

187 Alexander Stieglitz, son and successor of the St Petersburg financier Ludwig Stieglitz (who had died of apoplexy in March 1843 reputedly worth 75 million rubles). Alexander Stieglitz became Governor of the State Bank, from which he retired in 1867. However, he remained the close friend and adviser of Count Reutern, Finance Minister, in all his foreign operations.

188 Summarised in Henry Labouchère's two letters from St Petersburg, both dated 22 July 1861: Baring, HC 8.1. Labouchère was employed in an abortive attempt to secure the next Russian loan for Barings and Hope & Co. The loan finally went to Rothschild; it was not a success.

189 Henri Hottinguer to Thomas Baring, Paris, 4 April 1864: Baring, HC 7.1.

190 Stieglitz to Edward Baring, 21 February 1864: Baring, HC 10.1.

191 Stieglitz to Thomas Baring, 24 February 1864: Baring, HC 10.1.
192 M. Capefigue, *Histoire des grandes opérations financières*, Vol. III (Paris, 1858), pp. 75–6.
193 Minutes of Evidence, *Report of the Royal Commission on the London Stock Exchange*: P.P., 1878, XIX, Q.6984.
194 Crihan, *Capital étranger en Russie*, p. 250.

Chapter 4

Austria and Her Neighbours*

Foreign Finance in Middle Europe

Alexander Baring told the Commons in 1830 that Austria 'lagged behind every other nation in her financial system'.[1] Forty years later, Grant Duff, in an exasperated moment, asked whether any statesman, in or out of Europe, knew anything at all of the facts of Austria: 'It is a science in itself, nay, it is half a dozen sciences'.[2] Yet Austria, for all her disasters, was not a poor country, and neither were many of her Continental neighbours.

Obviously, some mid-European countries – Holland and Switzerland throughout the nineteenth century, Belgium before the 1830s, Belgium again and Germany in the later decades – were substantial *exporters* of capital. Contemporaries had a real respect for the quality and capacity of the Dutch market; to Alexander Baring the Dutch were a people who exhibited 'more good sense on financial matters than those of perhaps any other nation'.[3] After years of slow but steady accumulation (the product largely of accrued dividends) the Dutch came to hold an important position among foreign investors by the middle decades of the nineteenth century. The Austrian 'conversion' of 1868 showed Dutch holdings in Austrian state securities alone to have been worth nearly £33.5 million.[4]

However, more importance is often attached to Swiss than to Dutch foreign investment in the nineteenth century. Bertrand Gille, while conceding the importance of Swiss bankers for international finance in the eighteenth century, ignored the Dutch until well into the nineteenth century; he called attention to 'les deux pays exclusivement exportateurs [of capital], l'Angleterre et la Suisse'.[5] His priorities were wrong. Swiss investors, for example, might have been expected to have taken a strong interest in the securities of their neighbour, Austria. Yet the Swiss component of Austrian government securities held abroad in 1868 was just under 2 million florins (£157,000).[6]

* Austria: The par exchange was 10 florins to £1 sterling, although 11 florins is a more realistic rate for most of the period covered in this chapter. The rate in 1870 was 12.75.
Austria–Hungary: 24.9 crowns to £1 sterling (1870).
Italy: 25 lire to £1 sterling (1865).
North Germany: 6.8 thalers to £1 sterling (1870).

Switzerland, although much less important than Holland, was still a net exporter of capital. There were others, like Germany, in which 'capital was sufficient but not over-abundant'.[7] Germany may not have been 'chronically short of investment capital' before the middle of the nineteenth century,[8] but she was certainly content to draw on further capital from abroad, primarily from neighbouring states (France, Belgium, Switzerland and Scandinavia) to whom she herself sometimes exported capital in return. Germany built her own railways, with her own resources, and German capitalists, in 1848, were 'largely interested in railway undertakings abroad'.[9] About half of the capital for the railway systems of Germany (including Prussia) was supplied by the governments of the German states;[10] railways in Germany 'seemed to be a civilian branch of the army'.[11] Where the money was not supplied by the state, it came principally from the domestic investor.[12] By the end of 1850, the whole railway system of Germany (the largest on the Continent) had cost 800 million marks, more than 450 millions of which were obtained from Prussian investors.[13]

Foreign investment in Germany, such as it was, came principally from neighbouring states – Belgium, France and Switzerland;[14] Germany was the one exception cited by Dudley Baxter when he discussed the international need to seek assistance from the British capital market.[15] The Germans, by the 1870s, could well afford to handle their own government debts. The war credit of 100 million thalers (£14.7 million), issued in two tranches both in London and in Berlin (1870 and 1871), was taken enthusiastically in Germany.[16]

A shrewd commentator, writing in 1868, explained that the North German states had had no wants to date that could not have been satisfied at home, while Holland, Belgium and Scandinavia, 'second and third-class states', borrowed only to a modest extent 'just to show that they are alive'; their securities, even when issued in London, found their way to the Continent and were soon absorbed amongst investors in or near the home country.[17]

Whatever the importance of foreign capital, Hildebrand has explained that 'Scandinavian investment . . . was chiefly financed out of the savings of the domestic economy',[18] and a description of the four Scandinavian countries as dependent upon the leading money markets of Western Europe in the second half of the nineteenth century is likely to mislead.[19] Of course, all four countries imported capital to a greater or lesser extent, especially from Germany and later from France; and some parts of each economy drew more heavily on foreign borrowing than others. Sweden, in Sandberg's calculations, had lodged nearly 90 per cent of her government debt abroad in 1908, and 54–56 per cent of mortgage bank and local government borrowing; on the other hand, only 13 per cent of all other Swedish bond issues were foreign owned. Sandberg makes a useful point, of which contemporary borrowers were well aware: 'Thus a very large percentage of the capital needed for the construction of railways and cities was raised abroad, thereby freeing domestic savings for direct industrial and commercial investments.'[20] Nevertheless, the trend for Scandinavia was to draw first on domestic capital resources, supplemented, when necessary, from abroad. Norway, for one, made no important imports of foreign capital until after 1890.[21]

Nearly the whole of the Belgian railway system by 1850 was built by the government;[22] and, according to Lars-Erik Hedin, Swedish railways were 'mainly constructed with the aid of national capital'.[23] Ernest Seyd, writing in the mid-1870s, lists England, France, Germany, Holland, Belgium and Denmark as the nations that owned their own state debts:

> Although the French, Dutch and Danish debts are dealt in on other bourses, yet substantially these nations are internationally wealthy. The French debt is now almost entirely held in France and the English and German debts have always been kept at home.[24]

And the same was true for Belgium. In 1854, when the Belgian government asked for the small loan of 5 million francs, Belgians subscribed 172 million; there was, said *The Economist*, not only a great confidence in the government, but also 'great abundance of capital in the hands of numerous persons in Belgium'.[25]

European finance, when it could not be obtained on the domestic market, flowed readily between neighbours. For example, most of the foreign finance of Sweden during her accelerated development came from Hamburg and Frankfurt, right up to the point, in the years just before the First World War, when Sweden could command a surplus of capital and satisfy her own financial needs.[26] The attraction of investment in a neighbouring state was overwhelming. Berend and Ránki report that at the beginning of the twentieth century, when the foreign debt of Austria ran to 7 billion crowns (£280 million), Austria herself had a total of 5.2 billion crowns invested abroad, of which no less than 4.7 billion were in neighbouring Hungary and the rest, barely 500 million, mainly in the Balkans.[27] Of the twenty-one banks that formed the syndicate for the financing of Hungarian railways, fifteen were Austrian, and by 1873 the railway system had expanded to 6,253 kilometres.[28] Meanwhile, the Hungarians themselves, as they showed in their response to the first major foreign loan issued by the independent kingdom (£8.5 million of 5 per cents) in 1868, took and held a very large part of their own state debt.[29]

Germany was the best source of funds for Eastern Europe. In the late 1850s and early 1860s, engineers, contractors and financiers were interested in the first generation of Rumanian railways. But interest evaporated after 1866, and the amounts, in any case, were small; the first capital of the Danube and Black Sea railway was £300,000, while £45,000 was all that was raised initially for the Varna line.[30] The Rumanian railway loans of 1868 and 1869 were coldly received in London, but they were taken up with enthusiasm in Berlin and Vienna.[31] 'Les chemins de fer roumains', Jean Bouvier reports, 'sont entre des mains allemandes: le concessionaire et contracteur [Bethel Henry] Stroussberg trouve des crédits auprès des banques berlinoises.'[32]

The independent Kingdom of Rumania owed its existence, in large part, to Napoleon III, and foreign interest in Rumanian finance has traditionally been supposed to have been French. This was, no doubt, the case at the very beginning, and French interest was to increase from the 1890s; but the natural trade links were with Austria and Germany. Dorin Kastris has explained that the Rumanian financial market before the First World War was totally dominated by foreign capital and by foreign banks (more precisely, by Austro-German finance)[33], and it is probably true, as Berend and Ránki have argued, that before the first World War the Balkans never reached the financial independence achieved by Central Europe with the help (initially) of a boost from foreign capital.[34] Certainly, domestic banking in Rumania, Serbia and Bulgaria does not seem to have made substantial progress until after the turn of the century.[35]

As for Italy, there was ample reason for the foreign investor to hold back so long as the country remained a part of the Habsburg Empire. Neither were English investors interested in Italy's efforts to become free. They showed no enthusiasm for Cavour's Anglo-Sardinian loan of 1851, and the business, such as it was, passed from Hambros of London to the Paris Rothschilds.[36] *Independent* Italy was another matter. Foreign interest was delayed by continued uncertainties in the political and economic condition of the new kingdom before the position of Rome was established and the Austro-Prussian war brought Venetia into Italy. However, the speed of Italian development after independence (in railways particularly), and the gigantic deficits in government finance, made an appeal to foreign finance inescapable. It is probable that the new kingdom had not yet gained the complete loyalty and confidence of the domestic investor – Italians had been lending heavily abroad, especially in France. For the time being, if Italy wanted to maintain the momentum of development and to cover her deficits, she had to be prepared to draw a proportion of her financial needs from abroad.

In the early 1860s both London and Paris had shown a taste for the loans of the new government of Italy. The 1863 loan, issued abroad for about £8.5 million nominal, was wildly oversubscribed in both places.[37] But French interest had fallen off by the autumn of 1864, and English investors seem to have dropped Italian securities altogether by then.[38] It was now that the Italians themselves came to take an increasing interest in their own securities. Indeed, when James Rothschild pointed to the tendency of foreign securities generally, within a short space of time, to return to the natives of the borrowing nations (he was giving evidence to the Conseil Supérieur de Commerce in October 1865), one of his examples was precisely the return to Italy of the Neapolitan loans.[39]

This was true enough, and it would have been taken even further if Italy had not been borrowing on such a huge scale. Italy, said *The Times* in 1868, 'has gone at a geometrical rate of speed on her road to ruin'. Government revenues were increasing prodigiously at the time – from £18 million to £43 million in ten years (1862–71) – but they were as yet preceded by the expansion of government expenditure, and taxation was less than half the level experienced in Britain. The yearly deficit from 1860 to 1862 had ranged between £10 and £20 million; the funded debt (£84 million in 1861) had almost quadrupled in five or six years.[40] Foreign investors in Italy, *The Economist* thought in 1870, should be watchful, 'but there is ample excuse for Italian patriots being sanguine'.[41]

In the late 1860s it is difficult to see what attraction Italy might have had for the foreign investor. Italy, said 'Suum cuique' in 1868, had no chance of obtaining money on the London market.[42] In 1869 *The Economist* was deeply pessimistic about the state of Italian credit. Current efforts to raise money for loans to Italy were unlikely to succeed, and unless Italy could somehow achieve receipts level with expenditure, 'nothing short of a declaration of bankruptcy remains'.[43]

The French, perhaps as much for political reasons as economic, were more enthusiastic. The Italian tobacco loan of 1868 – 23 million francs (£9.5 million) in 6 per cents – was fully subscribed in Paris, although it was received less enthusiastically in London, Frankfurt and Berlin.[44] Characteristically, of the 592,000 obligations subscribed, the Italians themselves applied for 200–250,000, the French for nearly 200,000, and England and Germany for the remainder.[45] The Italians were (and continued to be) their nation's best creditors.

Italy borrowed extensively abroad, and in 1879 she was paying foreigners an annual interest of £2.5 million on her debt – 80 per cent in Paris, 13.5 per cent in London, 2.3 per cent in Berlin, and the rest in Vienna, Hamburg, Amsterdam, Frankfurt and St Petersburg.[46] Admittedly, this was a large amount (£41 million, capitalised at 6 per cent), but less so proportionately when the total public debt of Italy at the time, domestic and foreign, was £451 million.[47] Italian investors undoubtedly reabsorbed a large part of such debt as found its way abroad, and in practice, for lack of an alternative, Italians financed their government's huge deficits by bank advances, by the alienation of national property, lands, railroads and ecclesiastical estates, and by forced loans. Up to 1882, state and ecclesiastical property had been disposed of to the value of 888.4 million lire.[48] Much money was made by many. 'For years past', said *The Times*, '[Italy] has been a fine milch cow to the capitalist.'[49] Bloomfield acknowledges that Italy was a net capital importer in the 1860s and 1880s; for most of the other years up to 1914 she was a net capital exporter.[50] The Italian state found some of its resources through foreign loans; it built most of the railways itself, at a cost estimated at as much as £200 million by the end of the century.[51]

But a huge loan instantly raised, like the loan of 1881 (730 million lire nominal), was beyond the capacity of Italians unaided. McGuire, in fact, describes the 1881 loan (an appeal for a total of £21.5 million in cash), as 'the first large-scale foreign borrowing of the new Italian State'. French and English purchases of Italian securities took place in quantity for successive loans, but as McGuire explains, much was repatriated when, in 1906, to the disgust of the foreign investor, Italy converted her 4 and 5 per cent *rentes* to 3.5 per cents.[52] Even before, most must already have returned home. Bolton King, during the discussion that followed his paper on Italian statistics to the Royal Statistical Society in 1903, denied that Paris was the chief market for Italian securities: 'few of them are now held abroad, and the prices at Rome are those commonly quoted'.[53]

In both public and private sectors, Italian banks, as was proper for the birthplace of banking, were powerful and active. Even in the early years of independence, Sackville West reported (January 1862) that commercial transactions were not inhibited in Italy by lack of bank finance; existing capital was 'more or less abundant'.[54] At a later date Bouvier described the 'constellation' of Italian banks – the National Bank of Tuscany, the National Bank of Italy, the International Bank (Genoa), the Italian Crédit Mobilier, the Caisse Générale (Genoa), the Discount Bank of Turin – which, with the cooperation of the *haute banque* of Paris, took part in Italian government loans, railways, the tobacco monopoly and sales of state and ecclesiastical property. Three firms controlled all the great financial operations of the peninsula: the Rothschilds of Paris, the National Bank of Italy and the Italian Crédit Mobilier.[55] The plans of Count Digny, finance minister, for clearing arrears and paying Italy's way to the end of 1873, depended fundamentally on domestic resources – a 300 million franc advance from the company of the *Beni Demaniali* (backed, however, by foreign financiers) on the disposal of church property, a 100 million advance to the Treasury from the National Bank and the Bank of Naples (in return for the privilege of handling the Treasury account), and a forced loan (domestic) of 320 million francs.[56] When a London house like Barings took part in a large operation, as it did when it accepted, with Hambros, a third of the Italian Loan of 1881 (644 million lire), it joined a syndicate under the leadership of the Banca Nationale.

Britain and Austrian Finance

Austria lay at the heart of Continental Europe. She had the privilege of 'vast and varied' resources.[57] She could boast of 'the richest and most varied natural advantages'.[58] Count Mülinen may have been right to suppose that foreigners had more faith than its inhabitants in the riches of the Habsburg Empire, but he himself talked of 'les sources nombreuses de richesse qu'elle [Austria] cache dans son sein'.[59] Certainly there was a private financial sector, the *hofbankiers*, of some power and sophistication at Vienna.

In this respect Austria was like France, and she might have been expected to follow a pattern not dissimilar to France where foreign bankers and foreign capital merely primed the pump for a much larger flow of local enterprise and capital. This was often to be the case, and both the Austrian government and private entrepreneurs were able to draw on domestic capital to a far greater extent than their equivalents in Russia. But Austria, like Russia, had to depend on foreign borrowing to meet what appeared to be a permanent imbalance of expenditure over income, and for Austria the fear of political disturbance placed real limits on what might reasonably be expected from local taxation within an unruly empire.

The inability to raise revenue became very obvious after the disastrous domestic revolutions of 1848–9. At the end of 1848, the Austrian government, which had lost political control, approached London and Amsterdam with an appeal for 80 million florins (£7.3 million). Hope & Co. of Amsterdam were not interested, although anxious on the score of the heavy expenditure of the Austrian War Department. Barings reported that Austrian stock had never been of current sale in London, and nothing was ever done in it; they themselves had thrown cold water on all such proposals from European governments because they did not see their way clearly in European politics, and because they believed that they could hold US securities with greater safety and in some cases with as much profit. British investors, should they again become interested in Continental securities (after the shock of the revolutions of 1848), were more likely to prefer French to Austrian stock at the same price:

> France has perhaps double the amount of interest to pay annually but its resources are more concentrated and available. Austria drives a

> motley team of dependencies which may not move quietly together and she may have to go through some ordeals through which France has already passed.[60]

When Hope & Co. protested that Austria was more lightly taxed than France and that the political situation in France was very precarious, Barings replied that it would not be easy to establish a uniform system of taxation throughout the Austrian dependencies; it was sometimes more difficult to introduce and enforce moderate taxation in countries unused to it than to increase a heavier level of taxation in countries already much burdened.[61]

Austria was no favourite of the foreign investor. Britons were the least enthusiastic of all. When Philip von Krausz, Austrian Finance Minister, opened a subscription for 85 million florins (£7.7 million) in 5 per cents in September 1851, he offered it for sale in Amsterdam, Antwerp, Berlin, Brussels, Frankfurt, Hamburg, Paris and Vienna. London was deliberately omitted. At that moment, London prospects could hardly have been less promising. Kossuth, the Hungarian patriot, was expected in October, and popular feeling ran so high that General Haynau, the 'butcher of Hungary', was mobbed by the draymen at Messrs Barclay and Perkin's brewery; his visit was described as a 'wanton insult to the people of this country' in Palmerston's 'apology' to the Austrian ambassador. Kossuth was not forgotten. Austria's Rothschild loan of 1852, £3.5 million in 5 per cents at 90, was 'received very coolly by the financial community here [London]',[62] as it was by British investors at large; only the power of the name of Rothschild persuaded a few London bankers to be more receptive.[63]

The prime investor in Austrian government securities was still domestic. Britons in the 1850s invested modest amounts in such enterprises as the Empress Elizabeth railway (the Western of Austria) and the Tergove mines. British contractors and engineers took part in the construction of Austrian railways. Charles Waring, the well-known contractor, signed a contract with the Royal Hungarian government in November 1868 to build the Transylvanian system of railways (640 kilometres) with a government guarantee of interest.[64] But the money for the Hungarian railway loan of July 1868 (£6 million), originally contracted in Paris, seems very largely to have been raised in Austria and Hungary.[65]

British investors did not like autocrats, as the Tsar of Russia discovered. Nor did they like bullies. They took no part in the Austrian 'silver' loan of 1864 – 70 million florins (£6.4 million) issued in Vienna with interest payable in Amsterdam, Berlin, Frankfurt, London and Paris. British public opinion refused to leave what Charles Klein, Barings' Vienna correspondent, called 'its pets, the Danes' to the mercy of Prussia and Austria; British investors were not in the least inclined to help the Austrian government, already virtually bankrupt, to maintain its political influence by aggression and violence abroad.[66] Nor were they interested in private investment. Even during a period of exceptional enthusiasm in foreign banking securities, London investors 'were slow to take up the shares' of the Anglo-Austrian Bank when it came first to the market in 1863.[67] The 'extreme unpopularity' of the Habsburgs among Britons was remarked upon by *The Economist* some years later.[68] In common with Russia and Spain, Austria in 1867 'cannot borrow a sixpence in Lombard Street'.[69]

After decades of unsatisfactory business, Thomas Baring told Klein that British investors had never liked Austrian securities; by the summer of 1868 his own firm no longer held Austrian stock.[70] It was not so much that Britain had 'lost interest' in Austria and Italy after 1870;[71] she had never had any interest to lose. For Austria, or for anywhere else at the time, Hobson cannot be right in saying that 'British energy and the British purse were always available at a price'.[72] Sir Robert Giffen described Austria as one of the countries 'more or less formed by the capital of England and of other old countries', and by the investment of private English capitalists within their territories, principally in the form of English iron and manufacturers.[73] He thought that in 1878 about one-fifth of the public loans of Austria and Italy and as much as half of the Lombardo-Venetian railway were held in the United Kingdom.[74] This was not the case.

Philip Cottrell has written persuasively about the affairs of the Anglo-Austrian Bank, but perhaps the existence of a successful foreign bank, which brought little in the way of British capital into what was already a powerful financial market, does not, ultimately, tell us so very much about 'Anglo-European capital flows'.[75]

The Continent and Austrian Finance

Where, then, did Austria obtain such foreign finance as she needed? France, as a wealthy and powerful neighbour, was more obviously attracted to Austrian finance than Britain. French capital was deeply interested in Austrian railway development. Cameron reports that of the 200 million francs (£8 million) originally subscribed in the mid-1850s to the Austrian State Railway Company, 45 million were provided by Austrians and the rest by the Crédit Mobilier and by its associates in France.[76] Furthermore, he quotes James Rothschild as saying, at the end of 1858, that the French share in the 1 billion francs (£40 million) invested in the other great railway system of contemporary Austria (the Rothschilds' South Austrian, Lombardo-Venetian and Central Italian railway) was 600 million francs.[77]

Rothschild is an unimpeachable source, and the rivalry between the Rothschilds of Paris and the Crédit Mobilier must certainly have brought more French capital to Austria than would otherwise have been the case. Neither, however, was interested solely in the mobilisation of *French* capital for Austrian railways. James Rothschild himself preferred to attract domestic capital rather than foreign, in Austria as in contemporary Spain; an interest among domestic investors was more secure, and more helpful in defending an enterprise within domestic politics. The furious speculation that overtook Austrian railway investment in 1856 – the first year in which such railway securities appeared on the open market – was almost entirely Austrian and German.

The limitless resources released on the Vienna market during and after the autumn of 1855 were, of course, largely fictitious. It is enough to look at the subscription list for the Rothschilds' Credit Anstalt, a *crédit mobilier* type of concession won against the competition of Isaac Périère: 15 million florins were offered for sale in December 1855, and so feverish was the competition among subscribers that the police and army had to be called in to maintain order. The subscriptions, which closed after five days, reached the bizarre total of 644.5 million florins (£58.6 million).[78]

Viennese speculation reached its climax with the Credit Anstalt; it was North German capital that fed the flames during the subsequent speculation in Austrian railways. The new railway shares were not held in Paris, and only partially in Vienna; most of them found their way to Berlin, Breslau and other North German markets. When North Germany, glutted with Austrian railways securities and with new projects of her own, began to unload in the autumn of 1856, all the life went out of Austrian railway stock. A mass of Austrian paper was thrown back on the Vienna market.

Subsequently, Rothschilds and the Crédit Mobilier unloaded some part of this railway paper on Paris. But Roger Catin is wrong to imagine that French investors were really interested in Austrian state securities.[79] When Paris was approached early in 1864 for an Austrian state loan, Henry Hottinguer and his Paris friends agreed that a Paris quotation would be of use merely for speculation. The French public would not take an Austrian loan at any price: 'jamais et à aucune époque les fonds Autrichiens n'ont pu se vendre ici.'[80] It was not, in fact, until the following year (1865) that the French first showed interest in Austrian government securities.

An Austrian loan of 150 million florins nominal (100 million actual) was brought out jointly by the Comptoir d'Escompte of Paris and the Crédit Foncier Autrichien in the last week of November 1865. It was coldly received in London and in Amsterdam, and only 8 million florins were subscribed in Austria. But in France there was an astonishing reversal of public attitudes. On this occasion, with an ample disposable capital in France, the prospect of a real rate of interest of 8½ per cent and the aid of the Comptoir d'Escompte (with its mastery over the financial press and its loyal following among the trading community of France and the small capitalists), nearly the whole amount was taken on the first day, and the loan, when closed, was oversubscribed by 20 per cent.[81] For French investors the 1865 loan was not a particularly happy introduction to Austrian finance. The Austro-Prussian war put a stop to all business in 1866, mopped up the proceeds of the loan and put Austrian finances right back where they started. The only people to come out of it well were the promoters, whose profits (perhaps unrealistically) were calculated at 28.5 million florins (£2.6 million).[82]

Foreign investment in the Habsburg Empire came largely from Holland, Belgium and Germany. Frankfurt especially, but also Berlin, kept a close watch on Austrian securities. The Dutch were described as having a 'special predilection for Austrian securities'.[83] Ernest Seyd thought that the greater part of the Austro-Hungarian state debt (which he calculated at £346 million) was held abroad in 1876.[84] But this was an exaggeration, as was Giffen's estimate of a British share of 10 per cent of the Austrian debt in the mid-1880s – i.e. at least £30 million.[85] The real distribution was shown at the time of the 'conversion' of the Austrian public debt in 1868: the amount of the debt held abroad was 1,007.5 billion florins (£91.6 million), of which the Dutch held 426 million, the Germans 292 million, Belgians 156 million, French 109 million, and Britons only 17 million (£1.5 million).[86] The total debt, home and foreign, was about £300 million.[87]

Public Loans

Two-thirds, then, of the state debt of Austria at the end of the 1860s were owned by the Austrians themselves. By the end of the century, Austrians were described as holding virtually all of their *state* securities; Austria now had the means to finance her own government.[88]

In practice Austrians had always taken a large share of their state securities. The 1849 loan of 71 million florins was too expensive for London, at 85 for a 4½ per cent stock. It would not have sold to Britons even if Richard Cobden had resisted the temptation to describe it as an 'attempt to lay upon the earnings of peaceful industry the means of paying Haynau and his Croats for their butcheries in Brescia and their atrocities in Hungary . . . atrocities in which Haynau had surpassed everything that has occurred since the persecutions of the Middle Ages'.[89] Dutch investors were also to find the price too high, and such sales as were made were domestic.[90] Similarly, the Austrian loan of 1851 was a total failure abroad: almost the whole of the 56 million florins subscribed to the 85 millions requested was by the Austrians themselves.[91]

Austria came repeatedly to international markets, and in the early 1850s sales in Frankfurt and Amsterdam of Austrian 5 per cent silver florin stock, issued at exceptionally favourable terms in a desperate effort to raise foreign currency, went off briskly in both markets.[92] But these were small loans to cover short-term needs. The real test of Austria's ability to meet her mounting deficits (although not, as yet, to discharge her other objectives of currency reform, the resumption of cash payments and the completion of railways) came with the great national loan of June–September 1854: 500 million florins were to be raised in a single operation, and subscriptions by mid-September had reached 510 million (£46.4 million). The majority was for speculation, and the true limit to Austrian capacity was shown when the speculators, who were given a long period for paying up instalments, were forced even then to sell as instalments came due. The loan fell to a heavy discount. Between 200 and 250 million florins, more than half the net proceeds, had still to be paid in by November 1855.[93]

What was left to the government vanished in military expenditure, while Austria stood on the sidelines of the Crimean war. Three army corps were stationed in Hungary in the autumn of 1853, and four in Galicia from April 1854. By September, the Russians were collecting strong forces in Poland and evidently intended a demonstration on the Austrian frontier. After 2 December 1854 Austria was aligned with the Allies. She was still at peace, but her army expenses were nearly as great as if war had already broken out, and were said to exceed 25 million florins a month.[94]

So long as Austria remained politically disturbed, at home and abroad, foreign investors stayed clear. The Minister of Finance printed money, issued small internal loans at 9–10 per cent effective interest, suspended cash payments at the National Bank and diverted its resources to the government, and withheld interest on the national war loans. Austria stumbled from one expedient to another.

On 23 April 1860 Baron von Bruck was dismissed on suspicion of complicity in some gigantic frauds among members of the Trieste Exchange and in the commissariat for the Italian campaign; a few hours later, he cut his throat – 'a lamentable sacrifice to the fruitless financiering of that age'.[95] Bruck was a man of commercial experience and financial vision. His successor, State Councillor Ignaz von Plener, was unknown to the financial world.

The whole period 1857–66 has been labelled as the 'Plener Stagnation', which is true enough of the Habsburg economy as a whole, but which hardly describes the frantic and generally futile activity of the

Ministry of Finance. Plener and the head of his loan department, Baron Brentano, knocked at every door. They borrowed money at high rates of interest against the deposit of unsold stock in the 1864 silver loan (or against anything else that came to hand). They tried to sell the Crown Domains for 60 million florins to several different groups of financiers, one of which included Barings and Hope & Co.[96] They negotiated temporary loans of one kind or another from every quarter at practically any price. Klein reported at the end of May 1865 that estimates for the budget deficit ranged from 25 to 60 million florins, depending on whether the Minister intended to cover the deficit only for 1865 or also for 1866; a few days later, Plener was asking the Reichsrat for supplementary credits amounting to 117 million florins cash to cover his wants for 1865 and 1866, including the debt to the National Bank.[97] Thomas Baring, writing to thank Charles Klein for the difficult and disagreeable agency he had undertaken on Barings' behalf, added characteristically:

> It would seem to us that those who manage the finances of Austria wish to be too clever and to drive too hard bargains. They will treat with everybody and anybody and being suspicious of all none have any confidence in them, and the consequence is that in times of pressing emergency they have no friends on whom they can rely and must become the victims of those who know their wants, and choose to make the most out of them.[98]

Plener admitted to a government deficit of just under 117 million florins in his statement of 8 June 1865. An internal memorandum in the Baring papers points out that, under cover of the different headings in Plener's statement, about 28 million florins were required to meet secret debts unauthorised by the Reichsrat. With a rapidly decreasing income from taxation, and the interest to be paid on 117 million, the whole amount of the deficit would be brought to something not far short of 150 million, for which 250 million florins nominal would be required should it prove possible to issue a 5 per cent loan at 60.[99]

The memorandum proved remarkably accurate. Plener was dismissed when his Ministry resigned at the end of July 1865 in protest against the Emperor's conciliatory policy towards Hungary. The purpose of a floating debt, Mülinen explained, was to make resources available, at a given moment, when circumstances did not admit a regular appeal to national credit; Austrian finance ministers from 1848 to 1865 were often compelled to make this kind of indirect appeal to credit by issuing short-term Treasury bonds and by printing money.[100] Plener's successor, Count Johann Larisch-Mönnich, appointed Baron von Becke to Brentano's post and instructed him to re-open negotiations specifically with Barings for a London loan.

In a memorandum in which he set out the needs of the Austrian Empire, Becke explained that a net amount of 150 million florins would be required to restore an equilibrium between revenue and expenditure, of which 90 million had to be raised within the next few weeks, and 60 million could be brought out as a second series a bit later. Most of the loan was to be raised outside the Empire. Becke thought that although money in Austria was scarce the loan's 'highly patriotic character' would enable him to place 25–30 million florins among wealthy people in Austria.[101]

This at last was the comprehensive measure that Thomas Baring had been advising – sufficiently large to settle all outstanding claims, to put an end to the system of constant borrowing for short periods in all quarters, to cover the deficits for 1865 and 1866, and to restore confidence in the financial stability and credit of the Empire. Pending a loan, Barings, Hope & Co. and the Anglo-Austrian Bank agreed to advance £1.2 million, and they accepted the Minister's suggestion that they should unite with Rothschilds. Neither Barings nor Rothschilds were convinced in October 1865 that the time was ripe for a major loan. Baron James believed that very little support could be expected in France, while Frankfurt and Vienna were overloaded with Austrian securities. Furthermore, Rothschild used the opportunity, without consulting Barings, to demand twenty years of freedom from income tax for the Lombardy railway system of which he was president – a total of 28 million florins remission whether Rothschilds took the loan or simply made an advance. Becke, who had been approached by a number of financial groups in Paris while waiting six weeks for Rothschild to make up his mind, finally refused these 'exigences exorbitantes' and on 2 November gave the business to others.[102]

The Comptoir d'Escompte's loan of 1865 was, as we have seen, a great success with the French investor – the first of its kind. But this successful appeal to a new group of foreign investors was simply a flash in the pan. The great financial crisis of 1866 (the Overend-Gurney crisis) shut off the London market. The Austro-Prussian war closed the markets of the Continent. The forced conversion and partial repudiation of the Austrian public debt by the financial law of 1868 cut off Paris and Amsterdam, by now the most promising openings for new financial operations. The London Stock Exchange, too, was closed to Austrian securities. Austria, once more, was forced back on herself.

The profound pessimism of the foreign investor was not shared necessarily by the Austrians themselves. The government was always in trouble, and its deficits were notorious throughout Europe. But the economy experienced periods of industrial and railway investment in 1850–7 and particularly in 1867–73. Sustained growth, David

Good thinks, began with the 1860s.[103] Although much was fairy gold, and vanished with the collapse of the Vienna Stock Exchange in May 1873, there was a solid basis: exports of cereals from Austria–Hungary, which were a bare 4 million cwt in 1856, were estimated at 33–36 million in 1868; Hungary was building her own railways in 1868; payments on state guarantees to Austrian railways were reduced to £100,000.[104] In January 1870, *The Economist*, no friend of Austria, referred to 'the surprising material development of the Austrian States during the last three years'.[105] The splendid harvest of 1867 had 'at once repaired the losses of the Sadowa Campaign [the Austro-Prussian war] the previous year, and gave the country a start'.[106] *The Times* reported in January 1872 that Austrian state revenue had risen by 18 per cent since 1868 and that, unless there were further political disturbances, 'there is little doubt of the equilibrium between revenue and expenditure being permanently established'.[107]

Domestic Financial Resources

The chronic afflictions of the Austrian government, under-financed as always for the imperial role that it chose to maintain, should not be permitted to conceal the real strength of Vienna's private finance. The Viennese Stock Exchange had shown much spirit in the 1850s. During the second great boom of the late 1860s, *The Times* heard from its special correspondent at Vienna – 'not without surprise' – that Vienna, after London and Paris, was by then (1869) probably the first money market in Europe.[108] A huge Ottoman railway loan (£20 million) was reported in 1869 as very strongly supported in Austria.[109] Berend and Ránki have explained how, after 1848, Austria had begun to put her capital into Hungary, mainly into railways, navigation and mining; Austrian capital thus anticipated the flow of Western European capital to Eastern Europe by several decades.[110] Yet Austrian finance, at any rate before the world financial crash of 1873 (which originated, as it happened, in Vienna), was interested in great financial operations that lay well beyond her immediate neighbours. Reuters reported from Versailles on 9 November 1872 that representatives of all the great Austrian banking houses had arrived to offer M. Thiers a financial combination guaranteeing to Germany the fifth milliard (£40 million) of the war indemnity.[111]

The bankers of Vienna, the *hofbankiers*, which were family businesses, seem to Jean Bouvier (the historian of the Crédit Lyonnais) to have held on to their power against modern banks more effectively than the Parisian *haute banque*.[112] As far back as 1823 the Vienna houses, in collaboration with Salomon Rothschild (himself of

Vienna), were able to offer better terms than London for an Austrian government loan of 30 million florins.[113]

Indeed, it would have been difficult for a foreign banker to make much impression in Vienna before the 1840s. During the 1830s Baron Sina monopolised Austrian government finance, and he was said to have been worth nearly 20 million florins (£1.8 million) by the end of the decade; Arnstein and Eskeles, a rival Viennese house, had command of 3–4 million.[114] The resources of the *hofbankiers* were such that neither Hope & Co. nor Barings could be persuaded to enter into hostile competition when the charter of the Austrian National Bank came up for renewal; the management and direction, they argued, must evidently rest with influential resident bankers, and it would be both impolitic for the government to give a charter to foreign bankers and hazardous to undertake it without the cooperation of some strong national interest.[115]

In September 1840 a severe banking crisis in Vienna destroyed a number of the banks and permanently weakened others, notably Arnstein and Eskeles. Rothschilds, through their Vienna and Frankfurt houses, took the lead in Austrian government finance, although still working in association with the Viennese bankers. Further heavy losses were experienced in the collapse of railway speculation in Germany and Austria, which, in the mid 1840s, was described as having engrossed the minds of the community at large and distracted its attention from other, more legitimate pursuits. The shares of the Milan–Venice railway, for which only the Venice bridge and 13 kilometres had been completed after five or six years of work, had been puffed by speculation to a 33 per cent premium in 1845, and they were held almost entirely in Vienna. Others went much higher and, when speculation ceased, Viennese speculators and investors were left with depreciated shares on their hands, against which they had borrowed and on which much of the capital had still to be called.

Viennese bankers lost heavily by the failures at Karlsruhe and Frankfurt in January 1848 – Arnstein and Eskeles to the extent of nearly a million guilders in Frankfurt – and the fall and flight of Metternich in March 1848, with Vienna in the hands of the revolution until October, shattered whatever confidence remained. In the riots, mutiny and murder of early October 1848, Salomon Rothschild fled from Vienna, leaving his business in the hands of two clerks. He never returned. James Rothschild, himself shaken in confidence and fortune by the financial and political crises of 1848–9, continued to take an interest in Austrian affairs, but it was some years before the Vienna Rothschilds were re-established, under the leadership of Salomon's eldest son, Anselme.

Political disaster seriously damaged the *hofbankiers*; it did not destroy them. The Crédit Lyonnais thought seriously of doing business in Austria–Hungary at the end of the 1860s. But the competition of the private bankers of Vienna and of the great Austrian credit institutions was too formidable: 'on ne saurait attaquer de front une telle forteresse.'[116] Berend and Ránki date the new era in Austrian banking from 1855, the foundation of the Credit Anstalt:

> As in Germany, so also and even more in the cis-Leithan [Austrian] parts of the Monarchy, banks may be said to have been the primary force in financing the economic development and the modern economic transformation. The famous Austrian *haute finance* actually became the master of the economy.[117]

The figures are impressive. Total bank deposits in Austria and Bohemia in 1880 amounted to 1.5 billion crowns (£60 million); they were 2.6 billion (£152 million) by the end of the century.[118] In Hungary over the same period, bank deposits amounted to 610.5 million crowns (£24.4 million) in 1880, 1.1 billion in 1890 and 1.8 billion (£72 million) in 1900, when share capital and reserve funds added a further 833.4 million to Hungarian bank resources.[119] For Austria, the capital of the various joint stock banks, industrial undertakings, railways, etc. in 1870 was calculated at £104 million, which included neither debentures (nearly £60 million for railways) nor mortgages (£11.8 million for banks).[120]

With such resources it was natural that Austrian railways, more so even than Austrian state securities, were funded at home. By the end of 1847, Austria had 1,632 kilometres of railway in operation, almost as much as contemporary France (1,817 kilometres). It would appear that the capital for what was, in spite of an ultra-conservative system of government, a period of some progress in communications (road, river and railway), and in manufacturing industry generally, must fundamentally have been domestic.[121] The state owned 70 per cent of the railways by 1854, when the policy was reversed, state lines were sold off and private capital (subsidised by the state) took charge.[122] On 31 December 1875 the whole railway system of Austria–Hungary amounted to 10,217 miles, built at the cost of £229 million.[123]

Milward and Saul identify the great Credit Anstalt as a 'prime agent in financing the main line railways built before 1873', and they detect, as the main source of capital for railway development generally in the late 1850s and 1860s, 'investment banks based on the model of the Crédit Mobilier or the Darmstadter Bank'.[124] However, their conclusion that 'France was the major source of the capital flowing into the railway system, from the construction of the *Südbahn* onwards',[125] is less plausible, although shared by Rondo Cameron.[126]

Frenchmen played an important part in the construction and financing of Austrian railways, often indirectly through a credit institution like the Crédit Mobilier. But the ambition of the Paris Rothschilds was to mobilise *domestic* resources. Germany and Austria financed the greater part of their own and each other's railways. The Paris correspondent of *The Economist* reported in October 1868 that the shares of the Vienna–Prague railway (the North–West railway of Austria), of which much had been said for some time past in London and Paris, were so much in favour in Austria and Germany that they were not even advertised in Paris.[127] The experience was familiar. There was, it seems, an 'abundance of money seeking investment' in Austria in the late 1860s; *The Economist* reported in November 1868 that the latest issue of railway shares in Austria had been oversubscribed twenty-fold.[128]

Conclusion

Philip Cottrell expresses merely the conventional wisdom when he argues that, throughout the nineteenth century, the Habsburg Empire experienced a shortage of domestic capital, and that consequently both its government and indigenous industry were dependent on foreign funds. He cites the mounting total of state loans, which left the government, it seems, with an external indebtedness of £300 million in 1867.[129] Yet the figure for actual state indebtedness abroad, as shown by the 'conversion' of 1868, was only about £100 million, with a further £200 million of the state debt held within Austria herself. Clearly, the greater part of the state issues were taken at home.

All the same, Austria needed the assistance of foreign finance during these decades. *The Economist's* correspondent in Vienna reported in October 1852 that the government had borrowed so much of the disposable capital of the country that private individuals were having difficulty in finding loans.[130] It was a problem encountered so often elsewhere. Huge government deficits continued, totalling 575 million florins (£52.3 million) from 1860 to 1866. The Austro-Prussian war added 374 million florins to the consolidated debt and another 309 million to the unfunded debt. Should greater facilities have been afforded for the introduction on a large scale of foreign capital and enterprise? *The Economist* thought so. Austria, its correspondent said in 1867, had not obtained anything like the foreign assistance 'so lavishly rendered' to Spain and Italy, and yet she possessed far greater resources than either, and offered greater security.[131]

To some extent, Austria was slow to make full use of her own resources. A special correspondent of *The Times* in Vienna reminded his readers yet again in July 1869 of the marvellous boost to the economy delivered by the political settlement with Hungary – the Dual Monarchy of 1867. Two years earlier, Vienna had counted for nothing in international finance: 'nobody dreamt that there was any capital accumulated in the country, and everyone sighed after capital from abroad.'[132] Perhaps this was the reason why Austria borrowed more from abroad than she need have done.

London and Paris financial houses made substantial advances to the Austrian government. In May 1864, Barings alone were in advance to the Austrian government for as much as £746,000.[133] French credit institutions channelled French money indirectly into Austrian railways, although direct investment in Austrian public securities made no significant progress among Frenchman before 1865. Where foreigners took an interest in state and railway securities, they were likely to have been Austria's northerly neighbours – Dutchmen, Germans and Belgians. Austria, says Roger Catin, made many appeals to the Paris capital market after 1852, which 'jamais ne restaient sans echo'; Austro- Hungarian *rentes* from before 1870 were held in large part in France.[134] He was wrong. In spite of everything, state loans, banks and even railways were financed principally within the Empire, and there can be no doubt that land, building and manufacturing found their money at home.

Notes

1 *House of Commons Debates*, 15 March 1830, p.335.
2 Speaking in the Commons, 1869, and quoted by C. A. Macartney, *The Habsburg Empire, 1790–1918* (London, 1968), p.V.
3 *House of Commons Debates*, 2 March 1824, p. 691.
4 Comte de Mülinen, *Les Finances de l'Autriche* (Paris, 1875), p. 166.
5 Bertrand Gille, *La Banque et le Crédit en France de 1815 à 1848* (Paris, 1959), p. 226.
6 Mülinen, *Les Finances de l'Autriche*, p. 166.
7 L. Girard, 'Transport', in H. J. Habakkuk and M. Postan, eds, *The Cambridge economic history of Europe,* Vol. VI, (Cambridge, 1965), p. 238.
8 Tom Kemp, *Industrialisation in nineteenth century Europe* (London, 1969), p. 94.
9 Bernard Hebeler, 'Railways in Prussia and other continental states, at the close of the year 1848', *Journal of the Statistical Society*, 13:1 (February 1850), p. 79.
10 R. H. Tilly, 'Capital formation in Germany in the nineteenth century', in Peter Mathias and M. M. Postan, eds, *The Cambridge economic history of Europe*, Vol. VII, pt 1 (Cambridge, 1978), p. 415.
11 Girard, 'Transport', p. 238. H. M. Jagtiani includes a useful discussion of Prussian government policy towards railway development and finance in his book: *The role of the state in the provision of railways* (London, 1924). More recently, the stages in increased state finance for Prussian railways, culminating by 1914 in state ownership for practically the entire German railway system, have been described (for Prussia 1815–70) by W. O. Henderson, *The state and the industrial revolution in Prussia, 1740–1870* (Liverpool, 1958), pp. 150–89.

12 Girard, 'Transport', and Theodore S. Hamerow, *Restoration, revolution and reaction: economics and politics in Germany, 1815–1871* (Princeton, NJ, 1958, p. 6). The share of state investment in the financing, in Germany, of railways, canals, roads, river improvement, etc. is described by Wolfram Fischer, 'The strategy of public investment in XIXth. century Germany', *Journal of European Economic History*, 6:2 (Fall 1977), pp. 431–42.
13 Hamerow, *Restoration, revolution and reaction*, p. 8.
14 David Landes, 'Industrialisation and economic development in nineteenth century Germany', *First international conference of economic history* (Paris, 1960), p. 85.
15 R. Dudley Baxter, 'The recent progress of national debts', *Journal of the Statistical Society*, 37:1 (March 1874), p. 13.
16 *The Economist*, 17 December 1870, p. 1523; 14 January 1871, p. 46; 11 February 1871, p. 174.
17 'Suum cuique', in a long letter answering a leading article on rules for foreign lending: *The Economist*, 5 September 1868, p. 1023.
18 K.-G. Hildebrand, 'Labour and capital in the Scandinavian countries in the nineteenth and twentieth centuries', in Mathias and Postan, *The Cambridge economic history of Europe*, p. 607.
19 Arthur I. Bloomfield, *Short-term capital movements under the pre-1914 gold standard* (Princeton, NJ, 1963), p. 50.
20 Lars G. Sandberg, 'Banking and economic growth in Sweden before World War I', *Journal of Economic History*, 38:3 (September 1978), p. 655.
21 Arthur I. Bloomfield, *Patterns of fluctuation in international investment before 1914* (Princeton, NJ, 1968), p. 11.
22 G. R. Porter, *The progress of the nation* (London, 1851 edn), p. 366.
23 Lars-Erik Hedin, 'Some notes on the financing of the Swedish railroads, 1860–1914', *Economy and History*, 10 (1967), p. 19. As he says, some allowance must also be made for the foreign capital that reached Swedish railways through the medium of Swedish government loans.
24 Ernest Seyd, 'The fall in the price of silver, its consequences and their possible avoidance', *Journal of the Society of Arts*, 24 (10 March 1876), p. 309.
25 *The Economist*, 1 July 1854, p. 712.
26 Erin Elver Fleetwood, *Sweden's capital imports and exports* (Geneva, 1947), p. 27.
27 Iván T. Berend and György Ránki, *Economic development in East–Central Europe in the 19th and 20th centuries* (trans. New York, 1974), p. 98.
28 Iván T. Berend and György Ránki, *Hungary: a century of economic development* (Newton Abbot, 1974), pp. 36–8.
29 *The Economist*, 1 February 1868, pp. 116, 123; 5 February 1868, p. 152.
30 J. H. Jensen and Gerhard Rosegger, 'British railway builders along the lower Danube, 1856–1869', *Slavonic and East European Review*, 46:106 (January 1968), p. 119.
31 *The Economist*, 1 May 1869, p. 508.
32 Jean Bouvier, *Le Crédit Lyonnais de 1863 à 1882*, Vol. II (Paris, 1961), p. 510.
33 Dorin Kastris, *Les Capitaux étrangers dans la finance Roumaine* (Paris, thesis, 1921), p. 10. Kastris knew what he was talking about, but it seems that he underestimated French financial interest in Rumania for the decades before the war. Berend and Ránki have calculated that foreign financial credits to the Rumanian government had reached 1.7 billion francs (£68 million) by the outbreak of the war, of which 52 per cent was German, but a further 32 per cent French: *Economic development in East–Central Europe*, p. 106.
34 Berend and Ránki, *Economic development in East–Central Europe*, p. 111.
35 ibid., pp. 67–9.

36 J. D. Scott, 'Hambro and Cavour', *History Today*, 19:10 (October 1969), pp. 696–703.
37 Bertrand Gille, *Les Investissements français en Italie, 1815–1914* (Turin, 1968), pp. 182–3.
38 ibid., pp. 197–8.
39 Baron Rothschild's evidence was quoted in full in *The Economist*; this particular passage appeared in the issue for 3 March 1866, p. 255.
40 *The Times*, 22 January 1868, p. 8e.
41 *The Economist*, 30 April 1870, p. 536.
42 *The Economist*, 5 September 1868, p. 1023.
43 *The Economist*, 1 May 1869, p. 508.
44 *The Economist*, 10 October 1868, p. 1166.
45 *The Economist*, 17 October 1868, p. 1194.
46 Leone Levi, 'The economic progress of Italy during the last twenty years', *Journal of the Statistical Society*, 45:1 (March 1882), p. 14.
47 ibid., p. 12. Herbert Feis reports that the French owned over 80 per cent of the consolidated debt held abroad in 1884 (about 2 billion francs: £80 million): *Europe: the world's banker, 1870–1914* (New York, 1965 edn), p. 235. The figure seems implausible if Leone Levi was right for 1879.
48 Shepherd B. Clough, *The economic history of modern Italy* (New York, 1964), p. 50.
49 *The Times*, 29 April 1869, p. 10d.
50 Bloomfield, *Patterns of fluctuation*, p. 11. Bloomfield prints a table of net inflows/outflows of capital for Italy for the period 1861–1913 (his Appendix I).
51 Bolton King, 'Statistics of Italy', *Journal of the Royal Statistical Society*, 66:2 (June 1903), p. 224.
52 Constantine E. McGuire, *Italy's international economic position* (New York, 1927), pp. 360–2.
53 Comment and reply, King, 'Statistics of Italy', p. 271.
54 Mr Sackville West, Report on the Public Debt etc. of Italy: Parliamentary Papers (hereafter 'P.P.'), 1862, LVIII, p. 377.
55 Bouvier, *Crédit Lyonnais*, p. 532.
56 *The Times*, 29 April 1869, p. 10d.
57 *The Economist*, 10 August 1867, p. 907.
58 Report by Mr Fane, H.M.'s Secretary of Embassy, on the Manufactures, Commerce etc. of Austria: P.P., 1862, LVIII, p. 329.
59 Mülinen, *Finances de l'Autriche*, pp. 9, 144.
60 Barings to Hope & Co., 5 January 1849: Baring, PLB 1849.
61 Barings to Hope & Co., 13 January 1849: Baring, PLB 1849 (Hope & Co.'s correspondence is in Baring, HC 8.1).
62 Gresham Omnium, *A handy guide to safe investments* (London, 1858), p. 47.
63 *The Economist*, 3 July 1852, p. 734.
64 *The Times*, 7 November 1868, p. 5b.
65 *The Times*, 9 December 1868, p. 10e.
66 The correspondence with Barings for the silver loan of 1864 and for the subsequent issue (after the loan's complete failure) of exchequer bonds is in Baring, HC 8.1, HC 9.25, HC 9.26, HC 9.27 and PLB 1864.
67 P. L. Cottrell, 'London financiers and Austria, 1863–1875: the Anglo-Austrian Bank', *Business History*, 11:2 (June 1969), p. 113.
68 *The Economist*, 16 March 1867, p. 297.
69 *The Economist*, 14 September 1867, p. 1038.
70 Thomas Baring to Charles Klein, 23 May 1868: Baring, PLB 1868.
71 L. H. Jenks, *The migration of British capital to 1875* (London, 1971 edn), p. 281.
72 Hobson, *Export of capital*, p. 98.
73 Robert Giffen, *Essays in finance* (London, 1880), pp. 111–12.

74 Robert Giffen, 'Recent accumulations of capital in the United Kingdom', *Journal of the Statistical Society*, 41:1 (March 1878), Appendix V, p. 31.

75 Cottrell, 'London financiers and Austria', p. 114.

76 Rondo E. Cameron, 'The Crédit Mobilier and the economic development of France', *Journal of Political Economy*, 61:6 (December 1953), p. 466.

77 ibid., p. 469.

78 Bertrand Gille, *Histoire de la maison Rothschild*, Vol. II (Geneva, 1967), p.240.

79 Roger Catin, *Le Portefeuille étranger de la France entre 1870 et 1914* (Paris, thesis, 1927), pp. 18, 119. Berend and Ránki share the same view: *Economic Development in East–Central Europe*, p. 96.

80 Henri Hottinguer to Thomas Baring, 5 January 1864: Baring, HC 7.1.

81 Some correspondence for these negotiations is to be found in Baring, HC 7.1, HC 8.1, HC 9.26 and PLB 1865. Both Barings and Rothschilds had originally been approached to handle this loan, but had been supplanted, after much dithering by the Austrians, by the Comptoir d'Escompte.

82 *The Economist*'s Paris correspondent published an interesting comment on the new issue, 25 November 1865, p. 1427 ('any affair brought out under the auspices of the Comptoire d'Escompte is indeed sure of success').

83 Report by Mr Julian Fane, H.M.'s Secretary of Legation, on the National Debt of Austria, dated Vienna, 19 July 1860: P.P., 1861, LXIII, p. 181.

84 Seyd, 'The fall in the price of silver', pp. 309, 313.

85 Robert Giffen, *The growth of capital* (London, 1889), p. 161.

86 Mülinen, *Finances de l'Autriche*, p. 166. Mülinen's figures are preferable to some of the earlier statements since the conversion itself was not completed until 1 January 1874. Figures like those published in *The Economist* (6 March 1869, p. 271) turned out to be reasonably accurate for the British component (estimated at £2 million) but misleading for Holland (£100 million) and Belgium (£75 million). After the 1870s, French investors are said to have reached second place after Germany in their ownership of Austrian securities (Germany 48.5 per cent, France 32.8 per cent of Austro-Hungarian securities held abroad; Britons owned only 6.2 per cent): Bernard Michel, 'Les Capitaux français en Autriche au début du XXe siècle', in Maurice Lévy-Leboyer, ed., *La Position international de la France: aspects économiques et financières XIXe–XXe siècles* (Paris, 1977), pp. 227–8.

87 *Investor's Monthly Manual*, 28 December 1872, p. 409.

88 *Investor's Chronicle*, 7 (April 1900), p. 236.

89 Cobden's letter on the Austrian loan was reprinted in *The Economist*, 29 September 1849, p.1075.

90 Barings (London) and Hope & Co. (Amsterdam) were asked to take care of foreign sales. The correspondence is in Baring, HC 8.1, HC 9.22 and PLB 1849.

91 The correspondence for the 1851 loan is in Baring, HC 8.1, HC 9.22 and PLB 1851.

92 Ericksen to Barings, Vienna, 6 and 15 May 1854: Baring, HC 9.22 (Ericksen was Barings' correspondent in Vienna at the time).

93 Ericksen kept Barings informed of the progress of the domestic loan in his letters of June – September 1854. The amount still to be repaid was reported in his letter of 20 November 1855: Baring, HC 9.22.

94 Ericksen to Barings, Vienna, 18 December 1854: Baring, HC 9.22.

95 Max Wirth, 'The history of banking in Germany and Austria–Hungary', in Journal of Commerce and Commercial Bulletin, *A History of banking in all the leading nations*, Vol. IV (New York, 1896), pp. 71–2.

96 The extensive correspondence on the sale of the Crown Domains, which failed when the French bankers withdrew in June 1865 and when it became obvious that the government intended to raise a further large loan, is in Baring, HC 8.1, HC 9.25, HC 9.26 and PLB 1865. This was not the first incursion into Crown

lands. Crown lands to the value of 155 million florins (about £14 million) had been transferred by the Austrian government to the National Bank in 1855 to give value to its notes and enable it to resume cash payments: *Fenn on the Funds* (16th edn, London, 1898), p. 248.

97 Klein to Barings, 30 May and 8 June 1865: Baring, HC 9.26.

98 Barings (Thomas Baring) to Charles Klein, 1 March 1865: Baring, PLB 1865.

99 Internal memorandum (Barings) on Austrian government finance, undated and unsigned but probably by George White and prepared late in 1865.

100 Mülinen, *Les Finances de l'Autriche*, p. 140.

101 Undated memorandum, probably prepared for the Antwerp discussions between Barings, Hope & Co. and Baron von Becke, early September 1865: Baring, HC 9.25.

102 The correspondence for these negotiations is in Baring, HC 7.1, HC 8.1, HC 9.26 and PLB 1865. Baron von Becke sent Barings an interesting 'exposé des négociations avec le Baron James de Rothschild rélativement a l'emprunt de 150 millions de florins effectives', dated London, 10 November 1865, in which he told, with obvious indignation, the whole unhappy story, and excused himself for not having been able to conclude the negotiations with Rothschilds and Barings as he had always intended: Baring, HC 9.25.8.

103 David F. Good, 'Financial integration in late nineteenth century Austria', *Journal of Economic History*, 37:4 (December 1977), pp. 907–8.

104 *The Economist*, 6 February 1869, p. 156.

105 *The Economist*, 29 January 1870, p. 129.

106 *The Economist*, 23 September 1871, p. 1144. This was probably based on the report by A. G. G. Bonar, British Secretary of Embassy, on the Commerce, Industry etc. of Austria: P.P., 1868–9, LXI, p. 42.

107 *The Times*, 17 January 1872, p. 6c.

108 *The Times*, 23 July 1869, p. 9f.

109 *The Economist*, 14 May 1870, p. 606.

110 Berend and Ránki, *Economic development in East–Central Europe*, p. 100.

111 *The Times*, 11 November 1872, p. 5c.

112 Bouvier, *Crédit Lyonnais*, Vol. II, p. 513.

113 Karl F. Helleiner, *The imperial loans: a study in financial and diplomatic history* (Oxford, 1965), pp. 168, 172.

114 M. Sussmann to Barings, Vienna, 7 April 1840: Baring, HC 9.12.

115 Barings to Sussman, 10 January 1840: Baring, PLB 1840.

116 Bouvier, *Crédit Lyonnais*, Vol. II, p. 513.

117 Berend and Ránki, *Economic development in East–Central Europe*, p. 63.

118 ibid., p. 62

119 ibid., p. 65.

120 *The Economist*, Commercial History and Review of 1870 (11 March 1871), p. 36.

121 At least, Jerome Blum, who has studied the subject in detail, does not indicate otherwise: 'Transportation and industry in Austria, 1815–1848', *Journal of Modern History*, 15:1 (March 1943), pp. 24–38.

122 N. T. Gross, 'The industrial revolution in the Habsburg monarchy, 1750–1914', in Carlo M. Cipolla, ed., *The Fontana economic history of Europe: the emergence of industrial societies, Part I* (London, 1973), p. 260.

123 *Statistical abstract for the principal and other foreign countries in each year from 1865 to 1876–7*: P.P., 1878, LXXVII, p. 427.

124 A. Milward and S. B. Saul, *The development of the economies of continental Europe, 1850–1914* (London, 1977), pp. 320–1.

125 ibid., p. 322.

126 Rondo E. Cameron, *France and the economic development of Europe, 1800–1913*: (Princeton, NJ, 1961), p. 87.

127 *The Economist*, 24 October 1868, pp. 1220–1.

128 *The Economist*, 7 November 1868, p. 1280.
129 Cottrell, 'London financiers and Austria', p. 107.
130 *The Economist*, 30 October 1852, p. 1210.
131 *The Economist*, 20 July 1867, pp. 821–2. The figures for the deficits and war expenditure were taken from a report by Baron von Becke on the financial situation of Austria.
132 *The Times*, 22 July 1869, p. 5c, d.
133 Baring, French Accounts Current.
134 Catin, *Le Portefeuille étranger de la France*, pp. 15, 119.

Chapter 5

Spain*

Public Credit

Discussion of the Spanish economy in the nineteenth century, according to Jordi Nadal, must start with the assumption that domestic capital was scarce.[1] Yet when James Rothschild, the greatest banker of his day, was asked in the autumn of 1865 what had happened to Spain's foreign borrowing, he replied that five-sixths of Spanish loans contracted abroad had already returned to Spain.[2] The two statements are not necessarily incompatible, but the inference is plain. Rothschild, whatever he felt about the influence of foreign financiers in Spain, was not inclined to over-estimate the actual quantity of foreign investment in Spain. Nadal, following a different tradition, assumed that the 'greater part' of the resources administered by the Spanish credit companies in the 1860s was foreign, and that Spanish railways were 'brought in from abroad and set up by foreign resources'. Others believe that foreign capital, in one form or another, was indispensible for a poor economy like Spain's: 'chaque effort d'équipement ou d'industrialisation sera lié dans la peninsule a l'investissement financier venu de France ou Angleterre.'[3] It is a short step from here to the full armoury of the dependency theory. Spain, in the opinion of one of the most recent synthesisers, 'was converted into a satellite of the industrial metropolis of north-west Europe, which extracted often irreplaceable supplies of raw materials for its own use, sending back large quantities of manufactured goods and surplus capital'.[4]

As always, the real relationship was rather more complicated. Spain never quite lived up to expectations; even now, great wealth is not easily discernible in the barren, underpopulated and inhospitable territories of the interior. Yet Spain, said Bernard Cohen in 1822, was 'a country rich in all the elements of national wealth and prosperity'.[5] Robert Lytton, Britain's Secretary of Legation, concluded a pessimistic report on Spanish finance (November 1868) with the opinion that Spain was 'possessed of immense natural resources, of which

* The exchange rates in this chapter are £1 sterling to 25 pesetas or 100 *reales*. After the mid-1880s the peseta depreciated so that the rate of exchange, a decade later, was £1 sterling to 30 pesetas.

no mismanagement can altogether deprive her'.[6] The tone was set by a well-known British traveller, Richard Ford, in whose opinion 'it has, indeed, required the utmost ingenuity and bad government of men to neutralise the prodigality of advantages which Providence has lavished on this highly favoured land. . . .'[7]

Bad government, unfortunately, *was* endemic, although bad government was surely allied to insufficient resources. From 1834 to 1868, during the minority and reign of Isabella II, Spain had seventy-four ministers of finance, whose budgets were arranged generally 'to suit political objects of the moment'.[8] Between 1868 (when Isabella was exiled) and 1915, there were fifty-eight governments of Spain, eighty-three ministers of *Hacienda* (public finance) and eighty-five ministers of *Fomento* (economic development), quite apart from chargés d'affaires within the two ministries in the intervals between politicians (forty-three and fifty-four respectively).[9] Predictably, the result was administrative chaos. Señor Camacho was one of the better of the many capable finance ministers who wrestled briefly with the intractable problems of Spanish public finance. He calculated in his budget of May 1872 that the net deficit in government spending over revenue from the first published budget of 1850–1 to the budget of 1870–1 was no less than £70 million.[10]

The outcome of such deficits was default. The Spanish government was effectively in default from the mid-1830s to the 1870s; consequently it could no longer depend on international markets for assistance with its public loans. Certainly in Britain, but probably elsewhere in Europe (including France), the public credit of Spain never recovered. There is no accounting for the view, developed by Milward and Saul, that it was only *after 1867* (why 1867?) that the inflow of foreign capital became 'cautious and faltering and gradually less important'.[11] In fact, already by the early 1850s, Spanish bonds, even more than Pennsylvanian stock, were a 'byeword for an insecure and hopeless investment'.[12] In the mid-1850s it was 'scarcely possible' for the Spanish government to obtain the least assistance from London, Paris or Amsterdam.[13]

There were moments, like the dethronement of Isabella II (1868) and the accession of the young King Amadeus (1871), when the credit of the Spanish government experienced a revival. But the provisional government after the 1868 revolution was soon in default, and Spanish government securities collapsed on international markets when Amadeus left Spain in 1873; the months of rebellion that followed reduced the credit of the nation to its lowest ebb.[14] *The Economist* had warned its readers in October 1870, when the Duque D'Aosta accepted the throne of Spain, that Spanish stock was amongst the most dangerous securities in the market.[15] 'Beware of Spanish stock,' said Richard Ford; 'you cannot get blood from a stone; *ex nihilo nihil fit*.'[16]

Whatever the attraction to *speculators*, no *investors* (said *The Economist*) should have anything to do with Spanish bonds,[17] and it may be that historians of Spanish finance have not always observed the distinction between speculation and genuine investment. The volume of Spanish securities circulating in European markets had nothing to do with their popularity among investors. Transactions in Spanish stocks were very large in London at a low point in Isabella's reign, in January 1868, but the same was true of 'Turks'.[18] In the mid-1870s, Spanish 'passive' stock and certificates, Greek bonds and coupons, Mexican bonds, Italian state securities and Turkish *kaimés* shared the doubtful distinction of being the principal media for speculation in the London financial market.[19] At 30 or less for a 3 per cent stock, on which interest was known occasionally to have been paid, Spanish securities were a fair speculation, and the upheavals of Spanish politics provided all the alternations of despondency and optimism, the rise and fall in market prices that 'bulls' and 'bears' required. In fact, it is absurd to calculate the precise holdings of Spanish securities by different nationalities in the middle decades of the nineteenth century. They were substitutes for gambling chips, counters in the game of speculation. They responded instantaneously to the day's economic and political intelligence. They 'flit from one market to another', as events and credulity dictated.[20]

Such speculation and mobility in Spanish securities might suggest some doubts about those very precise estimates that now exist for French investment in Spain during the 1860s, not least because if Rothschild were right (and being who he was, he could hardly be wrong) the final 'flit' was from Paris back to Madrid. Spain was in default again by the mid-1870s, and it could not be otherwise. The Spanish national debt almost doubled in a single decade to £300 million in 1872,[21] only just short of Russia's £350 million, when Russia's population was at least four times as large and the Empire thirty-five times the area. Mulhall calculated that Spain's debt (home and foreign) had risen as high as £350 million by 1880, the highest ratio of debt to inhabitant in Europe.[22] With the climate of opinion that existed during the 1860s and 1870s, it is most unlikely that Spain's public debt was subscribed or held largely abroad.

British Investment

Although the volume of actual finance may not have been so large, foreign financiers were nevertheless active in Spain from the 1820s. Spain, according to the financial historian Capefigue, was 'une maitresse toujours trompeuse, toujours aimée'.[23]

Medley's assumption that, by the end of the 1870s, as much as two-thirds of Spanish government bonds had been issued and taken in London was unrealistic; his total of £110.8 million for British holdings of Spanish loans was entirely wrong.[24] Britons did take an interest in the Spanish government loans of the 1820s. They were heavily engaged in the £4 million Anglo-French loan of 1834, a large proportion of which went to London during the speculative mania of the early months of 1835. Until the spring of that year, 'hardly any packet arrived from the Continent which did not come loaded with every sort of foreign securities [principally Spanish] for realisation on the London Stock Exchange'.[25] But Britons took little interest in subsequent issues. Speculation in Spanish stocks collapsed in May 1835 when, in a sudden panic, Spanish stock fell on the London Stock Exchange from 72 to 50 in one week and 'nearly the whole Stock Exchange may be said to have stopped'.[26] The editor of the *Circular to Bankers* was less pessimistic; nearly one-half of the active members of the Stock Exchange would suffer loss. But he himself observed that no such ruin among individuals in one pursuit had occurred since Law's great bubble burst in Paris a century before.[27] Survivors looked elsewhere, and certainly no evidence exists of British anxiety to join in subsequent Spanish government flotations; rather the reverse, since Britons were reported as having 'absolutely rejected' the new issues of 1844 and 1845.[28]

Bravo Murillo's unfavourable 'conversion' of the Spanish debt in 1851 closed the London Stock Exchange to any new issues of government bonds. Gabriel Tortella describes it as poorly camouflaged bankruptcy.[29] Thereafter, apart from the activities of speculators, London left Spanish government loans entirely to themselves.

Fenn calculated that the foreign debt of Spain in 1855, including very large arrears of unpaid interest, came to about 6 billion *reales* (£60 million), of which 'the greater portion' was English.[30] But the British share must in fact have been much smaller. The main elements in Spain's foreign debt were the 'Cortes' loans of the early 1820s and the Anglo-French loan of 1834. In 1857, the distribution of 'certificates' of coupons on the 'active' bonds showed that the bonds were held to the extent of 40 per cent in Britain, 37 per cent in Holland and 23 per cent in Spain. No certificate holders were cited as registered in France, from which it may be deduced that bonds of these particular loans must already have departed by the late 1850s.[31]

The London Stock Exchange did not reopen to Spanish government loans until May 1868.[32] When it did, British investors were slow to come forward. The 8 per cent Spanish colonial loan for £2.3 million, contracted by Messrs Bischoffsheim and Goldschmidt in March 1868, was withdrawn after a dispute with the Spanish government. The revolution of September 1868, as the result of which Bourbon misrule was overthrown, brought new hope to the British investor.

Spain, said the *Bankers' Magazine*, was 'neither well nor favourably known among Englishmen, but the peaceful way in which the Revolution had been conducted had inspired the financiers and merchants of Europe with confidence'.[33] News of the revolution was greeted in London by a 30 per cent advance in Spanish funds,[34] but the revival was short-lived. By April 1869, when the Spanish government attempted to raise £10 million effective on the European money markets, the quotation had fallen from the highest point of 39 to 27½. London was asked to supply only about £2.4 million effective, and even then Britons were not interested. *The Economist* later described the loan as 'hardly saleable [in London] since its issue', and the price fell as low as 24.[35]

Nadal, relying on Jenks, calculates that from 1869 to 1873 Spain was second only to Russia in her claims on the British investor.[36] This was not the case. British investors had taken no share in the 1869 loan. A small loan in the summer of 1870, the Spanish quicksilver (mercury) loan for £2.3 million, closed in two hours on the London market. It was oversubscribed ten times, partly because of the security (the hypothecation of the Almadén mercury mines), but mainly because Rothschilds' name appeared on the prospectus.[37]

On only two other occasions did the British investor put aside his prejudices. Britons took an interest in King Amadeus' loan of September 1871 (£20 million nominal, £6.35 million effective); the popularity of the new monarchy, and the hope of a happier turn in the relations between Spain and her creditors, brought European investors flocking to the market, and the loan was eight times oversubscribed. Subscribers in London were allocated some £7.8 million nominal in the final distribution.[38] But almost immediately Ruíz Gomez, the Minister of Finance, lost office in a change of Cabinet, and his successor's plan to tax the dividends on the foreign debt once more destroyed the international credit of Spain. *The Times* believed that if this tax had been foreseen, the applications for the Amadeus loan in England and France (£7.2 million nominal in Paris) would have been 'almost *nil*';[39] *The Economist* reported that 'the old distrust of Spain has revived in full intensity'.[40] Nevertheless, on 12 December 1872 Amadeus managed successfully to float an underpriced loan for £10.6 million on European markets, after a further compromise with Spain's foreign creditors. The loan was covered three times over, and cash subscriptions in London amounted to about £3 million.[41] But in February 1873 King Amadeus abdicated; a republic was proclaimed, the debt was repudiated in June 1874, and public order was not restored until the return of the Bourbons (Alfonso XII) on the last day of 1874. The public credit of Spain was dead.

With the occasional exception, then, British investors were not attracted by Spanish government bonds. At the time, railways were the usual alternative to governments as the destination for major investment. In 1852, Spain had only 102 kilometres of railway in operation; by 1866 this had risen to 5,076 kilometres.[42] During the 1840s, British promoters and engineers were interested in a number of railway proposals, but investment was purely exploratory. The British railway mania, which in the 1840s had managed to surmount the Pyrenees, was, Ford said, 'confined rather more to words than deeds'.[43]

A royal decree opened the way to speculation among Spaniards ('un torrente de especulación y escasísima construcción'),[44] but Spain was a land of 'dehesas y desplobados', and Britons must have taken to heart Ford's advice not to invest one farthing in such 'imposing speculations'.[45] There is no evidence to suggest that Britons were active investors during the peak period of Spanish railway construction in the late 1850s and early 1860s. The closure of the London Stock Exchange to Spanish government loans after 1851 prevented the government itself from borrowing for railway construction, while naturally inhibiting the British promoter and investor. British capital and enterprise in Spanish railways was 'conspicuous by its absence',[46] and Henry Ayres was right to conclude that, in the absence of a state guarantee, 'railways, waterworks, gas, telegraphs, or canals, must remain in abeyance or be created by Spanish capital alone'.[47]

London financiers undertook some business in short-term loans to Spanish railways. In 1864 the International Financial Society, supported by a syndicate of London houses, made an advance of £400,000 at 7 per cent to the Málaga–Córdoba line, which was repaid by the end of 1865.[48] Others must have done the same. For the general investor, *The Economist* argued in 1867 that railway enterprise, which had given life in every other region of the world, 'in Spain has contributed an additional feature of disaster to the widespread discredit in which the country stands immersed.'[49]

Apart from the unfortunate investments in government bonds of the early 1820s and mid-1830s, and some relatively small investments in Spanish mines in the 1860s,[50] it may well be that the real contribution of *British* finance to the economic development of Spain lay both in the financing of commerce (normally confined to foreign trade) and in the considerable stake of resident Britons in certain areas of Spanish business. In spite of all the misdemeanours of the government – the defaults, the confiscations, the 'conversions' of the national debt – *private* trade and finance in Spain were high in character and reliability. During one of the worst periods of public discredit, *The Times* (October 1868) spoke of the 'extremely high' honour of Spanish merchants.[51] Two years later, after further disasters, a leading article in the same newspaper concluded that 'with all the havoc which centuries of corrupting misrule have wrought in the national character, nothing really lofty and generous ever comes amiss to the Spanish heart'.[52]

Much money was invested by Britons resident in Spain. In the autumn of 1868, the property of the twelve English houses in wine and land in Jerez de la Frontera alone was estimated at £2.2 million, while British property in Andalucía as a whole was said to be worth at least £5 million.[53] Spain at the time was by far the largest supplier of wine to the British market – an average of 6 million gallons annually between 1866 and 1870, by contrast with 3.9 million gallons imported from France and 2.9 million gallons from Portugal. Britons still preferred rich and heavy wines to the lighter wines of France, and they were consuming 90 per cent of the sherry produced in Spain.[54] The business was well established and it made heavy demands on capital. The French consul in Cadiz, writing to his Minister in the early 1870s at a time of revolutionary disturbances, deplored the possible destruction of *bodegas* at Jerez, where wines worth several hundred million francs were stored.[55]

By comparison, the activities of a few London financiers in advances and short-term loans to the government and railways may seem unimportant. Barings were sounded out privately in the summer of 1847 as to their disposition to enter into a £2 million loan to the official bank (the Banco de San Fernando). The money markets of Europe at the time were in too uncertain a state to justify further discussion, but Thomas Baring believed that 'for parties who would follow the matter up there is a good deal of money to be made in Spain and with more security than is generally supposed'.[56] High interest rates on short-term loans, with reasonable security, were obviously attractive to London financiers, even when no market could be found in the Stock Exchange for Spanish government bonds. British houses, in common with French, became deeply implicated in the short-term funding of Isabella II. Barings were nearly £1 million in advance to the Spanish government at the end of 1868.[57] But the money was lent for three months at a time; it was lost to the Spanish economy in current government expenditure and the servicing of previous debts. It was the kind of finance that was handled promptly and satisfactorily, although at far higher cost, by the Spaniards themselves.

Dutch Investment

The experience of Holland in Spanish finance was not dissimilar to Britain's, although the commercial and residential contribution within Spain was absent. The Dutch were the first foreigners to invest in Spain. Fenn quotes two 'Dutch' loans of 1804 and 1806 (£2.5 million and £800,000 respectively).[58] Dutch capitalists were interested also in the Spanish loans of the 1820s and 1830s and, as speculators, took part in the loans of 1844 and 1845 refused by investors both in London and Berlin.[59] In Amsterdam in the mid-1840s, Spanish loans, together with Portuguese and Mexican, seem to have been something of a favourite among speculators who showed 'a great disposition to go into any stock that [was] unusually depressed'.[60] The distribution of the 'certificate' debt shows that the Dutch followed closely on Britons as the principal holders of Spain's foreign debt at the time of the Murillo 'conversion' of 1851.[61]

The Amsterdam market, like London, was closed to Spanish government bonds from 1851; it did not reopen until after the revolution of 1868. Hope & Co. of Amsterdam refused to touch a proposed Spanish loan in 1853. They had lost a great deal of money, reputation and custom by Spanish stocks, and they wanted nothing more to do with them. But the partners of Hope & Co. were notoriously conservative, and their attitude was not endorsed elsewhere. William Borcki, Hope & Co.'s own broker, put himself down privately for £20,000 in Spanish bonds. Hope & Co., he said, knew as much about what was happening in Spain as they did about the moon. Borcki thought that he would be much mistaken if in Amsterdam, where capital was abundant at the time, plenty of money would not be prepared to go into Spanish bonds once it was seen that an international house of standing (Barings) had given their name to the revival of Spanish credit.[62] As it turned out, the loan contract was much criticised in the Cortes, the Cortes were suspended and the Ministry fell. A combination of Madrid capitalists was formed that offered more advantageous terms, and the idea of a foreign loan was abandoned. By the late 1850s, Dutch creditors were totally disillusioned with Spain's public finance.[63]

All the same, Dutchmen were more inclined to take an interest in Spanish railways than in government stock, especially the comparatively secure debenture issues of the 1860s. Belgians (who were often confused in the literature with the Dutch) were very interested in the stock of the Northern railway: the Société Générale of Belgium, with 20,000 shares, held a tenth of the share capital, and the Bank of Belgium took another 10,000.[64] Germany, too, took part in the market for Spanish securities – so much so that in the 1880s Germans were said to have taken the lead in promoting the rise in Iberian stocks.[65] There is clearly something wrong in Albert Broder's calculation that Dutch and Belgian capitalists took no part in the new Spanish debt of 1820–3, supplied only a total of 8.3 million francs (£332,000) to Spain over the whole period 1824–50, and took no part again between 1850 and 1865![66]

French Investment

Among foreign financiers and investors, the French played the leading role. They were the neighbours of Spain; they were actively concerned with political stability and economic development; they traded across the frontier. Their interest was obvious. But it is not at all obvious that Frenchmen took the share in Spanish finance that is assigned to them by their most recent and enthusiastic historian.[67]

The reality seems to have been that French investors were not deeply engaged in Spain until the 1850s. The 'Cortes' loans of the early 1820s were issued principally in Paris, but a fair proportion of the bonds found their way to London during the mania for foreign loans that culminated so disastrously in London's financial crash of 1825–6. Other Spanish loans of the period 'found a ready sale in Paris and Amsterdam'.[68] Still others were issued by London contractors such as William Haldimand and Campbell, Lubbock and Co., and were taken largely by British investors. The Anglo-French loan of 1834 found a market with British speculators, but, as far as the French investor was concerned, all that can safely be said is that these loans came eventually to be held in London, Amsterdam and Madrid.[69] A portion must have remained, held in part by rich Spaniards resident in Paris, like the Marqués de Casa Riera who specialised in Spanish financial operations. French investors themselves had better things to do with their money, and France does not seem to have provided a home of any importance for solid investment in Spanish securities. The Milward/Saul estimate of 500 million francs for French investment in Spanish government bonds between 1815 and 1851, although not in fact a very large sum of money (£20 million), is none-the-less implausible.[70]

It is true that, for a relatively short period, France *did* become the main source for Spain's borrowing abroad, although state loans were not important. For example, the real competition for the £3.24 million (net) loan floated by a shady Paris financier, Jules Mirès, at the end of 1856, came not from the Paris Rothschilds but from the financial houses of Madrid.[71] The loan offered a handsome return (about 25 per cent), and it has been assumed that, like other Mirès operations, it was a success;[72] in actual fact, the loan was reported to have failed.[73] Thereafter, there is no evidence to suggest that French investors were attracted by Spanish government loans. Indeed, the Paris Bourse was closed to further government issues from 1861, as a gesture of dissatisfaction with the treatment of the French holders of the 'passive' debt.

France's contribution to Spanish public finance took the shape of a considerable volume of short-term bankers' loans, both before and after the dethronement of Isabella II. Among the obligations outstanding when Isabella went into exile in the autumn of 1868 were short-term debts to foreign bankers amounting to over £3.4 million.[74] Much of these, although not all, was French.

The provisional government that replaced Isabella in 1868 was besieged with offers of temporary financial aid by the bankers of Europe. Rothschilds rescued the government by taking £1 million net in 3 per cents at 32 to meet the dividend on the foreign debt due on 31 December 1868, and in the same contract took another £2 million for the purpose of railway subsidies, debt servicing and general government expenditure. Throughout the *sexenio liberal* (1868–74), a period of disastrous default on the foreign debt, Spanish governments continued to draw on *cash* advances from abroad. In 1872, Amadeus faced severe problems with the Carlists, and he needed all the cash he could get. Bouvier quotes a list of advances falling due for repayment between 19 April and 15 June 1872: £650,000 to the Banco General de Madrid (Erlanger); £500,000 to Morgan (London); £450,000 to the Banque Franco-Egyptienne: £580,000 to the Fould group; £340,000 to Werner; another £100,000 to the Banque Franco-Egyptienne; and a contract of £1 million with the Banque de Paris and the Société Générale – a total of £3.62 million of advances to be repaid by the Spanish government to foreign bankers within a few weeks.[75]

It was not so much in government finance as in railways that French money made its mark. Cameron's claim that Spanish railway development was 'almost wholly a product of French capital and enterprise' is characteristically ambitious.[76] But the view is commonly held. *The Economist* in 1868 spoke of Spanish railways as 'almost exclusively executed by French capital' and 'still almost entirely in French hands',[77] and more recently Jordi Nadal, in a general overview of Spanish economic development, has described Spanish railways as 'brought in from abroad and set up by foreign resources'.[78]

The fault is one of emphasis – exaggeration rather than error. The important lines financed and constructed in Spain after the Railway Law of 1855 were the North of Spain (1858) and the Madrid–Zaragoza–Alicante railway (1857); the Norte was the child of the Crédit Mobilier group in Paris (through its Spanish offshoot, the Crédito Mobiliario Español), and the M.Z.A. of the Morny/Rothschild group, again of Paris. These two lines were joined by a third French enterprise, the Andalusian railway, in 1869. Although all three came to be legally domiciled in Spain, they originated in France. As late as the early 1920s, half of their *capital* could still be described as French.[79]

Tedde is right in saying that both the Norte and the M.Z.A. were tailored for the French market; they sold at 50 for a 3 per cent stock, thus offering 6 per cent interest and double the real capital invested on amortisation.[80] Between them the Norte and the M.Z.A. constituted a very large part of the Spanish network. Even in 1890, their paid-up shares contributed 56.4 per cent of the paid-up share capital of all Spanish railway companies. Tedde's own estimate, after considering the other estimates available to date, is that 57 per cent of Spanish railways in 1867 belonged to Frenchmen, and a similar proportion was still maintained in 1890.[81] Tedde's final conclusion for 1894 (the Norte, the M.Z.A., the Andaluces, and the remainder) is that something like 2.2–2.4 billion pesetas of Spanish railway securities were held abroad, mainly in France, which at 2.2 billion nominal (£88 million) in shares and debentures would constitute 60 per cent of the total issues, the rest being held in Spain.[82]

Tedde's percentage is too high, but even at the 40 per cent suggested later in this chapter the proportion of foreign investment in Spanish railway securities was still considerable. It would never have been so large if the decision had been left to the individual investor. The rates of interest and amortisation were popular on the Paris market, but the experience of Spain's public credit was depressing. If private investment had not been channelled through a few entrepreneurs – the new credit institutions of the 1850s and 1860s – the investment, for Frenchmen generally, would undoubtedly have fallen far below the level actually achieved. As it was, when the Crédit Mobilier of Paris finally collapsed in 1867, its lock-up was said to include 62,000 shares in the Norte, at a nominal value of £1.2 million, which by now 'could hardly be realised' on the Paris market.[83] Even greater support was supplied by the French credit institutions resident in Spain. Tortella estimates that possibly as much as three-quarters of the investments of the three French-supported credit companies, the Sociedad General de Crédito Mobiliario Español (Pereire), the Sociedad Española Mercantil e Industrial (Rothschild), and the Compañía General de Crédito de España (Prost), were devoted to railways during the first years of foundation.[84]

French interest in Spanish railways on the open market, on the other hand, was short-lived. The closing of the Paris Bourse in 1861 was directed simply at new *government* loans, but it must obviously have had a damaging effect on all Spanish securities indiscriminately. Spanish railway securities, for instance, fell dramatically on the French market. Norte shares, which were worth 472.50 francs in 1860, were down to 105 in 1865; M.Z.A. fell from 560 to 232. Even greater disaster was experienced with the securities of smaller and weaker lines: shares in the railway from Seville to Jerez, for example, dropped from 521.75 francs to 45.[85]

The distaste of the French investor (and of foreign finance generally) was shown also in the sharp decline in the importation of railway material into Spain. There must always be a lag in the response of imports of material to a cut-off in investment, but the figures are sufficiently dramatic. In 1864, Spain was still importing as much as 233 million reales (£2.3 million) of railway material; in 1865, imports sank to 68 million (£680,000), and in 1866 to only 29 million (£290,000).[86]

For lack of a genuine alternative, the financing of Spanish railways, in the early and mid-1860s, was undertaken by those banks that were already committed. Many bank advances were supplied by the banking system of Spain herself, but a number of Paris bankers had a heavy stake by now in Spanish railways and found themselves drawn further into the bottomless pit. The Compañía General de Crédito de España, an offshoot of the Parisian Crédit Mobilier, made loans of 324.8 million pesetas (£13 million) to companies – principally railways – in the five years 1862–6, when for the previous five years such loans amounted to only 95.1 million pesetas (£3.8 million).[87] Gille reports that the Société Générale of Paris was brought into a series of short-term advances to the Ciudad Real–Badajoz line from the beginning of 1865, from which it found no escape for the remainder of the decade.[88] So much was at stake in Spanish railways for Rothschilds and the Crédit Mobilier that there was talk, early in 1867, of a single large loan of 1.2 billion francs (£48 million) to bail out the railways and reconstitute the Spanish debt. The proposal failed; Baron D'Eichthal was right in asking whether anyone could be found in London or Paris to lend another penny to a government 'aussi abominable et aussi menacé'.[89] Nevertheless, out of the first international loan to reach Spain after the 1868 revolution (the £4 million Rothschild loan contracted in November 1868), a third was intended to salvage commitments to the Norte and the M.Z.A. of Rothschilds and the Crédit Mobilier.[90] The M.Z.A., according to the Paris correspondent of *The Economist*, had cost 50.5 million francs (£2.02 million) more than its issued capital. In 1868, the company was indebted for the completion of its works to the Paris Rothschilds, from whom it had received 42.8 million francs (£1.7 million) in advances.[91] By 1870, the other great line, the Norte, was in debt to the Compañía General de Crédito for 44.3 million pesetas (£1.8 million).[92]

Domestic Financial Resources

The nationality, character and distribution of such foreign finance as came to Spain in the middle decades of the nineteenth century may now be a bit more evident. Clearly, in one way or another, Spain made much use of foreign finance, and the use to which it put that finance illustrates what tended to be the case for the majority of the poorer economies of the Western world during the same period. Tortella argues rightly that Spain's experience could not have been otherwise, given the circumstances and the low level of domestic savings.[93] However, there is a gulf separating such a view, which is unexceptionable, from the argument that foreign finance took possession of the Spanish economy. Spain, in truth, was able to do much for herself.

In the middle of the nineteenth century the population of Spain was barely 15 million, widely dispersed and predominantly rural; prices were very low and the units of currency were *reales* (100 to £1) and *cuartos* (3 cents); a bread roll, for example, cost one cuarto.[94] In 1840, the population of Madrid, the economic centre of the country, was about 200,000 (a respectable figure), but the other cities, apart from Barcelona, were much smaller. Ringrose accepts unquestioningly the stagnation of the Spanish economy in the first decades of the nineteenth century, the reasons for which were 'the conservatism of the interior élites, the collapse of Spanish trade, the loss of the empire, the stagnant population, and the regression of urban life'.[95] Spain had suffered a huge deterioration in her revenue in the second and third decades of the nineteenth century when she lost her colonial trade and the tariffs that she derived from it. Government revenue, which had averaged 1.2 billion reales (£12 million) over the years 1785–1808, fell in 1814–20 to less than 700 million (£7 million).[96] If 100 were taken as the index number for the decade 1791–1800, government revenue had fallen to 77.2 for 1821–30.

A great improvement then took place. Revenue was up to 136.4 for 1841–50, 211.2 for 1851–60, and 303.8 for 1861–70.[97] Tortella points out that the commercial development of Spain was the most encouraging aspect of the mid-century economy.[98] Average annual imports for the five years 1850–4 were 732 million reales (£7.32 million); for 1860–4 they had risen to 1,812 million (£18.12 million). Exports over the same period rose from 668 million reales to 1,220 million.[99] *The Times*, in a leading article on 'the financial condition of Spain' (March 1869), found enormous increases in the value of external commerce over the previous twenty years, and a steady rise in revenue.[100]

The record of deficits in Spanish government finance was second to none: between 1850 and 1900 there were deficits for every year except four – an average deficit of 65 million pesetas (£2.6 million) annually.[101] The army was always a heavy drain on the exchequer – about 20 per cent of government revenue over the whole period 1850–1900. In the early months of 1868 – the last, most disastrous period of Isabella's unfortunate reign – there were 504 general officers on the army list.[102]

Admittedly, the government could draw on some exceptional domestic resources to help it through its many crises, and these reduced the need to borrow abroad. From 1837 the government raised a total of 257 million pesetas (£10.28 million) from the sale of Church property.[103] After the Ley Madoz of 1855, the disposal of property was extended to land held in mortmain, which in practice brought more money to the state than the more notorious expropriation of the Church, the *desamortización de Mendizábal*. Tortella argues that this whole operation, the consequence of which was to bring about a change of ownership of some 10 million hectares (approximately half of the cultivable lands of Spain), was perhaps the most important economic phenomenon of Spain in the nineteenth century – the other decisive step being the construction of the railway system.[104] Furthermore, Tortella has since calculated that the income received from the Ley Madoz over the forty years 1855–95 – some 2 billion pesetas (£80 million) – was not out of line with that obtained from the state lotteries (another extraordinary domestic resource) for approximately the same period (1850–90).[105]

The government could also call on the aid of at least five important items of revenue: the tobacco, salt and mercury monopolies, and the colonial revenues of Havana and Manila. These were sources of either cash or credit, and could be employed as securities, realisable outside Spain herself, for large advances from foreign financiers. Colonial revenues and advances were handled normally by the financiers of Madrid. The tobacco monopoly was largely a Spanish affair, negotiated by contract with domestic financiers. As for mercury (quicksilver), the contract was valuable. Mercury was the essential agent in the amalgamation process for the extraction of silver from its ores, and it remained so until amalgamation was replaced by the cyanide process at the beginning of the twentieth century. The Spanish government was the fortunate owner, at the mines of Almadén, of the richest source of mercury in the world. Almadén was worked with convict labour, and the cost of production of a quintal of mercury (101¾ English pounds at the time) averaged $18 (£4 10s).[106] The quantity mined at Almadén in the early 1830s was estimated at 20–22,000 quintals a year.[107]

The contract price of mercury negotiated with the Spanish government in 1830 by the 'Mexican' house, Inigo, Espeleta & Co., was $ Mexican 37.25 (£7.45) per quintal. Rothschilds took over the contracts from 1835, and by careful management pushed the price of Spanish mercury to its highest point on world markets. In the Rothschild contract of 1843 the price was set at $81.5 (£16.3),[108] which raised the government's gross annual revenue from Almadén to at least £326,000, by contrast with the 7 million reales (£70,000) estimated as the produce of the mines in the early 1820s.[109]

The price could not last. Competition from abroad, principally from new mines in California, brought the price down. At one point (April 1852), it dropped to $43 per quintal delivered in Guanajuato (Mexico).[110] Competing suppliers continued to be a problem for Spanish mercury, although the legend of the mercury contract in combination with the magic name of Rothschild was still sufficient, even in 1870, to persuade British investors, for all their distrust of Spain, to take up Rothschilds' 'quicksilver' loan of 1870 many times over.

Mercury remained a source of cash for the Spanish government, as did the revenues of the surviving Spanish colonies (when not in rebellion). Furthermore, the capital resources of Spain benefited generally, especially in the last decades of the nineteenth century, from the repatriation of capital by Spanish emigrants to the Americas, while more specifically the banking community of Madrid received welcome support from Spanish capital exiled from Cuba after the Spanish–American war of 1898.[111]

Extraordinary resources such as these could be only partial and erratic in their effect. They were useful, but in the two main areas of Spanish finance – government and railways – their contribution was modest. In both areas, more conventional varieties of domestic finance were of far greater importance.

The public debt of Spain on 30 September 1868, exclusive of the debts and engagements (mostly local) of the Treasury, was £240 million, of which £183.5 was internal and £56.5 foreign.[112] A proportion of the internal debt was non interest bearing, so that a more reliable indication of the relation between internal and external indebtedness was the commitment to interest payment. In the budget of July 1871, interest payable on the internal debt amounted to £5 million a year and on the external debt to £3 million.[113] Of course, a proportion of the 'external' debt was held in Spain, and the same was true, in reverse, for the 'internal' debt. But there is no reason to think that they cancelled each other out. Spanish holdings of the external debt were naturally higher than the share of foreigners in the internal debt. If Rothschild is to be believed, Spanish government bonds had largely returned to Spain by the mid-1860s.[114]

Indeed, there was even some evidence of substantial *exports* of Spanish capital in the mid and late 1860s. One Paris banker described the role of the Crédito Mobiliario of Madrid not as a recruiter of foreign capital to Spain but as the supplier of Spanish capital to its Parisian progenitor, the Crédit Mobilier: the Crédito Mobiliario was a branch establishment 'qui ne fait rien ou peu en Espagne, mais qui prête son argent à Paris'.[115] In the summer of 1865, Sackville West spoke of the injury done to Spanish finance by the 'excessive *exportation*' of capital,[116] and refugee capital was common enough during the stormy politics of the 1860s. *The Economist* reported in May 1869, some months after the ejection of the Bourbons, that 'a good deal of the wealth of the country has followed a crowd of fugitives into exile'.[117]

Nevertheless, there was money in Spain for public securities even after the revolution (1868). A national loan for £20 million, issued very soon after the expulsion of Queen Isabella, attracted only £4.4 million in domestic subscriptions, in spite of every appeal to the patriotism and interest of Spanish subscribers.[118] But at much the same time the Council of the Bank of Spain was resolving to issue a new domestic loan for the city of Madrid.[119] In spite of the empty Treasury and the 'utter confusion' of the Finance Department,[120] government stocks and mortgage bonds were selling at good prices in Spain. The problem was mismanagement and indecision within the government, rather than a shortage of domestic finance.

The accession of Amadeus to the Spanish throne early in 1871, marred though it was by the assassination of Marshal Prim (the leading figure in the provisional government), brought a new wave of confidence among domestic investors. In the summer of 1871, the Spanish government would have found it difficult to borrow abroad at terms better than 30 for a 3 per cent bond. But when foreign bankers were approached with a proposal for a loan of £6 million net, Madrid financiers came forward with an offer to take firm as much as two-thirds of the loan, the greater part of which was to be held for investment.[121] In the event, the Minister decided that he would prefer to borrow abroad, and made an appeal to the capital markets of Europe. Rothschilds and the Bank of Paris were the principal issuing houses in Paris, and Messrs Stern & Co. in London. The loan was heavily oversubscribed: 75 per cent was finally allotted equally to British and French subscribers.

Even then, for a loan designed specifically for foreign markets, the issue was well-supported in Madrid.[122] Immediately afterwards, the news of proposals to tax the dividends on the foreign debt once again destroyed foreign confidence in Spanish credit. Yet for the time being Spain's own investors continued to show their confidence in the future of the Amadeus government by buying national bonds, particularly those of the foreign debt.[123] Domestic investors had many reasons other than patriotism for holding some part of their money in bonds of their own foreign debt. There was a hiccup in 1874, when Spaniards refused to subscribe to the £7 million 'voluntary loan' (only £100,000 of which was applied for) – the failing government inspired no confidence whatsoever – but over the longer period domestic investors maintained their interest. After the Camacho conversion of 1882, they bought Spanish government bonds because interest was payable in foreign currency at a time when the peseta was depreciating.[124] And in any case, during the 1850s, 1860s and 1870s, the political anarchy of Spain was sufficient cause for wanting to buy and retain even national bonds abroad.

The Spanish Treasury, as was so often the case, found support more often in temporary loans on the domestic market than in heavy, long-term financial operations abroad. Even in desperate times, a home market could be found for Treasury bonds. In July 1854, a revolt of conservative generals at the head of a Madrid mob had exiled the Queen Mother and put her ministers to flight. The new Minister of Finance, Señor Callado, found the Treasury exhausted of funds. He proposed, as an interim measure, to attract foreign finance to an issue of 40 million reales (£400,000) of Treasury bonds at 8 per cent, so as 'not to embarrass the Madrid market'.[125] The future of Spain was too uncertain to recruit foreigners to a loan offering a bare 8 per cent without opportunity for capital gain, but the bonds were placed easily in Madrid.[126]

Big operations obviously stood less chance of success. On the scale required at the time, however, domestic capital was available in Spain at a reasonable price. In 1853, the government issued 20 million reales (£200,000) in *acciones de carreteras*, for the payment of road contractors. This extension of the Spanish floating debt was reported by *The Economist* as having attracted a comparatively high price in the domestic market (80 per cent and upwards), being of limited amount, duly authorised by the Cortes and bearing an interest of 6 per cent and a reliable sinking fund.[127] The pattern, for the small loans of the day, was followed subsequently. In the summer of 1871, for example, the Minister was able to negotiate a domestic issue of 30 million reales (£300,000) of the floating debt, with an interest rate of 10 per cent.[128] The rate of interest was not significantly at variance with the real rate of interest on the infinitely larger international loan of the same summer, the £6 million government loan, which was oversubscribed in Madrid.

Domestic Finance and Public Credit

To some extent, then, the Spanish government could borrow by the issue of bonds of the internal debt. In the decades before the evolution of an adequate banking system (and even after), the hub of domestic finance in Spain was the equivalent of the Parisian *haute banque* – the merchant bankers of Madrid. It has been suggested recently that very little importance need be attached to the Madrid group, at least until the mid-1840s. The Madrid houses included a few brilliant individuals, mainly Catalans, but 'sa partie dynamique et créatrice est singulièrement limité'; later, they came to take a hand in most of the great enterprises funded by foreigners in the 1850s and 1860s, although 'leur faible surface et leur penchant pour les opérations spéculatives handicapera gravement l'investissement autochtone dans les années soixante'.[129] This, surely, falls far short of the truth.

It is impossible to form an accurate idea of the actual resources of private partnerships. Ramón Canosa, although he calls attention to the existence of fifty-two merchant bankers in Madrid in 1857, and to the rise in their number to eighty-two by 1865–6 (just before the crash), does no more, unfortunately, than rank them without an estimate of their means.[130] Great fortunes were accumulated by resident bankers in their day-to-day dealings with the government, for which they occasionally chose to associate themselves with financiers abroad, more particularly with the group of wealthy Spaniards resident in Paris. The disposal of Church property, and of the national property generally, brought attractive opportunities for gain to the domestic financiers of Madrid. Hughes thought, in the early 1840s, that the fine carriages and establishments of the Madrid financiers and capitalists might be the reason why so little of the resources realised through the disposal of national property (to the extent of £30 million) ever reached the state.[131]

By any standards, the capital at the disposal of some of the Madrid houses was very considerable. Vicens Vives reports that Gaspar de Remisa's Madrid house, when it opened in 1827, had command of a capital of £500,000, together with a further £90,000 in customers' deposits.[132] The figures are implausible, since the Remisa house, with such resoures, would have ranked among the most powerful in Europe. But a handsome capital was available to Madrid financiers if they chose to act as a syndicate. The capital subscribed by the Madrid financiers and by their Paris associate, Pescatore, to the company that bid successfully for most of the government tobacco contracts in the late 1830s and early 1840s amounted to £1 million, which represented only a part of the resources that each individual could bring to bear in his normal business operations.[133]

The Spanish government could not afford to ignore such powerful financiers on its own doorstep, and much of its business was bound to be passed in their direction. The remainder, for which foreign finance was invited to compete, normally found its way to Rothschilds – not because they 'controlled' it, since the government was at liberty to invite rival tenders for a loan large enough to pay off Rothschilds' advances, but because no foreign house of sufficient stature was prepared to handle it.

Bertrand Gille, the historian of the Paris Rothschilds, admits that it is difficult to see why even the Rothschilds should have gone to so much trouble, since the 'désordre du pays n'était assurément pas pour encourager les banquiers'. Gille suggests that well-timed advances to the Spanish government may have been intended to forestall competition in the Spanish mercury contracts, without committing Rothschilds too deeply to government finance. He thinks also that what might, in other circumstances, have seemed a promising business, was adversely and unpredictably affected by political pressure from Rothschilds' Austrian connections and by Anglo-French diplomatic rivalry on the Peninsula.[134]

There may be a simpler explanation. Rothschilds had little to lose from a Spanish connection, and occasional opportunities for substantial gain. As Barings discovered in their own business, advances to foreign governments, normally well-secured, were not as hazardous as they might seem. The ordinary bond-holder in a large, government loan might find his bonds depreciated to nothing while for decades the government remained blatantly in default. No government could afford to behave so cavalierly to the capitalists, native or foreign, who supplied its short-term finance. If it did, it had nowhere else to turn.

Fortunes were not to be made by a foreign house, even by the Rothschilds, out of advances to the Spanish government. The money was safe enough, but for Rothschilds it meant locking up resources that could better be employed elsewhere, without even the prospect of a loan contract since international markets were closed to Spanish government loans. It must certainly have been irksome and humiliating for the Spanish government to find no one else to whom to turn abroad, even if Rothschilds' terms for periodical advances were no harsher than their foreign competitors' (and easier than the rates at which money could be borrowed in Madrid).

Meanwhile, the government continued to borrow at home. And, as Thomas Baring said to his old friend Ernest Sillem in September 1848 (when he heard that Sillem's son, William, was thinking of setting himself up in business in Madrid), he could not imagine a better theatre for talent and activity than Spain. The business, however, must be conducted from Madrid where, if it could be done with the participation of the Queen Mother, the door was open to all government transactions. Spanish business would have to be conducted in the Spanish manner, 'that is by exercising great patience under endless delays and obstacles, by extending credit and confidence where there is reason and a probability of safety (and there is a sort of Spanish honour which makes such engagements safe as risks), and by giving shares or their equivalent to the influential parties'. Thomas Baring thought that people who had been in Mexico would not be very squeamish on this last point, but he himself believed that most cases might be met without doing anything dishonourable; with talent and common prudence there was no better prospect of making a fortune.[135]

Thomas Baring was perfectly right and, in the midst of administrative chaos and corruption on a gigantic scale, a great deal of money was made. It was made, as he said, by the men on the spot – by the merchants and financiers of Madrid. Rothschilds had an advantage over Barings in that they kept a permanent representative in Madrid, but Daniel Weisweiller, a Jew and a foreigner, could not expect to act alone, and it was the Rothschilds' liquid resources, together with the influence, inside information and even the capital of their Madrid associates, that earned them, in the 1838 mercury contract, their richest rewards.

Antipathy to the foreigner, and suspicion of foreign control, characterised Spanish finance. Francis Falconnet, who had been instructed to suggest himself as Barings' agent and work directly *with* the Spanish contractors in winding up an unfortunate tobacco affair, reported that he had tried from the beginning to have such a course adopted. Spanish pride was a complete barrier: 'they would rather submit to any sacrifice than appear to be under the control of anyone, more particularly a stranger.'[136]

Wealthy as were the financiers of Madrid, the limit to what could be done through Spain's domestic finance was obvious. Spain in the 1850s and 1860s could not have replaced or even serviced her entire foreign debt from local resources, and each minister of finance had to start from the knowledge that large sums could not be obtained from abroad. On the other hand, if offered a sufficiently attractive interest rate and opportunities for related gains, Madrid financers could carry the government through its immediate needs. The capital at the disposal of the tobacco contractors, or of Madrid capitalists like Juan Manuel Manzanedo, José Manuel Calderón, Sanchez Toledo, the Duke of Sevillano, José Ibañez Moreno, Enrique O'Shea, and the Marqués de Salamanca (in the intervals between bankruptcies), suggest that even the largest of operations, such as the mercury contracts, were within their means.

The government's financial needs were insatiable, and resort to domestic or foreign finance was determined by a mixture of political and economic considerations; the business that the Madrid capitalists rejected for lack of an adequate return could sometimes be taken by a foreign house with the assistance of cheaper capital from abroad. In the last weeks of negotiation leading up to the mercury contract of 5 January 1850, a group of Madrid houses had no difficulty in making an advance to the government of 20 million reales (£200,000); it was for eight months only, at 14 per cent.[137] They could clearly have taken the mercury contract if they had been persuaded that there was enough in it for them, but they found better employment for their capital in shorter advances nearer to home.

The Spanish government was under no illusions. It knew perfectly well that it paid more for its money if the money had to be raised from the monopolists in Madrid. The government sent an agent, José Borrajo, to London in February 1850 to see whether there was any possibility of raising £600–800,000 in a foreign market; it wished to emancipate itself from the Madrid financiers, 'the more derogatory as the hard terms are enforced only by a few individuals'.[138] Borrajo failed, and over the years many attempts were made to draw foreign financiers more deeply into promising operations in Spain.

As a member of the syndicate led by the Madrid banker, Enrique O'Shea, Barings of London took part in several operations in government finance that gave an interest of 10–18 per cent; but they felt no enthusiasm for such business. The business was attractive to domestic capitalists for the opportunities it opened in government *pagarés* (promissory notes), Cuban and Manilan remittances, government bills, discounted stock, mortgages and depreciated securities of one kind or another – the expedients of a bankrupt government. The same inducements did not exist for financiers abroad.

The late 1860s were a sad time for Spanish financiers. Yet it was a Madrid group that offered, in the summer of 1871, to take £4 million of the £6 million required by the Minister of Finance. When the Minister decided to turn to a wider and more competitive market in the stock exchanges of Europe, it was Spanish investors who nonetheless subscribed more than the amount required. At the end of 1871, by which time borrowing abroad had once again become impracticable, a Madrid banking house, Urquijo y Aranzana, was able to lend the government £2.5 million for six months, at a relatively modest rate of 10 per cent per annum free from other charges and expenses.[139]

Tedde estimates the assets of the private banks of Madrid in 1874 at 113.3 million pesetas (£4.5 million); by 1914 their assets had risen to 486.5 million pesetas (£19 million). The assets of the private banks of Barcelona in 1874 were 87 million pesetas (£3.5 million); by 1914, they were 133 million pesetas (£5.3 million).[140] These were considerable sums for the day, not unlike the disposable assets of financial syndicates in many of the big money markets of Europe.

Powerful as were the merchant bankers of Madrid and Barcelona, they themselves were feeling the same pressure from developments in the banking system as their colleagues in the other financial capitals. Sánchez-Albornoz speaks of the very considerable mobilisation of unemployed capital that followed the immense expansion of the Spanish banking system in the decade before the financial crash of May 1866. In the main categories of banking institutions, no less than eighteen banks and thirty-seven credit institutions were founded in the years 1856–65, quite apart from branches of the Banco de España, a network of savings banks and the provincial dependencies of the Caja General de Depósitos.[141] The Caja de Depósitos, a government agency that attracted a large volume of individual deposits (entirely domestic), began life in December 1852 with a net specie balance of only 7.4 million pesetas (£296,000). By December 1860 this had risen to 259.5 million pesetas (£10.58 million), reaching a peak in December 1864 of 420.4 million pesetas (£16.8 million).[142] The issuing banks at the end of 1864 employed a capital of 306.4 million reales (£3 million); between them, the thirty-four credit institutions could mobilise a total employed capital of 1,134.8 million reales (£11.3 million).[143]

Most of the credit institutions were Madrid-based, but Barcelona (unassisted by foreign capital) had formidable resources. In 1864, two Catalan firms (the Crédito Mercantil and the Catalana General de Crédito) between them represented a capital of 15 million pesetas (£600,000).[144] The paid-up capital of the five credit institutions of Barcelona on the eve of the crash of 1866 was 160 million reales (£1.6 million).[145] Barcelona was not the only financial centre in the provinces. The investment portfolio of the Sociedad Valenciana de Crédito y Fomento in 1865 amounted to 7.3 million pesetas (£292,000); its assets were 18.7 million pesetas (£748,000).[146] The Crédito Castellano de Valladolid had a capital of 11.7 million pesetas (£468,000).[147]

It is true that the origins of the three leading credit institutions in Spain were French. But only one, the Crédito Mobiliario, was successful in raising much capital in France; the Sociedad Española Mercantil e Industrial, promoted by James Rothschild from Paris, aimed specifically at recruiting its funds in Spain. Harrison argues that 'the greater part of the resources mobilised by the credit institutions came from outside the Peninsula'.[148] However, the evidence suggests that, even on the most generous estimate for French participation, about half of the employed capital of the credit institutions must have been Spanish, while the 'French' component can easily be overestimated. Paris was the favourite *market* for Spanish securities, but this did not mean that Frenchmen held Spanish securities for investment. The Béistegui family, Mexican, financiers, owned over $Mexican 320,000 (£64,000) in the securities of Spanish banks and credit institutions, most of which were bought through Paris.[149]

The elaborate structure of domestic banking in Spain provided powerful support for the national government. In this respect domestic banking was far more effective than foreign finance. When Isabella II was expelled from Spain, the government's debts to foreign bankers, due for repayment by the end of December 1868, amounted to £3.4 million; in October 1868 the government owed the Caja General de Depósitos (only one, although the largest, of its domestic creditors) no less than £12.4 million.[150]

A state bank of one kind or another had existed in Spain since the late eighteenth century. In 1829, the Banco Español de San Fernando had surfaced from the reorganisation of the Banco de San Carlos. The main function of each was to advance money to the government. In 1855, the last year of the Banco de San Fernando, 229.3 million reales (£2.3 million) out of its total assets of 497.2 million (£4.97 million) took the form of Treasury bills and credits.[151] In 1856, the Banco de San Fernando was absorbed into the Banco de España, and Tortella calculates that from 1852 to 1873 the average end-of-year indebtedness of the government to the Banco de España was 82.1 million pesetas (£3.28 million).[152] For the last four years of Isabella's reign, 1865–8, the Bank of Spain had an average of 99.65 million pesetas (£4 million) of its assets (i.e. 68 per cent) engaged annually in the business of the state.[153] During the next quinquennium, although the average of assets employed by the state fell to 59.8 per cent, the sums employed rose to an annual average of 109.2 million pesetas (£4.4 million).[154]

The private sector was also a steady contributor to Spanish government finance. When the government was compelled to annul a contract with the Banque de Paris in November 1871, for an advance of £1 million on Treasury bonds, it was able to renegotiate substantial advances from Madrid financiers at very competitive rates. The advance of £2.5 million from Urquijo y Aranzana has already been mentioned above. It was a 10 per cent loan free of all charges, and it was supplemented by a further advance from the Bank of Barcelona of £500,000 at a mere 6 per cent. Between these two domestic operations, the Treasury was able to meet its obligations without further assistance from abroad.[155]

Domestic finance and the Railways

Domestic assistance was an essential element in Spanish government finance. As for the railways, it is often assumed that the greater part of Spanish railway development during the period was financed from abroad. The assumption is challengeable. Clearly, little enthusiasm was experienced for Spanish railways anywhere, in any quarter, at home or abroad. At the end of December 1875, Spain's railway system covered only 5,840 kilometres.[156] The first phase of railway development, as was always the case, was financed domestically. Foreign financiers, entrepreneurs and engineers took a share in the railway enthusiasm of the 1840s, but Wais is right to suppose that the major part of the capital required for the short, cheap lines that were actually constructed at this time was Spanish.[157] Spaniards again were the speculators in the railway boom of the early 1850s when, according to the *Clamor Público*, there was not a village in Spain to which a railway was not projected.[158]

The Railway Law of 1855 at last made the financing of railway construction in Spain an attractive proposition for the foreign investor. But such investment appealed equally, or more so, to the Spaniards themselves, who stood to benefit directly from the construction of lines. Spanish capitalists undertook a number of important railways such as those from Barcelona to Zaragoza, Bilbao to Tudela, Tarragona to Valencia and Almansa, and Barcelona to Gerona. Local banks, businesses and individual investors naturally took an interest in individual railway schemes within their own districts, but the national financial market for railways was Barcelona. Half of the capital invested on the Barcelona Stock Exchange in 1862 (in total 67.6 million duros, or £12 million) was in railway stock.[159]

Tortella points out that, by virtue of Spanish legislation in 1848, 1855 and 1856, banks and railways were the only enterprises that were able to organise themselves as joint stock companies, and the success of such companies in other parts of Europe meant that, in Spain, they enjoyed an almost unanimous confidence and high credit; they seemed to offer the ideal destination for investment.[160] To the Spanish investor, the securities of domestic railways and of the new credit institutions must have seemed an attractive alternative to government bonds at a time when the government was chronically unstable and could supply so little security on its own general debt.

Initially there can be little doubt that the biggest of the Spanish lines, the Norte and the M.Z.A., found their capital principally in France. But it is less likely that by 1867 as much as 57 per cent of Spanish railways were still owned in France. As Tedde himself says, Spaniards were most probably buying their own railway securities on the Paris market.[161] The return of public securities to Spain, which James Rothschild had noticed in the mid-1860s, undoubtedly occurred likewise with Spanish railway stock. A distinction, however, can be made. It was, it seems, the railway *debentures* which, in the early 1860s, were reported as almost entirely held in France, Holland and Germany.[162] The *ordinary* stock, about 40 per cent of the issued capital in 1864,[163] had not sold well abroad. The Crédit Mobilier and the Paris Rothschilds, together with the credit institutions formed in Madrid after 1856, found that much of their capital, foreign and domestic, was locked up in railway construction. Experience suggests that a far greater proportion of Spanish railway stock than is generally supposed, perhaps both of the debentures and of the ordinary shares, quite promptly found its way back to Spain, even if the initial finance, while Spanish investors were still feeling their way, was normally French.

Meanwhile, the railways had to continue operation and construction over a period, in the 1860s, when foreign markets were closed to Spanish government securities and closed similarly, by association, to most private securities as well. If Spanish railways were fortunate enough to be in contact with foreign finance, they turned to their foreign bankers for support–the Crédit Mobilier (which had backed the Norte) and the Paris Rothschilds (for the M.Z.A.). Loans to the Norte from the Crédito Mobiliario Español had risen by 1869 to 44.3 million pesetas (£1.77 million).[164] The remaining lines drew their support from domestic finance.

Tedde explains that the railway sector accounted for a large part of the portfolio of all the national and regional credit institutions before the crisis of 1866. In 1865, for example, three-quarters of the portfolio of the Sociedad Valenciana de Crédito y Fomento (7.3 million pesetas in all – £292,000) were tied up in railways, and as much again was out in the shape of a loan to José Campo, the director and entrepreneur of the Valenciana railway.[165] Domestic banks were as deeply engaged in railway finance as the credit institutions, especially in Barcelona. Tortella concludes that 'promoting railways seemed to be the easy way of doing business, and [Spanish banks] followed it blindly without analysing the economic soundness of their behaviour'.[166]

Finally, any calculation of the extent to which domestic finance contributed to railway construction in the nineteenth century, for Spain as for every country other than Britain, must allow for the contribution of the state. Some part of this inevitably took the form of government borrowing abroad, but in practice the Spanish government could borrow very little abroad after the 'conversion' of 1851. In fact, there is reason to believe that the money authorised by the Cortes in the late 1850s and early 1860s for the construction of roads and railways was obtained both from funds deposited at interest by corporations and individuals in the government's Caja de Depósitos, and by government bonds issued periodically on the domestic market in payment of subventions to railway companies. Still further assistance was received from the government in the shape of tax exemptions, particularly tariff concessions on imported railway material. Exemptions from customs duties on railway material cost the state a total of 69.89 pesetas (£2.8 million) for the three years 1861–3.[167]

As one might expect, the government contributed most during the years 1861–6, when the inflow of foreign capital for railway construction in Spain was in serious decline. Miguel Artola gives the figures for government railway subsidies, from which it appears that the total of subsidies at the end of 1866, incurred almost entirely within the previous five years, had reached just short of 300 million pesetas (£12 million).[168] Over the longer period to 1885, the Ministry of Public

Works calculated that the Spanish railway system, now 8,372 kilometres, had absorbed 637.6 million pesetas (£25.5 million) in government subventions.[169] No less than 26.34 per cent of the Norte's network (3,421 kilometres, at a cost of £56 million) was financed by government subsidies.[170]

In 1870, a total of 5,316 kilometres of railways were open to operation in Spain.[171] They must have cost about £50 million.[172] The contributions of Spanish investors, private bankers, issuing banks and credit institutions, and of the huge subsidy from the state, combine to suggest that Spain's share in the development and financing of her own railway system was considerable, probably as much as 60 per cent. This is half as much again as Tedde's estimate (40 per cent). The explanation for so wide a divergence may rest partly in Tedde's assumption that Spanish railway stock issued in Paris was held by Frenchmen, and partly in the need to make full allowance for Spanish government expenditure in any calculation of the total domestic contribution to the railway development of Spain.

Conclusion

Spain in the mid-1850s, says Gabriel Tortella, 'can be regarded as an underdeveloped country which had the ability to mobilise a limited amount of resources and which had a choice between alternative fields of investment'.[173] The 'Tortella thesis' is that these limited resources were drawn excessively into government loans and railway securities, at the expense of the development of a more balanced economy.

The deduction is obviously correct: domestic capital, which was relatively modest in dimensions, flowed naturally into the two giant whirlpools of nineteenth-century finance, the government and the railways, from which most of it never escaped. Henry O'Shea was right to complain of the volume of Spain's floating debt, which was so 'embarrassing to all Ministers', and which absorbed the means of Spain's 'monied men'.[174] However, it is not clear that there was a genuine alternative. Over the same period the public credit of developing countries like the United States and Canada was such that they were able to borrow abroad both for their governments and for their railways, thereby releasing a greater part of domestic resources for the development of home trade, finance, industry and agriculture. The state of Spain's credit abroad made a policy of this kind impracticable, and both the Government and the railways became dependent to a large extent on the resources of the domestic market.

Nor does it follow, necessarily, that money released from government bonds and railway securities must always have found a tempting outlet in the growth of domestic industry. Gerschenkron, when considering the parallel case of Italy, denies the assumed existence of a unified capital market. In Italy, both large and small investors looked to the security of their capital. While Italian investors were likely to be interested in government bonds and railways, short-term municipal loans and public works, they were reluctant to tie up their money in industrial ventures. 'The absence of large railroad investments', Gerschenkron concludes, 'did not necessarily mean increased capital availabilities to industry.'[175]

It may also be true that the volume of domestic investment in Spain's manufacturing industry is commonly understated, in part because it is estimated on the basis of the shares of limited companies and registered stock market securities at a time when manufacturing was seldom financed through the stock market. Even in an advanced country like Britain, unregistered and private family capital, reinvested profits and bank and commercial finance provided the bulk of the resources for the development of manufacturing right into the twentieth century. Cottrell concludes, in a recent study of Britain's industrial finance, that private and internal sources of finance were the stand-by for a considerable proportion of manufacturing concerns during the nineteenth century. He points, moreover, to the very low fixed capital requirements of firms outside the cotton, coal and iron industries before the last quarter of the nineteenth century.[176] If this were the case for Britain, how much more so was it for the development of manufacturing in Spain?

Nevertheless, and for whatever reason, it is undeniable that Spain's limited resources of disposable capital were channelled primarily into the state and Spanish railways when, under happier circumstances, they might have taken a larger part in the growth of the national economy. Meanwhile, foreign finance found a role in commerce (particularly in foreign trade) and in some specialised branches of Spanish industry, notably wine and the mines.

The closure of the British, Dutch and German stock exchanges to new issues of Spanish government loans meant that, after 1851, foreign capital was unimportant to Spain's *public* finance. Foreign bankers gave short-term support to the government, although never to the extent undertaken by domestic finance.

Foreign investment was, however, a principal element in the main railway and credit companies of the late 1850s. The Paris Bourse was closed to Spanish government securities from 1861. Although nominally directed only at the Spanish government, the Bourse's refusal to issue new government loans served as a severe check on private investment. When direct investment ceased, foreign financiers supported Spanish railways because they could not afford to do otherwise.

By 1870, perhaps 40 per cent of the Spanish railway system had been financed from abroad; the share of foreigners in Spain's public debt was proportionately very much less. When foreign finance was unwanted or unavailable, the balance, *faute de mieux*, was domestic.

Notes

1 Jordi Nadal, 'The failure of the industrial Revolution in Spain, 1830–1940' in C. M. Cipolla, ed., *The Fontana economic history of Europe: the emergence of industrial societies, part II* (London, 1973), p. 566.
2 Rothschild was giving evidence to the Conseil Supérieur de Commerce, 31 October 1865. The evidence was reprinted in full in *The Economist* early in 1866, from which this comment was taken (3 March, p. 255).
3 Emile Témime, Albert Broder and Gerard Chastagnaret, *Histoire de l'Espagne contemporaine de 1808 à nos jours* (Paris, 1979), p. 90.
4 Joseph Harrison, *An economic history of modern Spain* (Manchester, 1978), p. 54.
5 Bernard Cohen, *Compendium of finance* (London, 1822), p. 111.
6 Report by Mr Lytton, H.M.'s Secretary of Legation, on Spanish Finances, dated Madrid, 29 November 1868: Parliamentary Papers (hereafter 'P.P.'), 1868–9, LXI, p. 241.
7 Richard Ford, *Gatherings from Spain* (London, 1906 edn), p. 16 (first published 1846).
8 *Fenn on the Funds* (12th edn, London, 1874), p. 435.
9 Gabriel Tortella Casares, ed., *La Banca Española en la Restauración*, Vol. I (Madrid, 1974) pp. 41–2.
10 Quoted in *Fenn on the Funds* (12th edn, London, 1874), p. 439
11 A. Milward and S. B. Saul, *The development of the economies of continental Europe, 1850–1914* (London, 1977), p. 249.
12 *The Economist*, 17 September 1853, p. 1044 (in an angry leading article on 'Spanish barbarism').
13 *Fortune's Epitome of the stocks and public funds* (17th edn, London, 1856), p. 218.
14 *Investors' Monthly Manual* (Financial history for 1873), 27 December 1873, p. 411.
15 *The Economist*, 29 October 1870, p. 1321.
16 Ford, *Gatherings from Spain*, p. 49.
17 *The Economist*, 24 April 1869, p. 467.
18 *The Economist*, 18 January 1868, p. 67; 25 January 1868, p. 96.
19 'A sketch of the history of foreign loans', *Bankers' Magazine*, 36 (1876), pp. 427–8.
20 Charles A. Conant, 'Securities as a means of payment', *Annals of the American Academy of Political and Social Science*, 14:2 (September 1899), p. 47.
21 *Investors' Monthly Manual*, 28 December 1872, pp. 413, 415.
22 Michael G. Mulhall, *Balance-sheet of the world for ten years, 1870–1880* (London, 1881), p. 83.
23 J. B. H. Capefigue, *Histoire des grandes opérations financières*, Vol. III (Paris, 1858), p. 119.
24 George Webb Medley's memorandum on 'Loans to foreign states', *Report of the Royal Commission on the London Stock Exchange*: P.P., 1878, XIX, pp. 671–2.
25 J. Horsley Palmer, *The causes and consequences of the pressure upon the money market* (London, 1837), p. 28.

26 Joshua Bates' Diary, Vol. II, 31 May 1835: archive of Baring Brothers & Co. Ltd, Guildhall Library, London (hereafter 'Baring'), uncatalogued.
27 *Circular to Bankers*, 5 June 1835, p. 364.
28 From the 'Appeal by the Dutch creditors', printed in Henry Dashwood, *Spanish finance from 1820 to 1850: an appeal* (London, 1850), pp. 78–9.
29 Gabriel Tortella Casares, 'La economía española', in M. Tunon de Lara ed, Historia de España, Vol. VIII (Barcelona 1981), p. 144.
30 *Fenn on the Funds* (5th edn. London, 1855), p. 247.
31 The distribution is quoted by Henry Ayres, *Ayres' financial register of British and foreign funds, banks, etc. for 1857* (London, 1857), p. 366.
32 The Spanish government, by the law of 11 July 1867, had directed that the 'passive' stock (the bone of contention) should be converted into new 3 per cent stock. The terms offered were not entirely satisfactory, and it was not until May 1868 that the Committee of the London Stock Exchange reluctantly agreed to an official quotation of the new Spanish 3 per cents of 1867.
33 *Bankers' Magazine* (November 1868), p. 1127; (December, 1868), p. 1205.
34 Jean Bouvier, *Le Crédit Lyonnaise de 1863 à 1882*, Vol. II (Paris, 1961), p. 614.
35 *The Economist*, 23 October 1869, p. 1258.
36 Jordi Nadal, *El fracaso de la revolución industrial en España, 1814–1913* (Barcelona, 1975), pp. 31–2. Jenks never meant to imply that his list of authorised issues on the London Stock Exchange (1861–76) should be equated with British investment (although this is often taken to be the case): Leland H. Jenks, *The migration of British capital to 1875* (London, 1971 edn), pp. 421–4 (Appendix C); his revaluations in Appendix D make this clear. I cover some of this ground myself in my article 'British portfolio investment overseas before 1870: some doubts', *Economic History Review*, 2nd ser. 33:1 (February 1980), pp. 1–16.
37 *The Economist*, 4 June 1870, pp. 689–90.
38 *The Times*, 30 October 1871, p. 5a.
39 ibid., p. 6e
40 *The Economist*, 4 November 1871, p. 1332.
41 *The Times*, 13 December 1872, p. 7a.
42 Temime *et al.*, *Histoire de l'Espagne contemporaine*, p. 96.
43 Ford, *Gatherings from Spain*, p. 59.
44 Gabriel Tortella Casares, 'Ferrocarriles, economía y revolución', in Clara Lida and Iris Zavala, eds, *La revolución de 1868: historia, pensamiento, literatura* (New York, 1970), p. 130.
45 Ford, *Gatherings from Spain*, p. 59.
46 This was the view of a British railway engineer, George Higgin, writing in 1885. It is quoted by George L. Boag, *The railways of Spain* (London, 1923), p. 14.
47 Ayres, *Financial Register*, p. 366.
48 P. L. Cottrell, 'Investment banking in England, 1856–82: case study of the International Financial Society' (unpublished Ph.D. thesis, University of Hull, 1974), pp. 369–71.
49 *The Economist*, 30 March 1867, p. 358.
50 British interest in Spanish mines was largely a phenomenon of the mid–late 1870s, during which time between £8–9 million of British capital were said to have found a home in the development of Spanish mineral resources: Minutes of Evidence, *Report of the Select Committee on Wine Duties*: P.P., 1878/9. XIV, p. 544, Q. 6085.
51 *The Times*, 8 October 1868, p. 5b.
52 *The Times*, 5 January 1871, p. 7a.
53 *The Times*, 29 October 1868, p. 10b (reporting a letter from a correspondent at Cadiz).
54 Minutes of Evidence and Appendix No. 2, *Report of the Select Committee on Wine Duties*, pp. 552–3; QQ. 652, 3992.

55 Quoted by Nicolás Sánchez-Albornoz, 'Cadíz, capital revolucionaria, en la encrucijada económica', in Lida and Zavala, eds, *La revolución de 1868*, p. 105 fn. 55.
56 Barings to Hottinguers, 23 July 1847: Baring, PLB 1847.
57 Baring, Spanish Accounts Current, 1868.
58 *Fenn on the Funds* (London, 1837), pp. 88–9.
59 'Appeal by the Dutch creditors', Dashwood, *Spanish Finance*, pp. 78–9.
60 *The Economist*, 5 December 1846, p. 1592.
61 Ayres, *Financial Register*, p. 366.
62 William Borcki to Thomas Baring, 26 March 1853: Baring, HC 8.8.
63 *Fortune's Epitome*, p. 218.
64 Pedro Tedde de Lorca, 'Las compañías ferroviarias en España (1855–1935)', in Miguel Artola, ed., *Los ferrocarriles en España, 1844–1943*, Vol. II (Madrid, 1978), p. 27.
65 Arthur Ellis, 'The "quantitation" of Stock Exchange values', *Journal of the Statistical Society*, 51:3 (September 1888), p. 575.
66 Albert Broder, 'Les Investissements français en Espagne au XIXe siècle', *2nd colloque des historiens économistes français*, 4/5 October 1973, p. 164.
67 ibid., *passim*. Professor Broder has now defended his thesis (University of Paris X, 1982), and it may be that his sources, not given for the published paper of 1973, reveal more than I expect. Certainly his thesis, researched over many years, will have much to say for the details of French investment in Spain. I had not been able to obtain a copy at the time of going to press.
68 Dashwood, *Spanish Finante*, p. 7.
69 The evidence is unsatisfactory, but the conclusion is indicated by the distribution of the 'certificates' of coupons on the 'active' bonds as calculated in the 1850s: Ayres, *Financial Register*, p. 366, quoted above. It was the default of the 'passive' debt that closed the Paris Bourse to Spanish government loans after 1861. Even then, the *Bankers' Magazine* thought that 'the greater part of the passive debt . . . was held in London': 28 (February 1868), p. 90. This opinion is to some extent confirmed in *The Economist*, 5 October 1867, pp. 1134–5.
70 Milward and Saul, *Development of the economies of continental Europe*, p. 244.
71 As Bertrand Gille has explained, the Rothschilds had no faith in Spain's public finance from the 1830s to the end of the 1860s: *Histoire de la maison Rothschild dès origines à 1870* (2 vols, Geneva 1965, 1967), *passim*. James Rothschild's competition for the Mirès loan, often described as fierce, could hardly have been more than lukewarm. This is certainly the suggestion of the Paris correspondent of *The Economist* in the issue for 27 December 1856, p. 1434.
72 Redlich has given a good account of the operation of Jules Isaac Mirès in his article: 'Two nineteenth-century financiers and autobiographers: a comparative study in creative destructiveness and business failure', *Economy and History*, 10 (1967), pp. 38–66.
73 *The Economist*, 26 January 1857, p. 95.
74 Mr Lytton's Report on Spanish Finances, p. 221.
75 Jean Bouvier, *Le Crédit Lyonnais de 1863 à 1882*, Vol. II (Paris, 1961), p. 629 and fn. 1.
76 Rondo E. Cameron, 'The Crédit Mobilier and the economic development of France', *Journal of Political Economy*, 61:6 (December 1953), p. 470.
77 *The Economist*, 14 November 1868, p. 1305.
78 Nadal, 'The failure of the industrial revolution in Spain', p. 551.
79 Boag, *The railways of Spain*, p. 6.
80 Tedde de Lorca, 'Las compañías ferroviarias en España', p. 32.
81 ibid., p. 40.
82 ibid., p. 42.
83 *The Economist*, 21 December 1867, p. 1075.
84 Gabriel Tortella Casares, 'Spain, 1829–74', in Rondo Cameron, ed., *Banking and*

economic development: some lessons of history (New York, 1972), p. 109. Sánchez-Albornoz confirmed the overwhelmingly large interest of French capital in the three 'resident' financial institutions; they were, he said, 'asistidos por escasos capitalistas de nuestro país': Nicolás Sánchez-Albornoz, *España hace un siglo: una economía dual* (Madrid, 1977), p. 186.

85 Report by Mr L. S. Sackville West, British Secretary of Legation, on the Commerce, Statistics etc. of Spain: P.P., 1866, LXXII, p. 384.

86 Government trade figures: *Estadística de comercio exterior de España.*

87 Nicolás Sánchez-Albornoz, 'De los orígenes del capital financiero: el Crédito Mobiliario Español, 1856–1906', in his *España hace un siglo*, p. 175.

88 Bertrand Gille, *La Banque en France au XIXe siècle: recherches historiques* (Geneva, 1970), pp. 259–60.

89 A. D'Eichthal to Thomas Baring, 30 March 1867: Baring, HC 7.27.

90 Jean Bouvier, *Les Rothschild* (Paris, 1967 edn), p. 206.

91 *The Economist*, 27 June 1868, p. 738.

92 Sánchez-Albornoz, 'El Crédito Mobiliario', p. 176.

93 Gabriel Tortella Casares, 'El sistema bancario español en la segunda mitad del siglo XIX', in *Dinero y crédito (siglos XVI al XIX)* (Madrid, 1978), pp. 225–6. He puts it rather more strongly in another paper, where he claims that foreign bankers and capital were called on to play a *decisive* role in the formation of capital in Spain: 'La formación de capital en España, 1874–1914: reflexiones para un planteamiento de la cuestión', *Hacienda Pública Española*, 55 (1978), p. 411. I would not be inclined to follow him so far.

94 José M. Tallada Pauli, *Historia de las finanzas españolas en el siglo XIX* (Madrid, 1946), pp. 70–1.

95 David R. Ringrose, *Transportation and economic stagnation in Spain, 1750–1850* (Durham, NC, 1970), pp. 134, 139.

96 Josep Fontana, *La quiebra de la monarquía absoluta (1814–1820)* (Barcelona, 1971), p. 297.

97 Harrison, *Economic history of modern Spain*, p. 43.

98 Tortella, 'El sistema bancario español', p. 224.

99 Nicolás Sánchez-Albornoz, 'El trasfondo económico de la Revolución', in Lida and Zavala, *La revolución de 1868*, p. 73.

100 *The Times*, 2 March 1869, p. 4d.

101 Tortella, 'La economía española', pp. 135, 141.

102 *The Times*, 30 April 1868, p. 10b (i.e. 5 field marshals, 61 lieutenant generals, 121 major generals, and 317 brigadiers).

103 Temime *et al.*, *Histoire de l'Espagne contemporaine*, p. 82.

104 Tortella, 'El sistema bancario español', p. 222.

105 Tortella, 'La economía española', p. 139.

106 Falconnet to Barings, Mexico, 13 May 1849: Baring, HC 4.5.25. Barings' instructions to Falconnet of 30 May 1848 (Baring, PLB 1848) estimated production costs at Almadén at as much as $Mexican 27 per quintal, but Falconnet was more likely to be correct. Certainly Barings, when they wrote to O'Shea on 20 May 1853, had revised their estimate to $14 per quintal: Baring, PLB 1853.

107 Felipe Riera to Barings, 26 December 1833: Baring, HC 4.8.1.

108 At each of the periodical renegotiations of the mercury contract the prices were: $ Mexican 37¼ (1830), $54¼ (1835), $60 (1838), and $81½ (1843). The exchange was about five Mexican silver dollars to £1 sterling. These were quoted in an anonymous memorandum in the Baring archive: Baring, HC. 1.114. The wholly exceptional price negotiated by the Banco de Fomento y Ultramar for the 1847 contract ($86½ per quintal) proved unsustainable, and the contract had to be rescinded in May 1848.The contract seems simply to have been an attempt, at whatever the cost, to get the mercury business back into Spanish hands, supported and endorsed by the Minister of Finance. The 1850 contract, taken once

more by Rothschilds, was for $70. Barings of London were induced to take an interest in the negotiations for the mercury contracts from 1847 to 1849 (in the hope of breaking the Rothschild connection), and much useful correspondence on the subject is contained in their archives, mostly (for out-correspondence) in the Private Letter Books for 1847–9, in the private letters of their agent in Madrid, Francis Falconnet (Baring, HC 4.8.7), and in those of Thomas Baring to his partners from Madrid in 1849 (Baring, HC 1.20.4).

109 Cohen, *Compendium of finance*, p. 113.

110 Falconnet to Thomas Baring, Mexico, 3 July 1852: Baring, HC 4.5.25.

111 Tedde de Lorca, 'La banca privada española durante la Restauración (1874–1914)', in Tortella, *La Banca Española*, pp. 222, 452.

112 *Fenn on the Funds* (12th edn, London, 1876), p. 429. Seyd's estimate of £260 million for the public debt of Spain held abroad in 1876 is totally implausible: Ernest Seyd, 'The fall in the price of silver, its consequences and their possible avoidance', *Journal of the Society of Arts*, 24 (10 March 1876), p. 309.

113 *The Times*, 14 August 1871, p. 12c.

114 Source cited in note 2 above.

115 Henri Hottinguer to Thomas Baring, 27 April 1863: Baring, HC 7.1.

116 Mr West's Report on the Commerce of Spain, p. 446 (my italics).

117 *The Economist*, 22 May 1869, p. 604.

118 *The Times*, 19 December 1868, p. 9f.

119 *The Times*, 30 December 1868, p. 7c.

120 Reported by J. W. Birch, a London financier with a strong Spanish connection, to Kirkman Hodgson (Barings), Madrid, 10 November 1869: Baring, HC 4.8.24.

121 Birch to Barings, from Madrid. The correspondence for the loan proposal of 1871 is in Baring, HC 4.8.24.

122 *The Times*, 30 October 1871, pp. 5a, b.

123 *The Times*, 11 December 1871, p. 7a.

124 Tortella, 'La economía española', p. 145.

125 Henry O'Shea to Barings, 16 September 1854: Baring, HC 4.8.6.

126 O'Shea to Barings, 7 November 1854: Baring, HC 4.8.6.

127 *The Economist*, 23 July 1853, p. 818.

128 *The Times*, 7 August 1871, p. 5a.

129 Temime *et al.*, *Histoire de L'Espagne contemporaine*, pp. 70, 76–8.

130 Ramón Canosa, *Un siglo de banca privada (1845–1945): apuntes para la historia de las finanzas españolas* (Madrid, 1945), pp. 40–1. Tedde supplies slightly different figures for the number of merchant bankers (fifty-two rising to seventy-four in the decade 1857–67), but he may be allowing for the houses that collapsed during the financial crisis of 1866. Furthermore, he calls attention to another contributor to merchant banking in Spain – the private bankers (substantial houses) in operation simultaneously in Cataluña: 'La banca privada española', pp. 254–5.

131 T. M. Hughes, *Revelations of Spain in 1845* (revised 2nd edn, London, 1845), p. 359,

132 Jaime Vicens Vives, *Manual de historia ecońmica de España* (3rd edn, Barcelona, 1964), p. 659. This must be an error. Gaspar de Remisa was certainly a rich man, by any standards. But his total capital in 1822 was estimated by an official source at 15 million *reales* (£150,000): J. M. Ramón de San Pedro, *Don Gaspar de Remisa y Miaróns, Marqués de Remisa* (Barcelona, 1953), p. 14.

133 Henry O'Shea to Barings, 26 April 1844: Baring, HC. 4.8.6. Henry O'Shea's Madrid house (Enrique O'Shea y Cía.) had taken a sixth part in the tobacco company. O'Shea was Barings' correspondent in Madrid in the 1840s and 1850s. Although he was born British, he had come to Madrid during the reign of Ferdinand VII and, by the end of the 1850s, seems to have been second only in resources to Rothschilds' agents, Weisweiller and Bauer. Sir Henry Drummond Wolff,

who met him in Madrid in 1850, described him as having become 'almost a Spaniard'; as a leading member of the 'comerciantes capitalistas' of Madrid, he was no longer, in any real sense, a foreigner. No trustworthy figures exist, unfortunately, for the wealth of these houses, but the disposable resources of Enrique O'Shea y Cía are at least indicated by the ability of one of its partners to defraud the house of over £200,000 before he absconded in 1862.

134 Gille, *Histoire de la maison Rothschild, des origines à 1848* p. 257.
135 Thomas Baring to Ernest Sillem, 19 September 1848: Baring, PLB 1848.
136 Falconnet to Barings, Madrid, 5 November 1847: Baring, HC 4.8.7.
137 Henry O'Shea to Thomas Baring, Madrid, 17 December 1849: Baring, HC 4.8.6.
138 José Borrajo to C. de Murrieta, London, 8 February 1850: Baring, HC 17.141.
139 *The Times*, 22 December 1871, p. 5a.
140 Pedro Tedde de Lorca, 'Agregación regional de las principales magnitudes bancarias (1874–1914)' in Tortella, *La Banca Española*, Vol. II, pp. 502–4, 505–7.
141 Sánchez-Albornoz, 'El trasfondo económico de la revolución', p. 72.
142 Tortella, 'Spain, 1829–74', p. 104.
143 Nadal, 'The failure of the industrial revolution in Spain', pp. 547–9.
144 Tedde, 'La banca privada española', p. 237.
145 Sánchez-Albornoz, 'La crisis financiera de 1866 en Barcelona', in his *España hace un siglo*, p. 146.
146 Tedde, 'La banca privada española', p. 239.
147 Harrison, *Economic history of modern Spain*, p. 48.
148 ibid., p. 48.
149 Rosa María Meyer C., 'Los Béistegui, especuladores y mineros, 1830–1869', in Ciro F. S. Cardoso, *Formación y desarrollo de la burguesía en México* (Mexico, 1978), pp. 132–3.
150 Mr Lytton's Report on Spanish Finances, pp. 221, 234.
151 Rafael Anes Alvarez, 'El Banco de España (1874–1914)', in Tortella, *La Banca Española*, Vol. I, p. 115.
152 Tortella, 'Spain 1829–1874', p. 95.
153 Anes, 'El Banco de España', p. 119.
154 ibid., p. 119.
155 *The Times*, 29 November 1871, p. 5a; 22 December 1871, p. 5a.
156 Ramón Cordero and Fernando Menéndez, 'El sistema ferroviario español', in Artola, *Los ferrocarriles en España*, Vol. I, p. 324.
157 Francisco Waís, *Historia general de los ferrocarriles españoles* (2nd edn, Madrid, 1974), p. 159,
158 Quoted in *The Economist*, 18 September 1852, p. 1045.
159 Nadal, *Fracaso de la revolución industrial*, p. 37 fn. 49.
160 Tortella, 'Ferrocarriles, economía y revolución', pp. 131–3.
161 Tedde, 'Las compañías ferroviarios', pp. 40–3. The 57 per cent estimate is also from Tedde, p. 40. The three main lines, the Norte, the M.Z.A. and the Andalusian railway, calculated in 1892 that the annual interest on their foreign debt was more than 70.5 million francs (£2.8 million): Cie du Nord, *Procès verbaux des réunions du Comité de Paris* (5 February 1892). But these securities, although held abroad, were not necessarily the property of foreigners, and many had clearly been bought (and held) in Paris for Spanish account.
162 J. W. Birch to Thomas Baring, Madrid, 27 April 1864: Baring, HC 4.8.24.
163 Nadal, *Fracaso de la revolución industrial*, p. 43.
164 Tedde, 'La banca privada española', p. 249.
165 ibid., p. 239.
166 Tortella, 'Spain 1829–74', p. 121.
167 'Estado del material importado con destino a los ferrocarriles', *Estadística del comercio exterior de España, 1861–3.*

168 Miguel Artola, 'La acción del estado', in Artola, *Los ferrocarriles en España*, Vol. I, p. 353.

169 Ferrocarriles secundarias y carreteras', *Revista de Obras Públicas* (1889), p. 102.

170 *Compañía de los Caminos de Hierro del Norte de España (1858–1939)*, Vol. I (Madrid, 1940), p. 58.

171 Cordero and Menéndez, 'El sistema ferroviario', p. 324.

172 The final cost of Spanish railways is widely disputed. It has been placed as high as £16,250 per kilometre. But this is implausible, and the present estimate, at some £9,375 per kilometre, is based on Cordero and Menéndez, 'El sistema ferroviario', Table II:4, p. 265. Their figures are for the cost in pesetas per kilometre by 1896. I have taken the peseta at the depreciated rate (for 1896) of 30.065 per £1 sterling (for which I am indebted to the 1904 *Memoria* of the Norte and, besides much else, to Antonio Gómez Mendoza, formerly of St Antony's College, Oxford. Gómez has now published his research as *Ferrocarriles y cambio económico en España 1855–1915*, Madrid, 1982.)

173 Tortella, 'Spain 1829–1874', p. 96.

174 O'Shea to Barings, 16 September 1854: Baring, HC 4.8.6.

175 Alexander Gerschenkron, 'Notes on the role of industrial growth in Italy, 1861–1913', *Journal of Economic History*, 15:4 (December 1959), pp. 371–2.

176 P. L. Cottrell, *Industrial finance, 1830–1914: the finance and organisation of English manufacturing industry* (London, 1980), pp. 248, 256.

Chapter 6

United States*

Introduction

By contrast with the other countries studied in this book, there is no shortage of estimates for foreign investment in the United States. Many are reproduced in the four tables printed as appendices I–IV. Although superior in many respects to the estimates that exist for elsewhere, they must be treated with some caution. Bias could and did distort in either direction. *The Economist* once explained that the common 'guess' of $300 million for the quantity of American securities held abroad in 1853 was intended to 'strengthen the hands of the Protectionists, by showing the immense extent of American indebtedness, and so beget a desire to check imports'; it was probable that the real amount was not a third as much.[1] *The Economist* was an enthusiastic free-trader. The *Bankers' Magazine*, also of London, which was violently critical of the United States and obsessed by the drain of British capital to American railways, came to the opposite conclusion: $300 million was not enough. The estimate prepared by the US Secretary of Finance for foreign ownership of railway securities and bonds ($52.1 million) was much too low; English investors, and the railway securities currently circulating among British agents and brokers, must alone account for $90 million![2] In turn, US bankers were inclined to overestimate foreign sales so as to promote interest and speculation on the domestic market. . .

Even the most respected of statisticians have had a tendency to over-value foreign finance in the United States. C. K. Hobson reported an estimate of no less than $400 million (£80 million) of American railway securities held in Britain in 1857[3] (which was absurd). Leland Jenks thinks that British investment in US railways just before the First World War amounted to approximately $3 billion.[4] Britons bought many railway securities in the years just before the Great War, but only in 1911 John Maynard Keynes had expressed himself astonished at the $3 billion estimated by the distinguished statistician, George Paish. Such sums, Keynes said, may well have been subscribed originally, but the securities had since returned to the United

* It is convenient to take £1 sterling as the equivalent of $5 US, although in practice the par of exchange was reckoned to be 4s 6d to $1.

States; he did not believe that Paish's overall figure of £3.5 billion for British investment abroad 'ought to be regarded as supplying even a temporary estimate of foreign investments proper'.[5]

The automatic assumptions of an earlier generation of historians are illustrated in the remark that the United States owed her prosperity 'largely to the confidence placed in her integrity by foreign capital'.[6] It is true that before 1914 the United States was consistently indebted overseas; she became a net creditor only during the First World War, to the extent that she had extinguished her foreign debt and accumulated a credit of over $12.5 billion by the end of 1919.[7] But, as Kuznets says,

> Less widely recognised is the fact that neither the gross international indebtedness of this country nor the net (i.e., after deducting US claims upon foreign countries) has been large, either in comparison with the total pool of international capital investments, or in comparison with the total capital in this country owned by its residents. . .[8]

Foreign capital funds, he adds later, 'financed at best about a tenth of total capital investment within the country, and less in most decades'.[9] Naturally, there were significant differences between the experience of nations and, within nations, between periods. For Australia, New Zealand and Canada, the ratio between net capital imports and domestic savings sometimes approached 50 per cent during the half century before 1914, while for the United States it was usually below 5 per cent.[10] Although the 1830s brought much foreign capital to the United States, virtually nothing had arrived in the 1820s, and very little in the 1840s (more particularly after the state defaults). Irving Kravis calculates a modest 4 per cent as the contribution of foreign capital to US net capital formation from the 1820s to the 1860s, and a little over 6 per cent for the period 1869–1914.[11]

Foreign capital, for the United States, was the gilt on the gingerbread. It was at its most influential, relatively speaking, in the second and third quarters of the nineteenth century. But by the end of the century it was 'negligible compared with the level of internal savings'.[12] 'Independent growth' was certainly the experience of the United States, where the annual average of net national capital formation for 1834–43 was 9.5 per cent, rising to 17.8 per cent from 1869 to 1878.[13]

All the same, although the volume of foreign investment in relation to domestic investment was not impressive, the influence of foreign finance may still have been disproportionate. Experience varied with activity, time and place. Some forms of enterprise were naturally more popular with the foreign investor than others. Land and manufacturing attracted little money from abroad. Railway securities, on the other hand, were popular because they were familiar, and normally safe and remunerative. The westward movement of settlement and development, away from the older and more prosperous states of the East to the newly developing territories of the West, meant greater demands on external finance. Domestic finance in the East also helped to fund the West, but in reality there was no rush to invest in the West either from the East or from abroad. Local investment in domestic enterprise was eventually generated in the West as it had been in the East, but there was clearly a shortage both of domestic capital and of institutions capable of directing it into profitable uses;[14] in the South, local capital was not effectively mobilised until the twentieth century.[15]

Jenks is absolutely right to insist that American expansion would have taken place independently without a large injection of foreign capital, 'albeit at a slower rate'.[16] His reservation is all important, and it was well understood at the time. David Wells, formerly Commissioner of Revenue, emphasised the distinctive experience of the United States. The United States encountered rapid growth and forced development; the accomplishment of centuries became the work of years. While such conditions existed, the demand for new capital must always have tended to exceed domestic supply.[17]

The speeding-up of development, as a consequence of foreign finance, is unquantifiable – so many different factors are involved – but the whole process was certainly more significant than might be suggested by the 5 per cent estimated for the contribution of capital imports to the total increase in the 'durable tangible wealth' of the United States in the nineteenth century. The reason, as Raymond Goldsmith says himself, is that capital imports were concentrated in crucial areas of growth and, more particularly, because 'without them the development of the American railroad system, probably the main economic achievement of the second half of the nineteenth century, would have been slowed down considerably'.[18]

An acceleration of growth was what borrowers of productive capital came to expect. The United States never suffered from a shortage of entrepreneurs. She was, as Thomas Baring once said, a country of limited capital and abundant enterprise – the reverse of France. None-the-less, for the United States as for France, it may still be argued that the 'initial driving force towards capital formation' came in part from abroad.[19]

Given the shortage of domestic capital in the United States to meet every demand within an exceptionally active and expanding market ('ce qui manque actuellement [1870] dans ce pays, c'est l'argent'[20]), relatively small amounts of foreign finance could help to channel scarce resources into the most productive or profitable activities.

Douglass North, discussing the development of the West, notes the importance of foreign capital in directing real resources into transportation and plantation expansion, and in sustaining this expansion by making possible an import surplus.[21] The same was true for the East. The importance of foreign loans, Matthews argues, 'lay not so much in the provision of finance as in enabling the United States to run a heavy import surplus without suffering a deterioration in the foreign exchanges'.[22] During the post-bellum boom of 1866–73, foreign purchases of US government bonds undoubtedly *did* serve to release domestic savings and bank resources for railway, industrial and commercial promotion, and, for this reason amongst others, Jenks is probably right to conclude that the impact of foreign capital on the United States was never subsequently as momentous.[23]

Foreign finance proved its value to the domestic market in other respects. The New York money market may not have been quite so much of a 'poor country cousin' to London as Margaret Myers supposes. Securities valued at $3 billion were listed in New York in 1868, while the total was probably doubled by government and corporate bonds; annual transactions amounted to $17.5 billion.[24] Already by the early 1880s, a period of domestic boom, 'London was considered peripheral for most underwriters'.[25] But for an earlier date (for the 1840s) Myers explains the importance of the availability of foreign capital for maintaining stock prices – when supplies of capital from abroad failed, prosperity in the United States was not sufficient to maintain stock prices at home.[26] Similarly, interest rates in the United States were much influenced by foreign finance. It was the search for reduced domestic interest rates, which were 'much too high', that induced American railway entrepreneurs to look for money abroad, as much as it was a genuine shortage of domestic finance.[27]

Foreign Finance before the Civil War

Before the 1870s, commercial credit formed a substantial element in foreign finance world-wide. Nowhere was this more evident than in the United States. Although foreign commercial credit seldom reached as much as $100 million annually before the 1830s (a selection of estimates for the volume of such credit in the United States is printed below as Appendix IV), there is much to be said for North's view that the financing by foreigners of a substantial part of the American export trade, and of some domestic trade as well, could have been as important to the development of the US economy as long-term capital movements.[28] For example, Barings gave a credit of $1.25 million to the Bank of the United States.[29] For Jenks, the availability of the London money market as an element in the calculations of US entrepreneurs, together with the ease with which bills on London could be drawn on short term, 'may have been *of even more consequence* than the actual capital flows'.[30]

The scale was significant and the money exceptionally productive. As John Madden has explained, the British short-term capital market supplied working capital to American importers and exporters, it provided banks with the funds to carry inventories of gold or securities, it supplied exchange dealers with the sterling bills to reduce fluctuation in the value of the dollar, and it advanced the funds that enabled American railways to continue building while they mobilised longer-term support at home. Periodically the Continent gave a greater degree of short-term financial support to the United States than Britain, but it would, in Madden's opinion, be reasonable to believe that, in the 1860s and 1870s, about a quarter of US imports were financed in London.[31]

At an earlier period the proportion was probably much larger. In the autumn of 1836, the 'three Ws' – Wiggin & Co., Wildes & Co. and Wilson & Co., the leading British houses (after Baring Brothers & Co.) in the American trade – had aggregate debts of no less than £7 million ($35 million), and they still owed £5 million when they went into liquidation in 1837.[32] Barings themselves survived, but they lost a great deal of money and came under attack from the Governor of the Bank of England. A correspondent reported that Barings in April 1837 were under acceptance for £1.5 million of American paper.[33] Brown, Shipley & Co. of Liverpool, which by the 1850s had become the dominant firm in the US foreign exchange market, were relying on the discount market in 1854 (a peak period) for upwards of £500,000 a month.[34]

It was not surprising that Continental and Anglo-American houses held so strong a position in foreign trade. The rate of interest for commercial purposes, through all fluctuations, was consistently higher in the United States than it was in Britain. At the same time, resources of American commercial houses, at least until the 1850s and 1860s (when they matched British houses), were substantially lower; $200–300,000 was regarded as a large trading capital in the early 1830s, while $300–500,000 was 'very solid' in the late 1840s – although neither would have been considered particularly great in Europe. The resources of the London house of Baring Brothers & Co. were not only much larger than those of their American correspondents; they were also unrivalled among the 'American' houses in London. By the mid–1840s, Barings' capital was almost too large for comfort. It excited, Joshua Bates felt, envy and competition in the American trade, and he estimated that the capital resources permanently at Barings' disposal would enable them to buy out all competitors with £500,000 to spare.[35] Meanwhile, in the home trade, short-term credit was handled very largely by the domestic banking system, and had been so from the beginnings in 1782.[36]

Despite the domestic resources of the United States, the pace of American expansion in the middle decades of the nineteenth century was undoubtedly accelerated by financial assistance from abroad. The difference was that the United States, like France and the stronger economies of Europe, could take the initiative in marketing its own securities, and could normally count on placing the larger part of them at home. Madden is right to point out that 'the amount of federal bonds abroad before 1871 was much less than has usually been estimated'.[37] With few exceptions, US securities of every kind, federal, state and private, were put on the market first in the United States; it was the surplus – larger or smaller to the extent that the loan was intentionally suited to European tastes – that found its way abroad. Furthermore, before the Civil War (1861–5), the federal government had little occasion to look abroad for its money. Speaking in the Senate in 1872, Sherman recalled the traditional policy, uniformly maintained in peace, of paying off the public debt within the life of a single generation, or about thirty years.[38] After the war, the United States reduced her debt by $500 million (one-sixth of the total) in four years, despite all the burdens of rebuilding a devastated economy.[39]

Under ordinary circumstances, federal stock was held in the United States, just as consols were British-owned and *rentes* French; foreigners outbid Americans only when, as in 1830 and in 1848–9, they wanted to get their money out of Europe. The business was handled in the United States. In 1858, for example, Barings, together with friends in the United States, in London and on the Continent, thought seriously of tendering for a federal loan of $10 million. Domestic demand, however, excluded the foreign investor. The price discussed (before the tenders) was 105 for a 5 per cent stock, which was too high for Europe. Barings agreed with Hope & Co. to let the loan pass without their interference; it should satisfy local investors and leave the way open for a foreign tender when and if a second issue was required.[40] A federal loan of $21 million at 5 per cent was fully subscribed on the domestic market in the summer of 1860, shortly before the troubles began in South Carolina.[41]

In any case, the public debt of the United States was insignificant. In its first incarnation, the federal debt was paid off altogether by January 1835. It returned to a peak of $68.3 million in 1851, but at the equivalent of less than £14 million it was still incredibly small and was reduced successively over the years.

Two-thirds of what remained, according to one informed source, was held in Europe, principally on the Continent,[42] to which, presumably, it continued to be attractive as 'refugee' capital, supposedly safe from political misadventure. But the amount was not important – as little, perhaps, as $40 million (£8 million) in 1859 (Appendix II).

For some years before the Civil War, Barings and other foreigners were reducing their stake in American securities and sending the stocks back for sale to the United States. At the end of the 1853 boom in American securities, Barings had an American portfolio of £519,953 out of a total portfolio of £588,953; by the end of 1856, their American portfolio was reduced to £40,964.[43] With unimportant exceptions, Barings refused all new issues of American securities, even for favourite states, cities and railways, and sold what they could of the remainder.[44] The news of the surrender of Fort Sumter in April 1861 brought the sale of American securities in London to a complete halt. Many of Barings' friends were still interested, after years of investment, in federal and state stocks, but Barings themselves had reduced their portfolio by April 1861 to the bonds of the Hannibal & St Joseph's railway and to $250,000 in New Orleans City.[45]

Southern issues had been off the market for some time. Barings had never objected in principle to Southern finance if the security were sufficiently good, but from an early period they were aware that the price of Southern stocks reflected the reluctance of British investors to hold the bonds of slave states. In the years before the Civil War, slavery became an absolute disqualification, both for commercial dealings with slave owners and for the marketing of Southern securities. In December 1860, Barings were asked by the Bank of the State of South Carolina what England was likely to do if South Carolina seceded from the Union and established free trade. Joshua Bates replied that there was, as the Bank was aware, strong anti-slavery feeling in the United Kingdom. British laws were very severe: it was a felony to buy or sell a slave or to lend money to be employed either directly or indirectly in aiding the cause of slavery. A British subject was placed at a great disadvantage in dealing with a country in which the chief property of the inhabitants was in slaves, which he could not touch. So far as Britain was concerned, this had the effect of preventing the credit and general facilities without which extensive trade was impracticable. Should South Carolina attempt to negotiate a loan after secession, Bates thought it his duty to point out that 'apart from the Repudiation of Mississppi and Florida there has been for several years a growing indisposition with capitalists to invest in the Bonds of Slave States'.[46]

Foreign Finance during the Civil War

The Civil War was a new chapter in US public finance. South Carolina was the first state to secede from the Union, on 20 December 1860, and the other Southern states – Mississippi, Florida, Alabama, Georgia, Lousiana and Texas – followed suit within the next six weeks. Thomas Baring asked his partners whether South Carolina could issue letters of marque against Northern vessels; if so, he thought Barings might do a little privateering business.[47] It was no time for humour. Fort Sumter was the first engagement of the Civil War, and the Southern states were reinforced soon after by four of the border states – North Carolina and Arkansas, Virginia and Tennessee. Bates wrote in his diary that he feared a long and bloody war: 'It will be destructive of commerce and will materially reduce the profits of B.B. & Co.'.[48]

Already in 1860, when so much was to be expected from a rapidly advancing economy, 'all other considerations give place to that of the fearful calamity of impending civil war'.[49] The cost of the war was astronomical. Direct war expenditure during the four years 1862–5 reached $2.7 billion.[50] The public debt (less cash in the Treasury) rose from $87.7 million in 1861 to its highest point of $2.67 billion in 1865.[51] Later, the US Treasury calculated that the war and subsequent expenses paid by the Treasury and directly caused by the war amounted to nearly $6,190 billion (£1.2 billion),[52] without allowing for massive expenditure by the separate states (an accumulated state debt by the late 1860s of nearly $360 million).[53]

In the first years of war it may have been true that nearly half of the money required by the federal government was raised by printing money:[54] the rise of the gold premium to the extraordinary level of $1.85 in July 1864 (i.e. $1 gold equalling $2.85 paper)[55] reflected an alarming resort to the printing press. But this was not the whole story, and Fenn was wrong (except for the South) in describing the overwhelming expenditure of the Civil War as 'met for the most part by the issue of paper currency'.[56] The federal government decided from the beginning that the war was to be financed by loans rather than by taxation, so that the cost would be spread over present and future generations. Salmon P. Chase's first budget, published at the end of 1861, showed that for the first year of the war the United States was expecting to meet only 10 per cent of her expenditure through taxation.[57] As the war dragged on, this policy of deferred payment was abandoned, to be replaced by draconian taxes from the spring of 1864.

Meanwhile, the government found much of its finance through loans. These were taken almost entirely at home, where a combination of Jay Cooke's ingenious marketing with the attractive interest rate of 9 per cent on the biggest issue, the 'five-twenties', brought sufficient subscriptions from all levels of US society. In fact Cooke, who was responsible after October 1862 for the domestic sale of Chase's gigantic 5–20 issue of $500 million, made capital out of the fact that the country had been saved from the indignity of turning to European bankers.[58] The sales were concluded on 21 January 1864, by which time $510.8 million in 5–20s had found a market.[59]

The Confederates found it much more difficult to borrow. They financed themselves almost entirely by the issue of Treasury notes, which then served as the 'rebel' currency. Predictably, the South experienced disastrous inflation. By the end of 1863 (still some way from surrender), the confederate dollar had fallen to the equivalent of 5 cents gold.[60]

In whatever form, the Civil War was financed almost entirely within the United States and the contribution of foreigners was minimal. Contemporaries would have been puzzled indeed by Girard's opinion that a factor in the victory of the North was the 'influx of capital from the London market', as they would by a sum as large as Dunning's estimate for British investment in the United States, i.e. $234 million (£46.8 million) for 1861–5 inclusive.[61] Popular sympathy with the South and the advantageous terms offered for exchange against cotton brought a highly favourable response to the £3 million Confederate 'cotton' loan (7 per cent at 90, secured on cotton sales). It was all taken up after a subscription, in London (March 1863), of approximately £16 million – in two and a half days! But it was speculation, and the market collapsed.[62]

The 'cotton' loan was the only Southern loan to be floated in Europe, and no interest, naturally, was paid on the bonds after March 1865. It was, in any case, a paltry contribution: the final report on the loan showed that, after commission, support and repurchase, it brought the Confederacy little more than half of the face value of the loan, of which, in any case, a substantial part came not from British investors at all but from Erlangers, the Paris house originally in charge of marketing the loan.[63] The funded debt of the Confederate government, on 1 October 1864, was £107.9 million, together with unfunded liabilities (nominal) of £120 million.[64] The 'stupendous losses' that Nathaniel Bacon records for British ownership of Confederate bonds during the Civil War[65] can hardly have amounted to much more than a quarter of the 'cotton' loan.

The North floated none of its loans abroad. Some of the securities found their way into foreign markets, often for the purpose of speculation. When the victory of the North became a certainty, European investors recovered some interest in American securities. Foreign holdings of US securities in 1866, including pre-war investment, came to approximately $600 million (£120 million), but government bonds accounted for only $350 million (£70 million).[66] Foreign interest in the huge federal war loans of the day was obviously very small.

The reasons are plain enough. In 1861, the Trent affair threatened war between Britain and the North. Leonard Courtney, in an impressive paper delivered to the Statistical Society (London), explained that the act making government paper legal tender, which was approved by Congress in February 1862, contributed more than anything else to the great distrust of American securities experienced subsequently in Europe.[67] *The Economist* argued later that, but for the inconvertible currency and irredeemable paper circulated in the North, America 'might well have borrowed in London during the War'.[68]

Other factors were indicated in the response to the several attempts to negotiate Northern loans abroad. In the first months of the war, the Secretary of the Treasury asked the Rothschilds' representative in the United States (August Belmont) whether US stock might be sold in Europe. Belmont replied that it would be worse than useless to attempt to do so; Chase must raise the money himself on his own market.[69] Later, Chase sent a special agent to Europe (R. J. Walker, formerly Secretary of the Treasury under President Polk). Walker found hostility and strong distrust of US government credit.[70]

Early in 1863, yet another attempt was made to raise money in Europe (£10 million). The overtures were conducted by J. M. Forbes and W. H. Aspinwall, agents of the federal government and old friends and correspondents of Barings. Barings themselves were deeply committed to the North. Joshua Bates, the principal partner, was a Bostonian and an enthusiastic supporter of the Union; to him, all were traitors who talked of secession.[71] From the beginning Barings opened a regular credit for $2 million, at the request of the Secretary of War, to enable his agent, George L. Schuyler, to buy arms on the Continent.[72] At Schuyler's orders, they were also shipping rifles from Liverpool – 49,280 stand between May 1861 and March 1862. This was a very moderate amount, however, compared with some of their neighbours.[73]

Barings were anxious to do all that they could for the North, but the response of Continental financiers was dispiriting. Thomas Baring wrote to Hottinguers (Paris) and Hope & Co. (Amsterdam) to enquire whether a Northern loan could be placed in their markets. Henri Hottinguer thought that French investors, if they showed any interest at all in American stock, would find it more to their advantage to buy federal securities in New York, which at the current rate of exchange gave an interest of 8½ per cent. He doubted, in any case, whether the new 6 per cent bonds would be given a quotation on the Paris Bourse. The French government, on the pretext of neutrality, would refuse permission; the Emperor was vexed by the North's attitude to his Mexican adventure and favoured the South, 'et vous devez savoir que le Ministère est tout à fait guidé par l'opinion de leur chef'.[74] Hope & Co. were asked whether they might be able to place £3 million in Holland and Germany. Their reply was no more encouraging. Dutch investors had large sums locked up in the Southern states, particularly in Louisiana. Hope & Co. were reluctant to abandon their neutrality, and doubted whether a large amount of new bonds could be placed while the news from the United States was still so uncertain. They wished Barings well, but pointed out that there was a difference between their own position and that of Barings 'as the Bankers of the United States Government since a long period of years'.[75]

In Britain, the demand for government stock was limited to the Northern 5 per cents and in practice it was confined to commissions for Holland and Germany and for those Americans resident in Europe who had money and confidence in the North; the current price had dropped to 71 per cent. Thomas Baring told J. M. Forbes in August 1863 that no demand could be expected among the English for real investment while fears existed of some collision between the British and American governments during the continuance of the Civil War, with the still stronger apprehension that when the states had settled their internal differences they would turn their guns against Britain. Such cheap purchases as were made in London of American stocks, Thomas Baring thought, were for remittance to the United States.[76] Forbes and Aspinwall warned Barings that if the £10 million of federal 6 per cents could not be sold, the government wanted a loan of £1 million for one year secured on US stocks. Bates thought that a loan of £1 million would be a lock-up for Barings; they had so much due from the United States already that it would be putting too many eggs in one basket to take the £1 million themselves. Barings nevertheless agreed, after their unsuccessful soundings in Paris and Amsterdam, to lend the government £500,000 at 4 per cent interest and 1 per cent commission, to be disposed of as Forbes and Aspinwall directed, presumably for the purchase of armaments. It was a loan for six months in the first instance, but both the loan and account were extended until after Lee's surrender at Appomattox on 9 April 1865.[77]

In general, the London money market was interested neither in the North nor in the South. Repudiation was a live issue. 'Prudent Englishmen', said the *Bankers' Magazine* (London) in December 1862, '[will have] as little as possible to do either with the money matters of the North or South.'[78] It was delivering the same warnings a year later,[79] and although the violent anti-Americanism of its editor made its views less convincing than they might otherwise have been, the omens were never good for a return to US securities on the British market. In fact, English funds fell on the news of American peace negotiations in February 1865, since English investors believed that the United States and Britain would come to blows once the Civil War was over.

Barings continued throughout the war to sound out the market for US government stock on the Continent. They asked Hope & Co. early in 1864 whether Dutch and German investors might be attracted by the division of the bonds into smaller amounts and by the option to use the bonds in payment for government lands; the idea was that emigrants to the United States would be ready purchasers. Hope & Co. replied, very reasonably, that it would do no harm, but that if the intention were to sell a considerable amount, they doubted whether it would meet with much success since emigrants were generally poor.[80]

Morier Evans, writing in 1864, predicted that, after repudiation by some of the states in the early 1840s and the railway frauds, the Civil War would prove to be the third, and in all probability the final, blow to American securities on the London market.[81] In the short term, he was right. The Northern 5 per cents continued to sell to a limited extent on the Continent, but not in England. Even Continental interest has been overestimated. The figure of $200 million for US federal bonds supposedly distributed in Germany by the single firm of J. & W. Seligman of New York during the Civil War has been shown to be implausible.[82] Frankfurt certainly became the leading European market for US securities[83] – so much so that of the $320 million in Union bonds estimated to be held in Europe in March 1865 no less than $250 million were said to be German or Dutch[84] – but by the end of 1864 the Frankfurt and Amsterdam markets were reported to be overloaded. Northern 5–20s were down to 51.5 per cent in February 1865, while the only real activity in 1864, again simply on the Continent, was a feverish speculation in heavily depreciated Confederate bonds: some $100 million of Southern internal bonds were hawked around the Continent in 1864 at between 6d and 8d per dollar.[85]

Morton Peto was only slightly exaggerating when he said that US financiers during the Civil War were in no position to negotiate their securities outside their own country, except at excessive and unreasonable rates; 'the whole of the debt incurred had, therefore, to be raised within the territory'.[86]

The Restoration of Public Credit

American public credit abroad took long to recover. Patterson reckons that 'the credit of the government was not fully restored until fourteen years after the war was ended'.[87] In France, sympathy with the South and continued irritation at the Federals' attitude to French intervention in Mexico, reduced popular interest in American stock. For some time to come, Frankfurt and Amsterdam continued to be virtually the sole markets for US securities in Europe, and it was not until the Franco-Prussian war that German and Dutch holdings of Civil War securities found their way in numbers to the London market. British investors remained cautious. Russia, at the end of 1866, could borrow in London at 6 per cent; the United States, by contrast, had to pay about 8.3 per cent.[88] US securities were distrusted in part because of America's reputation for repudiation, but more because the very real danger existed that the principal of the main war debt (the 5–20s) would be paid off not in gold but in depreciated 'greenbacks'. The protracted attempts to impeach President Andrew Johnson in the early part of 1868, although unsuccessful, did nothing to endear federal securities to the foreign investor. To *The Economist*, 'President Johnson is so odious that anything coming from him is apt to be received with disfavour on that account'.[89] In his Message to Congress at the beginning of 1869, Johnson actually advised his countrymen to repudiate the national debt.

The result of this and other misfortunes was that, although American public securities rose considerably in favour after the Civil War, in January 1869 they were still priced at less than half the level of the British debt: US 6 per cents stood at 86, while British consols (3 per cents) fetched 92. In the opinion of *The Economist*, as late as March 1869, American commerce and finance could never be regarded as in a sound condition until the greenback paper dollar was called in and cancelled: 'as matters now stand, American credit does not enjoy the favour or occupy the position to which the vast resources of the United States justly entitle it.'[90] In fact, Frank Evans, an English associate and agent of Jay Cooke, told Cooke in February 1869 that, as a result of the Erie disclosures (the fraudulent financing of the Erie railway), the British public was thoroughly frightened off US securities.[91]

Attitudes changed only in the second and third quarters of 1869. The revival in foreign interest was associated with a number of separate developments, such as stable government and a strong Union under a new president (General Grant from March 1869), the declaration that the principal on US government securities would be redeemable in coin (the Public Credit Act, also of March 1869), burgeoning trade, budget surpluses and a steady reduction in the national debt. It took some time to acclimatise British and Continental investors to the 5–20s, but by early 1870 they were returning, and *The Economist* reported them to have 'found their way into almost every portfolio'.[92]

The restoration of credit was still incomplete. Repudiation was at issue in the House of Representatives as late as December 1869. The Alabama claims were not referred to arbitration until 1871. The Erie scandal threw doubt on all US railway securities. *The Times*, in a stern leader on the battle between the English shareholders and the 'Erie ring' – Britons were said to hold no less than $50 million of the $70 million of Erie railroad stock – concluded that the standard of commercial morality in New York was lower than anywhere else in the civilised world.[93] The US 'sixes', among the earliest of the Civil War loans, were the first of American securities to reach par, in February 1870.[94] 'The truth is', said *The Times* in December 1869, 'the bonds of the United States are still looked upon in Europe as somewhat uncertain forms of investment.'[95]

None-the-less, European holdings of US government securities, which were estimated at around $350 million in 1866, have been thought to have risen to as much as $1 billion in 1869 (Appendix II). This estimate is probably much overdone. *British* investors at any rate showed little taste for them, and Philip Cottrell is mistaken in implying the contrary.[96] The French market certainly bought federal bonds from the closing stages in the Civil War, at a time when Britain was still apprehensive of an Anglo-American conflict. In 1870, a Paris banker was reported as saying that American securities were now sold principally in Paris.[97] Large quantities of US securities, chiefly 5–20s, undoubtedly crossed the Atlantic in settlement of an endemic deficit on the US balance of payments. The New York *Journal of Commerce* reported in December 1869 that ever since the end of the Civil War American exports of produce and specie combined had averaged $60–100 million below imports and interest obligations to Europe.[98] *The Times* noticed that for the fiscal year 1868 the imbalance of imports and exports had been settled by the export of £16.8 million in specie and £20 million in national bonds and other paper.[99] All the same, there is little evidence of direct investment in federal securities on the London market, even during the heady days that preceded the international financial collapse of September 1873. Madden has rejected the Cairncross estimate of £160 million of federal bonds in British hands at the end of 1870; his own, more plausible, estimate is about £33 million ($165 million), or approximately 30 per cent of foreign holdings ($518 million).[100]

The market improved – Madden calculates British holdings of federal bonds in December 1874 at $420 million, by contrast with the $220 million held in Germany and Holland – but it was never brisk. It could offer few attractions to the foreigner. From the autumn of 1869 George S. Boutwell, Secretary of the US Treasury, was considering the possibility of refunding the federal debt (mainly in 6 per cents) at 4.5 per cent, and *The Economist*, in a rare moment of enthusiasm for American credit, agreed that no nation should be able to borrow more cheaply.[101] *The Times*, on the other hand, thought that there was no chance of success.[102] It was right, and when the refunding proposals, even at a more modest level, were finally brought forward in 1871, the initial reaction was decidedly cool. A strong syndicate of international bankers failed to place the first London issue of the US funded loan in March 1871; 5 per cent at par was too high a price, and the Americans themselves were the principal subscribers. The

American Secretary of Finance was trying to reduce the interest on government securities from 6 to 5 per cent, but only $75 million were subscribed to the $200 million on the market, and the subscribers were Americans.[103]

A few months later (August 1871), Jay Cooke negotiated a successful issue of the funded loan, again supported by a powerful syndicate of European bankers. He succeeded in placing $75 million on the London market, and the loan was taken up entirely by a combination of British, Continental and US investors.[104] But the same syndicate was unsuccessful in placing the remaining portion of the 5 per cent funded loan in London in February 1873; only $28.5 million of the $300 million on offer were sold in Europe, and very much less in the United States.[105]

The financial crisis that followed in the autumn of 1873 cut off further foreign investment, and no bonds were sold at a lower rate than 5 per cent until 1877.[106] Subsequent attempts during the 1870s to reduce the rate to 4 per cent were a failure; American credit would not support it. John Philip Trew, a dealer on the London Stock Exchange whose business was entirely American, told the Royal Commission on the Stock Exchange in December 1877 that he did not know of a single transaction in American 4 per cents. The 4.5 per cent loan had gone off well, but the attempt to reduce the borrowing rate of the US government to 4 per cent had resulted in a complete fiasco.[107]

It was as true for the United States as it was, say, for France that public credit was stronger within the country than abroad, and that domestic investors were prepared to pay more for government securities than they would fetch in foreign markets. By the end of the century United States bonds were almost all owned at home, in common with state, county and municipal bonds, bank stock and industrial securities. Foreign interest was limited to railways.[108] In one estimate, railway securities formed as much as four-fifths of American securities held abroad before the First World War.[109] But it was only under the most exceptional circumstances that the national *government* had to look further than the domestic investor.

Foreign and Domestic Finance in US railways to 1853

Although, on the figures we have, the amounts of capital were smaller for foreign investment in railways than they were for US government bonds ($1 billion in government bonds in 1869, by contrast with $243 million in railways: see Appendices II and III), the consequence of direct investment in railways was clearly greater for the development of the American economy. It would, however, be unreasonable to take this contrast too far. Attitudes towards one kind of investment were shared, naturally, with those towards another, and in any case they overlapped. Neither US government bonds nor railway securities were particularly popular abroad. There were too many unwarranted assumptions in C. K. Hobson's view that, by 1869, 'by far the greatest share' of foreign investment in the United States was British, and that British capital, after the crisis in state borrowing of 1838, flowed as steadily into American railway securities as it had previously into state bonds.[110] Hobson's estimate of £80 million ($400 million) for American railway securities held in Britain in 1857 in unreasonable (alternative estimates are given in Appendix III). Nor is it right to conclude that the American railway network was 'to a large extent financed by British capital', so that 'in the same way as in Europe, American railroads were largely the product of the influx of foreign capital and generous subsidies in land'.[111] It is useful to keep some sense of proportion. When the Secretary of the Treasury obtained an estimate of American securities held abroad in 1853, the total ($222 million) amounted to about 18 per cent of all the American securities then outstanding.[112] Leland Jenks, taking an overall view, calculates that British investment in American railways can never have been more than 3 per cent of US national wealth, and that in boom years the US supply of capital was augmented some 10 per cent by British investment. On the other hand, as he says, it is clear that investment in an industry with such extensive leverage effects had a disproportionately large influence in accentuating booms and slumps and intensifying their effects.[113]

Muriel Hidy once remarked that the safest generalisation for the source of American railway capital was that 'the hundreds of railroads got it where and when they could',[114] But there was a general rule that normally determined where and when railway capital was brought in from abroad. Barings, still the principal 'American' house in London, took no part in US railway issues until the early 1850s, except indirectly in the form of state or municipal bonds brought out in favour of a particular enterprise. Barings' argument was always that certain classes of American securities were as safe and as competitive as any on the market, and that the discredit attached to a few should not be allowed to injure the rest. Sales became feasible, however, only within fairly tight limits. If offered a sufficient return, the American home market would take off most, if not all, American issues. European investors likewise preferred their own stocks, and customarily paid more for them than for anything from across the Atlantic. The margin between the price at which Americans would let their stocks go overseas and the level at which Europeans would begin to buy was not large.

English investors were in the middle of their first railway boom in the 1830s when American stocks flooded the market, and they had to be tempted from home railways to foreign stocks. Even if state repudiation had not so fearfully damaged American credit after 1842, England's second railway boom would have mopped up any surplus capital in the years leading up to the financial crisis of 1847. British railways were again absorbing domestic capital in the early 1850s. US railways became very attractive to the British investor in 1852–3. From the mid-1850s, however, political trouble abroad and the financial collapse of 1857 cut off Britain's foreign investment, so that at a time when money was cheap and plentiful the attention of British investors was concentrated on home and colonial stocks and British and Indian railways.

Simply as a rule of thumb, it might be said that British capital ceased to migrate whenever it could get 5 per cent at home. US federal government stock could attract domestic investors at less than 5 per cent, and so could some of the best state and municipal stocks. Capital had to be particularly cheap in England, and state, municipal and railway securities more than usually abundant in the United States, for the trans-Atlantic market to operate. Conditions such as these certainly existed from time to time, and the flow of capital could be very large. But Jenks is surely right when he says of American railways before the Civil War that in only a few cases was foreign investment an initiating factor in development.[115]

The early history of foreign financing in US railways illustrates the point. Europeans showed little interest in direct investment in American railways during the first decades. Although some railway shares found their way to Europe, the great majority was subscribed locally, not so much by simple investors as by local manufacturers, farmers, landowners, bankers, merchants and contractors, all of whom stood to gain immediately and directly from a new railway. The 'financial rock' of the Western Railroad Corporation of Massachusetts during the 1830s was the 'Boston industrial community, particularly that part of it involved in the Springfield factories', although, characteristically, when the Commonwealth of Massachusetts was persuaded to take a one-third partnership in the railway, the Commonwealth's contribution was financed not from tax revenue but by 'state scrip sold in London as each assessment fell due'.[116]

This pattern of shared domestic and foreign contributions to railway finance was more true of the Eastern states than it was for the Western; but the principal railway development during the first half of the century took place in the East, and the conclusion is inescapable that 'until some time in the fifties' (more precisely, until the short boom of 1852–3) funds for railway development came 'chiefly from local sources, whether private or public'.[117]

Foreign finance, so far as it reached the first railways, was recruited indirectly through state loans – as it was in the case of the Western Railroad Corporation mentioned above. Of the $172 million outstanding of state debts in 1838, $42.9 million had been allocated to railways; in turn, about half of the state debts was said to be held in Europe.[118] The contribution of state governments to canal construction was even greater, at $60.2 million by 1838.[119] For the whole period 1815–60, Cranmer has calculated that, of the $195 million allocated to canal construction, $121 million was spent by state governments and $74 million by private companies.[120] Some part of state funding of canals, as of railways, was financed by the sale of state securities abroad, but it is unlikely that Margaret Myers is right in saying that nearly one-third of all funds used in canal construction by both public and private agencies, mostly between 1825 and 1840, came from foreign investors.[121] When the Secretary of the Treasury considered foreign ownership of canal and navigation companies at 30 June 1853, it appeared that, out of a total of $58 million in stocks and bonds, only $2.5 million were held by foreigners.[122]

Carter Goodrich, the authority on this subject, calculates that state governments, in the period before the Civil War, allocated some $300 million in cash and credit to internal improvements, while local governments (municipalities, etc.) contributed more than $125 million. The federal government, by land grants, by the distribution of surplus revenue to the states and by the reallocation of the proceeds of the direct sale of public lands, 'made much larger sums available to the States'. During the 1850s, no less than 9.11 million hectares of public land were distributed and sold for the financing of public improvements.[123]

Foreigners were not *directly* interested to any extent in US railway securities until the beginning of the 1850s. During the 1840s, foreign investors had placed money privately in US railway securities, although more so on the Continent than in Britain. Throughout the 1840s *The Economist*'s listing of American securities included only two railways, the Camden–Amboy and the Philadelphia–Reading.[124] *Barings' Circular* for the end of 1851 explained that the bonds of American railway companies had not yet obtained much currency in the London market; where investment was desired, orders were transmitted to the United States.[125] Barings took part in the purchasing of iron rails for US companies in the 1840s, in return for which US railway bonds reached European markets; but they made their first attempt to bring US railway securities directly to the London market only in the autumn of 1852.[126]

Barings and Rothschilds, amongst others, had nursed American credit so that by the late 1840s and early 1850s British investors were ready once more to place their money in America. In and after the European revolutions of 1848, a great deal of Continental capital sought refuge overseas. The experience of Barings with consignments of American securities in July–September 1848 was that 'far more than half the sales were made to residents on the Continent, chiefly in France and Switzerland'.[127] British investors, who were under less political pressure at the time, were slower to react, but money was abundant, and a bewildering quantity of US securities was sent to London in the early 1850s. The difficulty was not to attract sales but to control the flood. Past experience was no guide. Joshua Bates could give no advice to Thomas Baring on the eve of Baring's visit to the United States in the late summer of 1852. Bates did not know what to think of American securities, railways in particular. Coleridge or some other writer, he said, had compared experience to the stern lights of a ship that illuminated the path behind. This was true of himself, since his whole experience (of forty years) was useless in judging things now, and the Californian gold discoveries had thrown him out in all calculations: 'You must find out on the other side what we are to do, and be safe.'[128]

Thomas Baring was revisiting America after twenty-three years. He was overwhelmed with information, assured on all sides that everything was sound, that there was wealth enough to hold what was afloat and even to take up what might be returned from Europe, that there was no large circulation of bank notes and no inability to meet a sudden call for the settlement of pending engagements. He could not quite see it that way. Two thousand miles of railroad were planned for the single state of Illinois, and the state was borrowing on its notes of hand from six months to six months at 6 per cent: 'This can go on as long as Californian gold and a demand abroad for Bonds and Stocks continues but if a panic comes. . .' Barings' policy, Thomas Baring concluded at the end of his tour, should be to take only what was really good, stocks that could be held, even if sales were stopped, with perfect security. He advised against the more remote railway and city securities; many of the city bonds were very good, but they fell like a Scotch mist – 'a constant shower, looking so small and thin that it cannot hurt and yet *c'est la petite pluie qui perce*'. Barings ought to buy and sell securities that they could positively recommend, so as not to keep themselves out of the market and out of the world. But they should always resell at prices that would give a good profit, remembering that a time might come when they would need their money to help those friends in the United States who now looked so independent.[129]

Meanwhile, in the United States the annual total of railway investment rose from $37 million in 1849 to a peak of $111 million in 1854.[130] The *Bankers' Magazine* calculated that, between 1 July 1848 and 1 July 1852, £12 million ($60 million) were invested by foreigners in American railways securities and in municipal bonds issued in favour of American railways, in addition to which a further £5.2 million ($26 million) were invested by Europeans in American state bonds, a part of which was issued on behalf of the railways.[131] Even at this period, however, the bulk of the new securities – state, municipal and railway – was taken up within the United States. Foreign assistance was desirable, but not essential. California's gold was sufficient in itself to balance large import surpluses, and Sobel is right in thinking that at this juncture, for railways, there was still enough local money to keep the market busy so that, for a while, no great importance was attached to the loss of foreign finance after the financial crisis of 1853.[132]

Foreign and Domestic Finance in the US Railways since 1853

Direct comparison between the foreign and domestic financial contribution to American railways is not straightforward. However, the Secretary of the Treasury calculated that in June 1853 foreign ownership of railway securities and bonds represented 10.8 per cent of the total of paid-up capital and bonds outstanding (that is, $51.9 million out of $480 million).[133] By 1856, foreign holdings in US railway securities were estimated, again by the Secretary of the Treasury, at $83 million (see Appendix III). Few state stocks were sold in Europe after 1839, so that state financing through foreign borrowing (perhaps $25 million at its peak) ceased and, in the mid-1850s, the federal government was not borrowing abroad. The capitalisation of US railways in operation in 1861 is commonly estimated at $1,145 million, to which governmental agencies had contributed 25–30 per cent.[134] Even allowing for the imperfections of these figures, it might not be completely implausible to estimate the contribution of foreign finance to the development of the US railway system before the Civil War at not much more than 10 per cent (i.e. about half of Jenks' estimate).[135]

There was so much trans-Atlantic traffic in American securities, in both directions, that it is impossible to supply a precise figure for the quantity of foreign capital engaged at any one time in the great railway expansion of the 1850s; parcels of securities were sold and resold, often in small quantities and for every kind of enterprise. For a short period, US railway securities were indeed the 'prime glamour issue' in London: it has been calculated that, by 1853, 26 per cent of all American rail bonds were in the hands of foreigners.[136] Much of the enthusiasm for American railway securities went out of the London market after the autumn of 1853; by November the demand in London had come temporarily to a complete stop.[137]

Schulyer's 'gigantic frauds and forgeries' in the New York and New Haven Railroad, which came to light in the early months of 1854, checked any renewal of foreign investment.[138] Further frauds associated with Kyle (Harlem) and Crane (Vermont Central) railways deepened the wound. Apprehensions throughout 1853 of a European war, followed by its outbreak in the Crimea in March 1854, suspended dealings almost entirely in American securities. The United States herself experienced a severe financial crisis in 1853, comparable in some degree with the crisis of 1837, and she shared the international financial disasters of 1857. As late as 1861, on the eve of the Civil War, *Cassell's Handbook* was warning British investors to be very cautious with the American railway bonds that reached the London market.[139]

After the 1853 crisis; the market for American railway securities was in fact overwhelmingly domestic in composition and management, and so far beyond the capacity of a London financial house like Barings as to make it foolhardy beyond belief to throw British resources into the unknown. Good business was still possible, and Ralph Hidy is probably overstating his case when he talks of the 'virtual retirement of the Barings after 1853 from the field of marketing American securities'.[140] But he rightly calls attention to a policy of increased caution and restraint. As he says, few of the more important railways in the United States and Canada failed to appear, in some form or another, in Barings' correspondence over this period. In practice, Barings took responsibility only for those in which they felt the utmost confidence – the Eastern, Pennsylvanian, Michigan Central, New York Central and Panama. Samuel Gray Ward, T. W. Ward's son and successor as Barings' agent in the United States, was instructed in July 1853 not to contract for any shares or bonds in the United States except where the continuance of former connections made it necessary to take some part of an issue, or where an engagement to take a portion would help to maintain the value of securities already held by Barings.[141]

For the market in general, Dorothy Adler has explained how interest in US railway securities in London was deepening rather than widening; attention was concentrated on a few major lines.[142]

A long time-lag is bound to exist between capital issues and actual railway construction, but it is clear that the financing of United States railway construction during its most dynamic phase – from 30,000 kilometres in 1855 to 50,000 kilometres in 1860 – must have been overwhelmingly domestic.

After the Civil War, foreign interest in US railways revived. *Poor's Manual* calculated the total funded debt of the railways of the Northern and Western states at $662 million in 1870.[143] The actual amount of money diverted to railway development was very much larger.

Indeed, the stock, mortgage bonds, equipment, obligations, etc. of US railways in 1869 were valued in total at just over $2 billion.[144] Foreign holdings of US railway securities were calculated by the Special Commissioner of the Revenue in 1869 at $243 million (see Appendix III), which is 12 per cent. If some allowance is made for indirect investment through federal and state municipal loans, the foreign contribution, even then, worked out at about one-sixth of the total (16.7 per cent). This was for a period, prior to 1870, when perhaps 40 per cent of the costs of all construction were taken by national and local governments.[145] A popular observation in the American press during the summer of 1871 was that over the previous decade Congress had given away to railway corporations as much land as the whole area of the original thirteen states of the Union.[146]

It is probable that the notoriety attached to speculation in the Illinois Central and Erie shares, favourites at one time in London, has given an impression of activity on the London market that is not justified. This would certainly seem to have been the case in the late 1860s and the early 1870s, when public opinion and the press were obsessed with a few dramatic scandals. Bernard Cracroft spoke of the two 'parrot cries', the Erie and the Atlantic & Great Western, but, of the 96,560 kilometres of US railway operating in the early 1870s, the Atlantic & Great Western, the Erie and the Illinois Central (another scandal) accounted for scarcely 4 per cent.[147]

The length of railways in operation in the United States rose from 56,466 kilometres in 1865 to 119,241 in 1875 and 150,090 in 1880.[148] Total financing for railway securities, mortgage bonds, equipment obligations, etc., which stood at $1,172 million in 1867, had increased to $4,658 million in 1875.[149] An expansion of this size and speed obviously required the assistance of foreign finance even if, taken at a slower pace, no difficulty would have been experienced in raising the money at home.

Numbers have their own magic and some sense of proportion is needed. Jenks quotes Schumpeter's view that during the railway boom of 1866–73 the doubling of US railway mileage was financed entirely from abroad, to the extent of $2 billion; Jenks himself does not believe that the foreign contribution was more than about $500 million.[150] And certainly the estimates for foreign investment is US railways cited in Appendix III suggest a rise from $50 million in 1866 (Myers), to $243 million in 1869 (Wells), and to $500 million in 1876 (Adler). Foreign finance was clearly an element in the railway boom, but foreigners did not lead the field, nor were Britons (at this point) the principal foreign investors; it is difficult to accept Saul's view that British capital in America reached its most important phase in the middle decades of the nineteenth century.[151] Holland and Germany, in fact, were the popular markets for US rails until the early 1870s, as they were for US government bonds.

The outbreak of the Franco-Prussian war put a stop to Continental purchases, but Dolores Greenberg is a year or more ahead of the times when she places the major British purchases of US rails in 1871.[152] A London partner of Jay Cooke, writing in October 1872, complained that the British market in American railways had been most unsatisfactory for over a year.[153] There is no basis for Sir George Paish's view that Britain, with Holland, was the main European investor in US government and private securities in the 1850s, 1860s and early 1870s.[154] Britons were demonstrably uninterested in major investment in federal state and municipal stock. The repudiation of state debts in the early 1840s had a totally shattering effect on European markets for US state and municipal securities, and the collapse of confidence spread well beyond the repudiating debtors themselves. James Capel, a leading broker on the London Stock Exchange during the 1840s and a specialist in foreign issues, mentioned United States stocks, along with Spanish, Portuguese and South American, as the cause for the 'great distaste' currently felt by British investors for all foreign funds.[155]

The boom in American rails that captured the Continent from 1868 to 1870 did not reach London until the autumn of 1871.[156] It was short and sharp, confined largely to 1873. London was a better market than the United States for American rails throughout 1874, but the international financial crisis of the previous September finally took its toll. America's domestic market was at once prostrated; it was 'not until the fall of 1879, after the resumption of specie payments on January 1, that the recovery of clearings and security prices was complete'.[157] Dorothy Adler concludes that 'the 1880s was the first decade in which American railway securities gained substantial popularity in London'.[158]

An important element in British finance that does not appear in the estimates for direct investment was the exchange of railway and state bonds for British rails. Back before the Civil War, Samuel Ward had thought that as much as half of the $70 million of European investment in American railways in 1853 took the form of railway bonds given to iron masters as payment for rails.[159] The railway contractor Morton Peto calculated that during his own period (the late 1850s and early 1860s) the largest proportion of construction costs on American lines was to be accounted for by iron, in the form of rails usually obtained from Britain.[160] Such payments continued. Although British investors showed little interest in the US railway mortgage bonds that flooded Dutch and German markets in 1870, it was still true that large shipments of rails left England and Wales for the United States in exchange for mortgage bonds.[161]

Nevertheless, the conclusion must be that foreign finance was far less influential in American railway development that it is often declared to be. During the earlier phases, US authorities took advantage of foreign technical and operational experience, but they did not ask for British money.[162] Railway projects and proposals were initiated by domestic entrepreneurs, and only then, if necessary, sold to foreigners. The first resort, from the beginning, was to domestic finance. The railway securities that actually reached Europe were the discards of American money markets. '*None* of our securities', said the American *Railroad Journal* in 1852, 'are taken abroad by *first* hands, that can find a market at fair rates *here*; the only reason why they are taken abroad is that they will not sell *at home*.'[163] Boston replaced Philadelphia as the main market for US railway securities in the 1840s, and it was Bostonian capital that financed the railways in and out of New England. In 1835, twenty-one US railways traded their securities on the New York Stock Exchange; by 1856 this number had doubled, to forty-two.[164] From the end of the 1840s, New York was 'the only American city with funds available for large-scale railroad construction': the great expansion of US railways in the 1850s, was 'financed through New York City'.[165] In the 1850s, it was funded to the middle of the decade with material help from Europe; thereafter it drew principally on its own domestic resources.

Conclusion

From time to time the United States offered great attractions to the foreign investor. Alexander Baring, a knowledgeable proponent of foreign finance in the United States, once explained that it was in a rising country that capital could best be employed; in a country where growth was as rapid as it was in the United States, capital could be placed at an advantage 'almost incredible to Europeans'.[166] The advantage was mutual. For the United States, access to foreign finance, while not indispensable, was always a convenience: it cheapened credit and it accelerated growth. At the same time, foreign finance was only one element in the contribution from overseas, and not necessarily the most important. The London money market has been described, after 1839, as 'definitely bearish toward the United States – and with reason'.[167] And the preoccupation of the most professional study of British investment for the period was to establish 'why the British investor *failed* to purchase American securities before 1870'.[168] Ultimately, Raymond Goldsmith concludes, international trade and mass immigration made a greater contribution to the economic development of the United States than foreign investment[169] – and one is bound to agree. The immigrants were not insignificant for the importation of foreign capital resources. Their labour was their greatest contribution, but they came in their millions and, at least in the earlier decades of the nineteenth century, they may have brought with them as much as £15 per head.[170]

The United States enjoyed a multiplicity of advantages, the most important of which were the talent and energy of her people. Resources of land and minerals seemed inexhaustible. In the eight years that followed the first gold discoveries in California in 1848, it was calculated that California had furnished world markets with gold to the face value of £60 million ($300 million). The production of gold in the peak year 1854 was valued at no less than £13.6 million ($68 million).[171] By contrast, the production of gold in the mid-1860s by Russia, one of the main traditional suppliers, averaged only £3.3 million ($16.5 million) annually.[172] Between 1850 and 1873, the net outflow of specie from the United States was just under $1.1 billion ($962.5 million of which was in gold).[173]

Again, state valuations of real property in the United States, at the nearest date to 1860, show a total of £1.86 billion ($9.3 billion). In Britain, the richest country in the world, real property was valued (on similar lines) at £3.15 billion ($15.75 billion).[174] The Civil War was a serious interruption, but the 'amassed wealth of the United States', as calculated by the US Census Bureau, was reported at $30.07 billion in 1870, and it had grown at a phenomenal rate (from $7.1 billion in 1850 and $16.2 billion in 1860). The $30 billion for 1870 was almost exactly the fiugure estimated by D. A. Baxter for contemporary Britain. The figures, of course, are curious and not strictly comparable; *active* capital in Britain exceeded the United States, where the chief investment was locked up in land and buildings.[175] All the same, they are sufficiently impressive. George Norman, reflecting on the same census figures for the United States in 1870, began his paper to the (London) Statistical Society with the observation that there had 'probably never existed upon earth a nation so favoured by Providence as the Anglo-Americans'.[176]

Simply in the area of private finance, there is something to be said for John Knapp's view that the growing indebtedness of the United States in the nineteenth century, rather than indicating an inability to match current investment by current saving, may merely have reflected the underdeveloped state of the domestic banking system and capital market: reliance on foreign borrowing was 'nothing much more than a costly process of satisfying her preference for liquidity'.[177] US banks were not foreign-owned. State and private banks were domestic enterprises, and Mulhall calculated that of the 7 million national bank shares in circulation in the early 1880s, only 26,000 were held in Europe (7,000 in Britain).[178] The expansion of the American banking system was as extraordinary as anything else in the development of the American economy. Davis and Gallman report the existence of fewer than 1,000 banks in 1840, with assets of under $750 million. Rapid growth was experienced from the 1860s. There were 174 state banks in 1870 with assets of about $149 million, and 1,612 national banks with assets of $1.6 billion. By 1910 there were 13,257 state banks with assets of $24.5 billion, and 7,145 national banks with assets of $9.9 billion – that is, total assets for state and national banks combined of $34.4 billion (£6.9 billion).[179]

It is suggested, therefore, that US government securities were almost entirely taken and held at home, and that the foreign contribution to US railways before the Civil War, even allowing for federal and state assistance partially financed from abroad, was no higher than 10 per cent. In the post-Bellum boom, the proportion may briefly have reached 16.5 per cent. Any simple deduction from these figures is likely to mislead, since even small amounts of foreign financial assistance might have had a disproportionately large effect. But foreigners were not influential in domestic banking, commerce and finance. Madden finds that British investment in banks, land companies, ranching, real estate and industry was unimportant for the period he examines (1860–80); Britons took an urgent interest in gold, silver and oil, but the estimated nominal value for British investment in US minerals for Madden's whole period was a mere £5.6 million.[180] By contrast, the contribution of foreigners (British and Continental) to short-term credit, both in overseas trade and in the expansion of communications, was important.

In general, foreign finance was influential in enabling the diversion of scarce domestic resources towards productive investment, and, above all, in accelerating the astonishing growth of an already remarkable economy. As early as 1854 *The Economist*, by no means an enthusiast for the United States, had concluded that the 'rapid progress and the greatness of the Americans, like their clipper ships, are, in the main, their own and chiefly due to themselves . . . They seem certain to become the greatest and most powerful nation that ever existed'.[181]

Notes

1 *The Economist*, 23 April 1853, p. 462.
2 *Bankers' Magazine*, 14 (November 1854), p. 605
3 C. K. Hobson, *The export of capital* (London, 1914), p. 128.
4 Leland H. Jenks, 'Britain and American railway development', *Journal of Economic History*, 11:4 (Fall 1951), p. 375.
5 Discussion on George Paish's paper 'Great Britain's capital investments in individual colonial and foreign countries', *Journal of the Royal Statistical Society*, 74:2 (January 1911), pp. 195–6. Keynes' views had been anticipated during the discussion of a previous Paish paper to the Royal Statistical Society. On that occasion, C. Rozenraad, president of the Federation of Foreign Chambers of Commerce and an authority on US finance, thought that the £600 million supposedly invested by

Britain in American railway securities was a mistake – 'They [the securities] were only issued here, America being in constant relations with the English money market, having sent in subscriptions here': discussion on G. Paish, 'Great Britain's capital investments in other lands', *Journal of the Royal Statistical Society*, 72:3 (September 1909), p. 494. I have discussed some of these overestimates in an article on 'British portfolio investment overseas before 1870: some doubts', *Economic History Review*, 2nd ser. 33:1 (February 1980), pp. 1–16.

6 Harvey E. Fisk, *The inter-ally debts* (New York, 1924), p. 312, or, for the ante-Bellum years, that 'the key to American growth . . . must be sought in European, and largely British . . . capital resources': Frank Thistlethwaite, *The Anglo-American connection in the early nineteenth century* (Philadelphia, 1959), p. 10.

7 Simon Kuznets, 'Foreign economic relations of the United States and their impact upon the domestic economy: a review of long-term trends', *Proceedings of the American Philosophical Society*, 92:4 (1948), p. 237.

8 ibid., p. 233.

9 Simon Kuznets, *Modern economic growth: rate, structure and spread* (New Haven, Conn., 1966), p. 332. Kuznets calculates that the inflow of foreign long- term capital into the United States, 1850–73, averaged $42 million annually: *Capital in the American economy: its formation and financing* (Princeton, NJ, 1961), Table 10, p. 121.

10 Arthur I. Bloomfield, *Patterns of fluctuation in international investment before 1914* (Princeton, NJ, 1968), p. 13.

11 Irving B. Kravis, 'The role of exports in nineteenth-century United States growth', *Economic Development and Cultural Change*, 20:3 (April 1972), pp. 403–4.

12 S. B. Saul, *Studies in British overseas trade, 1870–1914* (Liverpool, 1960), p. 66.

13 Lance E. Davis and Robert E. Gallman, 'Capital formation in the United States during the nineteenth century', in Peter Mathias and M. M. Postan, eds, *The Cambridge economic history of Europe*, Vol VII, pt 2 (Cambridge, 1978), p. 2.

14 Arthur M. Johnson and Barry E. Supple, *Boston capitalists and Western railroads: a study in the nineteenth-century railroad investment process* (Cambridge, Mass., 1967), *passim.*

15 Lance E. Davis, 'Capital immobilities and finance capitalism: a study of economic evolution in the United States, 1820–1920', *Explorations in Entrepreneurial History*, 2nd ser., 1:1 (Fall 1963), pp. 93, 97.

16 Leland H. Jenks, *The migration of British capital to 1875* (London, 1971 edn), p. 73.

17 Letter quoted and commented on in *The Times*, 18 May 1871, p. 10d.

18 Raymond W. Goldsmith, 'The growth of reproducible wealth of the United States of America from 1805 to 1950', in Simon Kuznets, ed., *Income and wealth of the United States: trends and structures* (Cambridge, 1952), p. 285.

19 Saul, *Studies in British overseas trade*, p. 66.

20 Édouard Kleinmann, writing to the Crédit Lyonnais from the United States, 4 April 1870: Jean Bouvier, *Le Crédit Lyonnais de 1863 à 1882*, Vol. II (Paris, 1961), p. 563 fn. 2.

21 Douglass North, 'International capital flows and the development of the American West', *Journal of Economic History*, 16:4 (December 1956), p. 500.

22 R. C. O. Matthews, *A study in trade-cycle history: economic fluctuations in Great Britain, 1833–1842* (Cambridge, 1954), p. 55.

23 Leland H. Jenks, 'Railways as an economic force in American development', *Journal of Economic History*, 4:1 (May 1944), p. 9.

24 Joseph Edward Hedges, *Commercial banking and the stock market before 1863* (Baltimore, Md., 1938), p. 147.

25 Robert Sobel, *The big board: a history of the New York stock market* (New York, 1965), p. 116.

26 Margaret Myers, *The New York money market: origins and development* (New York, 1931), pp. 40, 42.

27 *American Railroad Journal*, 3 July 1852, reproduced in Alfred D. Chandler, Jr, comp.

and ed., *The railroads: the nation's first big business* (New York, 1965), p. 61.
28 North, 'International capital flows and the American West', p. 494.
29 R. W. Hidy, 'The organisation and functions of Anglo-American merchant bankers, 1815–1860', *Journal of Economic History*, 1 (December 1941), Supplement, p. 62.
30 Jenks, 'Britain and American railway development', p. 382.
31 John J. Madden, 'British investment in the United States, 1860–1880' (unpublished Ph.D thesis, University of Cambridge, 1957), pp. 150–6.
32 *Circular to Bankers*, 17 April 1846, p. 331.
33 *A portion of the journal kept by Thomas Raikes from 1831 to 1847*, Vol. III (London, 1857), p. 157.
34 Edwin J. Perkins, 'Managing a dollar–sterling exchange account: Brown, Shipley & Co. in the 1850s', *Business History*, 16:1 (January 1974), p. 55.
35 R. W. Hidy, *The house of Baring in American trade and finance: English merchant bankers at work, 1763–1861* (Cambridge, Mass., 1949), p. 371. Bates was the leading partner in Barings at the time. He may well have underestimated his rivals, although he was not in the habit of doing so. Clearly, the Anglo-American house of Brown Brothers & Co. was a formidable competitor: Edwin J. Perkins, *Financing Anglo-American trade: the house of Brown 1800–1880* (Cambridge, Mass., 1975), *passim*.
36 Bray Hammond, *Banks and politics in America from the Revolution to the Civil War* (Princeton, NJ, 1957), pp. 673–4.
37 Madden, 'British investment', p. 400.
38 Quoted in *The Times*, 5 April 1872, p. 12f.
39 *The Times*, 20 May 1869, p. 8d.
40 Barings to Hope & Co., 2 and 12 July 1858: Baring papers, Public Archive of Canada, Ottawa (hereafter 'Ottawa'), frame nos 74203–4; Hope & Co. to Barings, 15 July 1858: archives of Messrs Baring Brothers & Co., Limited, Guildhall Library, London (hereafter 'Baring'), HC 8.1.
41 *The Times*, 21 October 1870, p. 4a.
42 *Bankers' Magazine*, 20 (January 1860), p. 51. The informant had had access to the books of the Sub-Treasury in New York where, it seemed, seven-eighths of the public debt of the US was then paid.
43 Baring, Accounts.
44 Hidy, *Barings in American trade and finance*, pp. 471–2.
45 Barings to Ward, Campbell & Co. (New York), 27 April 1861: Baring, PLB 1861.
46 Barings (Joshua Bates) to the Bank of the State of South Carolina (Thomas Waring), 15 December 1860: Ottowa, frame no. 74943, and Baring, PLB 1860.
47 Thomas Baring to Barings, 20 January 1861: Baring, HC 1.20.4.
48 Joshua Bates' Diary, 28 April 1863: Baring, uncatalogued.
49 Report by Mr Archibald, British Consul at New York, on the Trade of his Consular District for the year 1860: Parliamentary Papers (hereafter P.P.'), 1862, LVIII, p. 775
50 Davis Rich Dewey, *Financial history of the United States* (New York, 1922 edn), p. 329.
51 National Monetary Commission, *Statistics for the United States, 1867–1909* (Washington, DC, 1909), p. 239.
52 *The Times*, 5 August 1880, p. 6a.
53 *Investor's Monthly Manual*, 30 December 1871, p. 403.
54 Report by Mr W. Stuart, H.M.'s Secretary of Legation, on the Finance, Public Credit, etc. of the United States, 22 February 1864: P.P., 1864, LXI, p. 737.
55 Charles J. Bullock, John H. Williams and Rufus S. Tucker, 'The balance of trade of the United States', *Review of Economic Statistics* (July 1919), p. 222.
56 *Fenn on the Funds* (9th edn, London, 1867), p. 480.
57 *The Economist*, 23 December 1871, p. 1564.
58 Henrietta Larson, *Jay Cooke: private banker* (Cambridge, Mass., 1936), p. 129.
59 ibid., p. 148.
60 James L. Sellers, 'An interpretation of Civil War finance', *American Historical Review*, 30:2 (January 1925), p. 282.

61 L. Girard, 'Transport', in H. J. Habakkuk and M. Postan, eds, *The Cambridge economic history of Europe*, Vol. VI (Cambridge, 1965), p. 234. Dunning's annual totals are a distillation (and adjustment) of Matthew Simon and Albert H. Imlah: John H. Dunning, *Studies in international investment* (London, 1970), Table 3, p. 155.
62 Robert Cecil Todd, *Confederate finance* (Athens, Georgia, 1954), p. 183.
63 ibid., pp. 183–4.
64 *Fenn on the Funds* (12th edn, London, 1874), p. 496.
65 Nathaniel T. Bacon, 'Capital invested in the United States from abroad', *Yale Review*, 9 (November 1900), p. 283.
66 Myers, *New York money market*, p. 289.
67 Leonard H. Courtney, 'On the finances of the United States of America, 1861–67', *Journal of the Statistical Society*, 31:2 (June 1868), p. 175.
68 *The Economist*, 30 October 1869, p. 1278.
69 Larson, *Jay Cooke: private banker*, p. 117.
70 Dewey, *Financial history of the United States*, pp. 354–5.
71 Joshua Bates to Barings, 2 October 1861: Baring, HC 1.20.8.
72 Barings to G. L. Schuyler, 28 August and 2 October 1861: Baring, PLB 1861.
73 Barings (Liverpool) to Barings (London), 30 March 1863: Baring, HC 3.35.
74 Henri Hottinguer to Thomas Baring, Paris, 8 March and 7 May 1863: Baring, HC 7.1.
75 Barings to Hope & Co., 14 April 1863: Ottawa, frame nos 75465–6; Hope & Co. to Barings, Amsterdam, 16 April 1863, and Henri Labouchère to Thomas Baring, 25 April 1863: Baring, HC 8.1.
76 Thomas Baring to J. M. Forbes, 29 August 1863: Baring, PLB 1863.
77 Joshua Bates' Diary, 7 April 1863: Baring, uncatalogued: Barings to Aspinwall, 17 April and 29 June 1863 and 5 May 1865: Baring, PLB 1863 and 1865.
78 *Bankers' Magazine*, 22 December 1862, p. 785.
79 *Bankers' Magazine*, 23 October 1863, pp. 811–12.
80 Barings to Hope & Co., 8 February 1864, and Hope & Co. to Barings, 10 February 1864: Baring, PLB 1864 and HC 8.1 respectively.
81 D. Morier Evans, *Speculative notes and notes on speculation* (London, 1864), p. 127.
82 The figure is cited in Vincent Carosso, *Investment banking in America: a history* (Cambridge, Mass., 1970), p. 18, but it has been questioned more recently by Dolores Greenberg, 'Yankee financiers and the establishment of trans-Atlantic partnerships: a re-examination', *Business History*, 16:1 (January 1974), pp. 25–6.
83 Larson, *Jay Cooke: private banker*, p. 208.
84 Cleona Lewis, *America's stake in international investments* (Washington, DC, 1938), p. 54.
85 Barings kept Aspinwall and Ward, Campbell & Co. up to date with the demand for US stocks, Northern and Southern, in England and the Continent for 1864 and 1865: Baring, PLB 1864 and 1865.
86 Sir Samuel Morton Peto, *The resources and prospects of America* (London, 1866), pp. 8–9.
87 Robert T. Patterson, 'Government finance on the eve of the Civil War', *Journal of Economic History*, 12:1 (Winter 1952), p. 37.
88 *The Times*, 16 January 1867, p. 8e.
89 *The Economist*, 26 December 1868, p. 1474.
90 *The Economist*, Commercial History and Review of 1868, 12 March 1869, p. 37.
91 Quoted by Larson, *Jay Cooke: private banker*, p. 475 fn. 87.
92 *The Economist*, Commercial History and Review of 1869, 12 March 1870, p. 46.
93 *The Times*, 19 May 1870, p. 9b.
94 *The Times*, 11 March 1870, p. 4d.

95 *The Times*, 8 December 1869, p. 9b.

96 P. L. Cottrell, 'Investment banking in England, 1856–1882: case study of the International Financial Society' (unpublished Ph.D. thesis, University of Hull, 1974), p. 581.

97 Cited by the Paris correspondent: *The Economist*, 20 August 1870, p. 1035. It is quite clear, however, that this was a development only of the second half of the 1860s. The massive investment by Frenchmen in 5–20s, described by Catin, is implausible: Roger Catin, *Le Portefeuille étranger de la France entre 1870 et 1914* (Paris, thesis, 1927), pp. 15, 18.

98 Quoted in *The Economist*, Commercial History and Review of 1869, 12 March 1870, p. 66.

99 *The Times*, 1 March 1869, p. 4c.

100 Madden, 'British investment', pp. 12–13, 20.

101 *The Economist*, 30 October 1869, p. 1278.

102 *The Times*, 8 December 1869, p. 9b.

103 *The Economist*, 19 August 1871, p. 998.

104 *The Economist*, 26 August 1871, p. 1029. It turned out not to be quite the success it seemed. In Germany, for instance, the funded loan was only partially successful and the scrip fell to a small discount on par. It was, however, successful in the United States: *The Economist*, 9 September 1871, p. 1096; 16 September 1871, p. 1123.

105 Larson, *Jay Cooke: private banker*, pp. 395–6.

106 Dewey, *Financial history of the United States*, p. 356.

107 Minutes of Evidence, *Report of the Royal Commission on the London Stock Exchange*: P.P., 1878, XIX, p. 522.

108 The division of interest, foreign and domestic, is explained fully in Bacon, 'American international indebtedness', pp. 264–6.

109 Bullock, Williams and Tucker, 'The balance of trade in the United States', p. 245.

110 Hobson, *Export of capital*, pp. 134, 115–16.

111 Girard, 'Transport', pp. 232, 251.

112 Margaret Myers, *A financial history of the United States* (New York, 1970), p. 119.

113 Jenks, 'Britain and American railway development', p. 382.

114 Editor's introduction to Dorothy Adler, *British investment in American railways, 1834–1898* (Charlottesville, Virginia, 1970) p. vii.

115 Jenks, 'Railroads as an economic force in American development', p. 8 fn. 19.

116 Stephen Salsbury, *The state, the investor, and the railroad: the Boston and Albany, 1825–1867* (Cambridge, Mass., 1967), pp. 137–47. The degree of municipal assistance is described usefully in Carter Goodrich and Harvey H. Segal, 'Baltimore's aid to railroads: a study in the municipal planning of internal improvements', *Journal of Economic History*, 13:1 (Winter 1953), pp. 2–35.

117 George Rogers Taylor and Irene D. Neu, *The American railroad network, 1861–1890* (Cambridge, Mass., 1956), p. 6.

118 Adler, *British investment in American railways*, pp. 9–10.

119 ibid., p. 10.

120 H. Jerome Cranmer, 'Canal investment, 1815–1860', in National Bureau of Economic Research, *Trends in the American economy in the nineteenth century* (Princeton, NJ, 1960), p. 558.

121 Myers, *Financial history of the United States*, p. 112.

122 General summary, printed as Appendix A, Cleona Lewis, *The international accounts* (New York, 1927), p. 140.

123 Carter Goodrich, *Government promotion of American canals and railroads, 1800–1890* (New York, 1960), p. 268.

124 Adler, *British investment in American railways*, p. 53.

125 Quoted in ibid., p. 19.

126 R. W. Hidy, 'A leaf from investment history', *Harvard Business Review*, 20:1

(Autumn 1941), p. 72. Also R. W. Hidy and M. E. Hidy, 'Anglo-American merchant bankers and the railroads of the old North-West, 1848–1860', *Business History Review*, 34:2 (Summer 1960), pp. 150–69.

127 Hidy, 'A leaf from investment history', p. 69.

128 Joshua Bates to Thomas Baring, 27 August 1852: Baring, Northbrook Papers, Letters to Thomas Baring, unnumbered.

129 Thomas Baring's letters from the United States, September – November 1852, are in Baring, HC 1.20.4.

130 Albert Fishlow, *American railroads and the transformation of the ante-bellum economy* (Cambridge, Mass., 1965), p. 117.

131 *Bankers' Magazine*, 28 October 1854, p. 1182, and Adler, *British investment in American railways*, p. 52.

132 Sobel, *The big board*, p.59.

133 Quoted by the *Bankers' Magazine*, 14 (November 1854), p. 605.

134 Goodrich, *Government promotion of American canals and railroads*, pp. 270–1. The total 'stock, mortgage bonds, equipment, obligations etc.' of US railways in 1860 were calculated elsewhere at $1,149 million: US Department of Commerce, *Historical statistics of the United States of America, 1789–1949* (Washington, DC, 1949), p. 201.

135 It should be said, however, that Jenks is considering *ownership* of securities, bonds, etc. ('one fifth of the nominal value of American railroads was foreign-owned in 1873') rather than the actual contribution of foreign and domestic finance: Jenks, 'Railroads as an economic force', p. 9.

136 Sobel, *The big board*, p. 57.

137 Joshua Bates to Joseph Howe, 25 November 1853: Ottawa, frame no. 72521.

138 *Bankers' Magazine*, 14 (November 1854), pp. 601–8.

139 *Cassell's Handbook of Investments* (London, 1861), p. 43. It was a view shared by other contemporary handbooks for British investors such as *Fortune's Epitome of the Stocks and Public Funds*, Gresham Omnium's *Handy Guide to Safe Investment, Fenn on the Funds*, etc.

140 Hidy, *Barings in American trade and finance*, p. 476.

141 ibid., pp. 423, 428.

142 Adler, *British investment in American railways*, pp. 66–7.

143 *Poor's manual of American railroads* (New York, 1870 edn), quoted by *Chadwicks' Investment Circular*, 3 September 1870, p. 6.

144 US Department of Commerce, *Historical Statistics*, p. 201.

145 Sobel, *The big board*, p. 88.

146 Quoted in *The Times*, 26 July 1871, p. 4b.

147 Foreword to a pamphlet in 'Cracroft's Investment Tracts': Robert Giffen, *American railways as investments* (London, 1873), pp. vii, viii. The detail for these events is supplied efficiently by Julius Grodinsky, *Jay Gould: his business career, 1867–1892* (Philadelphia, 1957).

148 US Department of Commerce, *Historical statistics of the United States: colonial times to 1970* (Washington, DC, 1975), p. 731.

149 ibid., p. 734.

150 Jenks, 'Railroads as an economic force in American development', pp. 8–9.

151 Saul, *Studies in British overseas trade*, p. 66.

152 Greenberg, 'Yankee financiers and the establishment of trans-Atlantic partnerships', p. 30.

153 Larson, *Jay Cooke: private banker*, p. 385.

154 George Paish, *The trade balance of the United States* (Washington, DC, National Monetary Commission, 1910), p. 173.

155 M. C. Reed, *A history of James Capel and Co.* (London, 1975), p. 49.

156 Adler, *British investment in American railways*, p. 75.

157 Ada M. Matthews, 'New York bank clearings and stock prices, 1866–1914', *Review of Economic Statistics*, 8 (1926), p. 186.

158 Adler, *British investment in American railways*, p. 143.
159 Hidy, *Barings in American trade and finance*, pp. 428–9 and p. 605 fn. 17.
160 Peto, *Resources and prospects of America*, p. 272. Peto was chairman, at the time, of the London Board of Control of the Atlantic & Great Western Railroad, and had visited America to inspect the line. He was exaggerating. Cost depended, after all, on the terrain. An 1844 report for the cost of construction of the Central Railroad of Georgia showed 'iron rails, spikes, and plates' as taking up $476,081 of the total construction costs of $2,205,509, by far the largest element of which ($975,898) was for grading: E. R. Whicker, 'Railroad investment before the Civil War', in National Bureau of Economic Research, *Trends in the American Economy in the nineteenth century* (Princeton, NJ, 1960), p. 522.
161 *New York Times*, quoted in *The Times*, 20 April 1870, p. 7a.
162 This is explained by Robert E. Carlson, 'British railroads and engineers and the beginnings of American railroad development', *Business History Review*, 34:2 (Summer 1960), p. 138.
163 Extracted from an article on 'Negotiation of railroad securities at home and abroad', published on 3 July 1852, and reprinted in Chandler, *The railroads: the nation's first big business*, p. 62.
164 Myers, *New York money market*, pp. 431–3.
165 Chandler discusses this transfer of railway finance between domestic markets (Philadelphia, Boston and then New York): Alfred D. Chandler, Jr, 'Patterns of American railroad finance, 1830–50', *Business History Review*, 28:3 (December 1954), *passim*.
166 Alexander Baring to Henry Hope and John Williams Hope, Philadelphia, 10 January 1797: Baring, DEP 3, Pt III.
167 Walter Buckingham Smith, *Economic aspects of the Second Bank of the United States* (Cambridge, Mass., 1953), p. 96.
168 Madden, 'British investment', pp. ix–x.
169 Goldsmith, 'Growth of reproducible wealth', p. 285.
170 Jenks, *Migration of capital*, p. 363, fn. 48.
171 *The Economist*, 6 September 1856, p. 977. Pierre Vilar reports that California produced 752,400 kilos of gold in the nine years 1848–56, representing a value, in the money of the day, of about £100 million. His estimates are generally too high, and *The Economist* is probably the more reliable source: Vilar, *A history of gold and money 1450–1920* (trans., London, 1976), p. 326.
172 Charles Jutting to Barings, St Petersburg, 2 and 18 March 1864: Baring, HC 10.28.
173 Bullock, Williams and Tucker, 'Balance of trade of the United States', p. 222.
174 Cornelius Walford, 'Recent financial and taxation statistics of the United States', *Journal of the Statistical Society*, 26:2 (June 1863), pp. 162–3.
175 *Shipping and commercial list* (New York), quoted by *The Times*, 1 May 1872, p. 5b.
176 George Wade Norman, 'The future of the United States', *Journal of the Statistical Society*, 38:1 (March 1875), p. 64.
177 John Knapp, 'Capital exports and growth', *Economic Journal*, 67 (September 1957), pp. 433–4.
178 Michael G. Mulhall, *Mulhall's dictionary of statistics* (London, 1884), p. 38.
179 Davis and Gallman, 'Capital formation in the United States', p. 65.
180 Madden, 'British investment', pp. 73–5.
181 *The Economist*, 18 March 1854, p. 281.

Chapter 7

Conclusion

Much of the argument of this book has turned on the ability of domestic resources to meet a major part of capital requirements. This was not necessarily a matter of choice; there were no massive surpluses of capital for export, and, perhaps, no compelling reasons for borrowing. Even the exporting countries had much, like their own railway systems, to keep their capital where in any case they preferred it to be – at home. Once real surpluses developed, fluctuations in the terms of trade must indeed have supplied at least a partial explanation for the distribution of investment between home and abroad. It becomes possible to identify the inverse character of the long swings (eighteen to twenty years) in such important areas as the home investment of the United Kingdom and the United States.[1] For the middle decades of the nineteenth century, however, when capital exports were determined much more individually and piecemeal, it was the curiously uniform ten-year cycle in international finance – from boom to slump to boom again – that affected the will to borrow and invest.

This is no exercise in theory, nor does it examine, except in passing, some of such important consequences of the movement of international capital as the transfer of technology, or the benefits and losses to be experienced by the capital exporter. Uniformity cannot be expected. In some countries, and for short periods, 'foreign loans might finance up to half of domestic investment' but, at least for Continental Europe, 'over considerable periods of time, capital imports were always less important than domestic savings'.[2] What is suggested here, beyond the often surprising capacity of domestic finance even in such unlikely territories as Bourbon Spain, is some explanation for the capital movement that actually existed at the time – how much, for what and from whom?

The rapid development of large railway systems made demands on the domestic capital supply after the middle of the nineteenth century that could only sometimes be met – by Britain and France, of course, and also by Northern and Central Europe, Russia and the United States. But local finance, in all save the poorest countries, was sufficient to build railways to meet purely local needs. Even in Ireland, just over half of the total private investment in railways by 1850 was domestic (£4.4 million out of £8.7 million).[3] Richer, industrialised regions like Lancashire and Cataluña were not, after all, so different in their ability to raise money locally, while the piecemeal extension of local lines in North America, financed by local interests, is well understood.[4]

Apart from any other convenience that they might offer to businessmen and landowners, railways under the right conditions could be an excellent investment. In 1844, at a time when the yield on consols (British government securities) had fallen below 3 per cent, home railways – even the less successful – could offer a better return, while the most successful of the British lines paid 9–10 per cent.[5]

National governments took a heavy share in domestic railway finance. Since they borrowed abroad, their resources were in part foreign; more often, they derived their income from national taxation or from the sale of state property. Railway subventions from the government of Italy were reported as costing over £2 million a year at the end of the 1860s,[6] and every country except Britain gave substantial government aid (local and central) to the construction and operation of its railways – whether directly or by guaranteed dividends, special exemptions on taxes and tariffs, ear-marked taxes on the public or land grants. The British government was more generous to colonial than to home railways; the government of British India undertook, by an agreement in 1849, to guarantee interest at 5 per cent on Indian railway securities. Between 1850 and 1900 this guarantee cost £50 million, on a total investment in Indian railways (by 1902) of £236 million.[7]

Too much attention is paid to the major capital markets – London, Paris, Berlin and Vienna. The growth of industry for all countries in the nineteenth century, as it was for Britain from the eighteenth century, was 'primarily provincial and local, from very small-scale beginnings with equally local, small-scale financial resources sustaining it . . . By far the greatest source of finance for capital investment in industry was retained profit.'[8] Provincial capital financed local industry and railways; it occupied itself, too, with the purchase of land and with the mortgage market.

The nineteenth century opened unexpectedly large resources of capital. In France the mobilisation of petty capital in railways, in *rentes*, in Parisian municipal loans and in financial societies like the Crédit Mobilier and the Société Générale, was taken further than anywhere else. But the tendency to open up the market to a wider subscription was general. The Northern railway of France had no less than 20,000 shareholders.[9] The railway system of Britain was financed by 'an outpouring of mass investment'.[10] Monied investors continued to hold the greater part of British railway shares long after the 'attorneys' clerks, college scouts, coachmen, dairymen, beer sellers, butlers, footmen, and mail guards' had lost their money during the railway 'mania' of the mid-1840s.[11] But it is interesting that already by 1830, out of the 274,823 stockholders of public funds then on the books of the Bank of England, 250,000 did not receive more than £100 as their half-yearly dividend, while the number of half-yearly dividends of £500 or more was no greater than 2,000.[12] France experienced the same phenomenon. In 1830, 195,000 individuals owned French government *rentes*, averaging £1,230 per head. By 1870 there were 1,254,000 *rentiers*, with average holdings of only £360.[13] In the early 1860s, the introduction of limited liability in England mobilised capital everywhere and at all social levels: 'anybody could get a million or so for anything'.[14]

Small, individual capitalists provided the base for an immense expansion of banking systems. Bank resources were largely domestic, since foreign banks like the Rothschilds in Spain and Austria aimed rather at mobilising domestic deposits than at importing capital from abroad. Local financiers showed themselves peculiarly well-placed to handle government business and state monopolies, not only among the elite (the *haute banque* of Paris and the *hofbankiers* of Vienna) but also among the private bankers of smaller capital cities like Madrid. Later, the modern financial institutions of Paris (from the early 1850s) and of London (from the 1860s) brought money to the market, while huge capital and deposits were attracted by the new generation of commercial, joint stock banks.

The old bankers could not ignore the new. James Rothschild and the Crédit Mobilier fought for business, but neither Barings nor Rothschilds could ultimately withstand the power of these new institutions, sustained as they were by their ability to attract mass investment. James Rothschild admitted, as early as 1856, that it was impossible for his house to abstain completely from the new finance: 'nous sommes en effet trop profondément mêlés à toutes les affaires financières de l'Europe pour rester étrangers aux combinaisons qui touchent au crédit public et privé'.[15] The Rothschilds did not disappear, far from it; but there can be no doubt, said Jean Bouvier, that, 'leur royauté financière n'est plus'.[16]

Domestic financiers were not always so powerful. Berend and Ránki may well be right in their belief that domestic banking in the Balkans did not take off until the turn of the century.[17] It took time to build up bank deposits even in stronger, new economies. But the power of domestic finance lay not so much in the scale of its resources as in its friends in office and, above all, in its instant availability. So long as the needs of the governments themselves were limited, domestic finance might have sought *aid* from abroad, but it took management and direction for itself.

After all, there may not have been much surplus capital for export in the mid-nineteenth century. From the 1880s, Britain disposed of a substantial surplus in search of profitable employment overseas. The same, however, cannot so easily be argued for periods prior to the 1860s.[18] C. K. Hobson is confident that British investors 'managed even during the 'forties to spare large sums for investment on the Continent',[19] but the evidence does not support him. The £259 millions spent by Britons on their own railways in the fifteen years from 1843 were indeed 'a striking testimony to the investment effort in only one section of the British economy in this short period',[20] and they left little for investment overseas. French experience cannot have been so different. France had paid for the vast part of her own railways launched during the boom of the 1840s. New investment was brought to a halt by the financial crisis of 1847, followed by the political revolution of 1848; but it had picked up again by the early 1850s. During 1857–9, concessions were granted that implied an annual outlay of very nearly £20 million. Thomas Tooke thought that if the relative resources of the two countries were compared, this £20 million must impose just as severe a strain on France as the £30 million spent by Britons on their own railways for 1848–9.[21]

The capital of British railway companies (shares and loans) is said to have risen from a total of £48.2 million in 1840 to £239.4 million in 1850, and to have reached £529.9 million by 1870.[22] A. G. Kenwood has argued for the 1840s that huge commitments at home must have dried up funds in Britain for overseas investment. Capital, he thinks, began to flow into foreign railways again in the 1850s.[23]

To some extent this was true – Indian railways are said to have attracted £50 million of British capital between 1862 and 1872[24] – but the figures are not entirely convincing. It is difficult to see how such enormous surpluses of capital for export could have been achieved. If £529.9 million had genuinely been raised by British railway companies by 1870, the amount exceeded a recent estimate for Britain's entire portfolio investment overseas, colonial and foreign, everywhere and for everything. And this was not the end of it. More than half of the existing joint stock companies in Britain in the 1860s had been brought into existence in that decade, while immense funds were attracted to banking and other classes of enterprise. Deane and Cole describe the 1880s as the peak of capital formation in British railways, so that by 1885 railways accounted for about 12½ per cent of the national capital.[25] As late as the 1860s, home investment was absorbing the major part of whatever surplus of capital existed within the British economy. Perhaps this was the case even during the most spectacular of boom periods in foreign investment – the first half of the 1820s. During the build-up to the great crisis of 1825–6, a substantial investor, the cotton manufacturer Samuel Greg put a large proportion of his surplus into the securities of foreign governments. But irrespective of his substantial holdings in mills and land and of foreign government securities, he still retained nearly 70 per cent in British Consols.[26]

Home rails were always favourites among British investors, and deservedly so.[27] A mortgage on British railways, said *The Economist* in 1866, was 'one of the very best securities which exist'.[28] In 1869 the *Investors' Chronicle* was still advising British investors to direct their permanent investment in preference towards colonial funds, Indian government loans and railways, and British railway debentures.[29] The largest and best of the English lines – the London and North Western, the Lancashire and Yorkshire, the Great Western, the Midland, the North Eastern – were solid securities. The investor 'may rest satisfied that in purchasing Railway Debenture Stock, he has fulfilled his desire of making the best and most permanent provision for the future'; even preference shares in the great British railway companies were safer than foreign government bonds.[30]

On the broader issue of the priority given to home over foreign investment, A. R. Hall has established that, contrary to the usual supposition that preference was given to foreign issues on the London market, new capital issues for *home* investment were normally larger, and sometimes much larger, than overseas capital issues right up to the end of the nineteenth century.[31] The 1850s and 1860s were for Britain (the principal foreign investor of the day) a period of very rapid expansion at home. David Landes reports, for instance, that the extent of railways in the United Kingdom rose from 10,945 to 24,374 kilometres (1850–69), coal consumption from 37.5 million metric tons to 97.1 million, steam power from 1.3 million horse power to 4 million (1850–70), pig-iron output from 2.2 million metric tons to 5.4 million, and raw cotton consumption from 266,800 metric tons to 425,800.[32]

While so much of the capital resources of the Western World continued to be tied to its own development, finance was unlikely to flow freely abroad. There was, in any case, a tendency for good railway securities either to be taken from the beginning in the railway's own territory, or soon to return to the domestic investor. Ordinary shares were a gamble – the 'speculative sauce which seasons the investment salad' – while debentures, sufficiently covered by income and property, carrying foreclosure rights and redeemed by a sinking fund, were 'a real investment'.[33] Railway debentures were the sound, relatively risk-free investment of the day, and they served as the obvious destination for whatever money the domestic investor might have to place. As for Continental railways, Robert Lucas Nash noticed in 1880 how their securities were 'yearly becoming more and more "home investments", and offer less inducements to the English capitalist, apart altogether from possible political embroilments'.[34]

'Political embroilments' were clearly a major disincentive for some species of foreign finance, while distance and inaccessibility were others. Hartley Withers, writing in 1916, remembered 'old-fashioned stockbrokers' who maintained that no investment was better than home rails because domestic investors could always take a look at their property, which could not run away. Withers dated a comprehensive change in attitudes only from the mid-1900s, from Lloyd George's budgets and the cry for tariff reform to save Britain's 'dying industries'.[35] At the height of the foreign investment boom of the early 1870s, *The Economist* was *still* disinclined to recommend investment abroad: the best class of British industrial securities – the ordinary stocks and shares of the leading British railways and banks – were 'decidedly preferable, as they are more secure and yield a better return'.[36]

Advice to the British investor was strongly biased against foreign investment throughout the middle decades of the nineteenth century. The *Bankers' Magazine* asked its readers in 1859 whether it was not better to 'retain our gold at home, employ it in our own investments, where profit will not be much if at all less, and the principal will be much more secure?'[37] The relative condition of national credit was indicated by bond prices on the London Stock Exchange. In 1873, Britain and Denmark alone could borrow at 3 per cent; Holland, Belgium, the German states, India, Canada, Australasia and Sweden paid 4 per cent. Others paid more, from 5.1 per cent (the United States), 5.3 per cent (Russia and France), 6.3 per cent (the Argentine), 6.7 per cent (Portugal), and 7.5 per cent (Austria), to 16.5 per cent for Spain and 66 per cent for Honduras! All could be bought in London, from totally secure investments at low interest rates suited to trustees, to every variety of unsafe investment at high interest rates preferred by 'those most incautious and rash of all investors – clergymen and widows'.[38]

The Stock Exchange made up its mind as to the security of alternative forms of foreign investment – 'current quotations indicate pretty closely the intrinsic merits of each stock'.[39] The investing public might well have paid more attention. Sir Robert Giffen, who had spent eight years as a financial journalist and editor (he was assistant editor of *The Economist* under Walter Bagehot) complained that he had been asked hundreds of times whether such and such security, paying 6 or 7 per cent or perhaps even higher, was 'safe', to which he had replied with 'the disagreeable doctrine that no security was absolutely safe'.[40]

The Economist was right to feel that foreign government securities should be dealt in only by those with some knowledge of the political and financial condition of the borrower; knowledge of foreign countries, however, was 'not a thing for which any class of Englishman will be apt to take credit'.[41] Some months before, the same journal had already concluded that, in a fortune of several thousand pounds, a moderate stake in foreign bonds might do no harm and might serve to raise the average rate of interest on the whole portfolio. One practical piece of advice should, however, be given; namely, that 'clergymen, widows, old maids, pensioners, clerks, and small capitalists, have no business to put their money into any sort of foreign loans or speculations'.[42] There was much to be said, indeed, for what Disraeli called the 'sweet simplicity of the three per cents'.

All the same, money drifted abroad, and it went, as Hobson says, because the 'principal motive which influences investors is the hope of obtaining a higher money return than could be obtained by investment at home'.[43] J. Horsley Palmer dated the migration of British capital in search of higher interest to the peace of 1815,[44] and it is true that the yield on British government consols had fallen to a level where shareholders were virtually compelled to look for more remunerative investments. At the beginning of April 1823, 3 per cent consols were on sale at 73½,[45] The price was abnormally depressed even for that time, but throughout the nineteenth century the net yield on consols seldom approached 3½ per cent; between 1885 and 1898 it fell from 3 to 2 per cent. Home railway debentures declined during the final quarter of the nineteenth century from about 4 per cent to 2½ per cent, and first-class mortgages from 4½ to 3½ or even to 3 per cent.[46]

Under these conditions, there was certainly an incentive to export. *The Economist* noticed in July 1868 (just as the tide was turning again in favour of foreign securities) that the difficulty of employing money in Britain left almost no alternative to investment in the securities of foreign states.[47] The Royal Commission on the London Stock Exchange (1877–8) concluded that the 'craving for high rates of interest' was a 'leading cause' of the export of enormous sums of money since the 1850s.[48] Low interest rates at home could indicate only an over-supply of capital; more capital existed in Britain than could find remunerative investment. It is this condition that for J. A. Hobson forms the 'taproot of imperialism'.[49]

A British government guarantee gave a promise of security to stocks, which enabled colonial governments to reduce their interest rate but which attracted the conservative investor. Canadian government securities benefited in this way, and so did those of the government of India. Indian 5 per cents, with a British guarantee, sold at par. Five per cent on Indian stock was better than consols and gave almost the same security, and in the early 1860s, when no investments in the United Kingdom yielded such good interest with sound security, Indian 5 per cents were favourites.[50]

The Overend-Gurney crisis of 1866 dealt a shattering blow to confidence on the London Stock Exchange. It put a stop to overseas investment for at least three years. *The Times* (October 1867) spoke of a lock-up of £70 million.[51] In September 1868, capital was still 'on strike'.[52] The discount rate in 1867–8 remained at 2 per cent for longer than ever before.[53] Recovery was slow, and it was destroyed by the Franco-Prussian war. It was not until 1871 that the market really picked up again, in time to come to grief in 1873.

W. P. Kennedy has recently challenged the notion that foreign investment automatically offered higher rates of return than British, and in individual cases he may well be right.[54] But there is no doubt that the contemporary assumption was that better yields were obtainable overseas than at home. In 1871, *The Economist* calculated the return on colonial and foreign stocks at 6–7 per cent, which by then was a yield unobtainable on good securities in Britain.[55] High-risk domestic investment, in manufacturing, mining, construction and financial services, naturally paid better than sound, foreign government securities and railway debentures. But, in Kennedy's argument, like was not being compared with like. Experience in fact showed that foreign government securities realised average returns well above home funds; it was the averaging of risks between different classes of investments and between home/foreign securities that attracted so much interest in the higher yields promised by the trust companies and financial institutions of the 1860s.[56] Lehfeldt made the proper distinction when he noticed that the return on British investments in 'safe' British *colonial* securities was very little higher than that on home investment; the advantage was far more evident between home and *foreign* securities when the differential in favour of foreign securities averaged 1.7 per cent between 1898 and 1910, and about 1.25 per cent thereafter (until the end of 1912).[57] The differential might, indeed, have been even more.

Foreign finance was obviously less critical for economic development than it has often been made out to be. Correspondingly, the tendency has been to undervalue the domestic contribution. But something still needs to be said. Foreign finance fulfilled a limited role – we have seen the results for a number of separate countries, on both sides of the Atlantic. But what, in general, did it achieve?

Sir Alexander Cairncross is very much to the point when he explains that the significance of foreign investment 'lay not so much in the proportionate addition to domestic savings which it yielded, as in its impact on the sectors of the economy which were critical to further growth'.[58] Furthermore, it is clear from each of the countries and areas examined that the role of foreign capital was transient. Although less transient in some countries than in others (some 35 per cent of *all* Austrian shares and securities were said still to be foreign-owned in 1900),[59] Berend and Ránki point to what was in fact a common experience even for the countries of Western Europe (which came to finance themselves much earlier). Foreign capital in

Austria, as elsewhere, was concentrated within two areas – state loans and transport – and these were of declining relative importance. Foreign participation in industry and banking was always small:

> Foreign capital was used chiefly in the initial development of the modern economy, with a dominant function in building up the infra-structure. In branches which were increasingly dynamic, foreign capital was of less significance.[60]

At the same time, it is clear that states and railways were the great consumers of capital in the middle decades of the nineteenth century. Both classes of securities shared a tendency to drift back to domestic investors, but at least a proportion of the huge sums required over the first decades had necessarily to be raised abroad. Domestic capital, Sir John Habakkuk explains, was able to some extent to satisfy normal commercial demand in mid-century Australia, but 'the loans for large scale construction had to be obtained from London'; before 1870, England supplied her colonies with all their long-term capital.[61]

Sir John's conclusion is not entirely sustainable, but it is near enough. The priorities that determined the distribution of foreign and domestic capital in British colonies – at least, in those with any wealth of their own – were evident in the experience of mid-century India. During the 'guaranteed' phase of development (1849–69), railway securities were bought almost entirely by Britons.[62] Between 1845 and 1875, when India was supplied with a basic network of communications, British companies invested some £95 million in Indian guaranteed railways, towards which the contribution of Indian investors was negligible:[63] of the £76 million railway capital raised up to the beginning of 1868, only £750,000 was subscribed in India.[64] Clearly, even a guaranteed 5 per cent on railway securities was insufficient to attract the domestic investor, although guaranteed Indian rails were popular in Britain. But Indian investors in search of *absolute* security (trusts, banks, retired people and 'unenterprising zemindars') went heavily into the 3½ per cent stock of the government of India, so that in 1870 £73 million of the government's debt was held in India (much by resident foreigners) while only £35.2 million was domiciled in Britain.[65]

Investment in Indian securities (government and rails) made considerable demands on Britain at a time when investment abroad was far from popular. But it must all the same have been true that the mass economy of India – land, trade, commerce, industry, construction – was locally financed, while the most productive areas of foreign finance, beyond the creation of a basic system of communications, took the form of short-term credits on India's external trade and the development of production in such agricultural and processing areas as indigo and tea. The government of India continued to borrow abroad, although no longer necessarily in Britain (the first rupee loan of 1880; was taken, in large proportion and at a very high price, by Parisian houses).[66] But the total government debt of India, on 30 September 1880, was £71.3 million for loans raised in England (although sometimes held elsewhere), and £86 million for loans raised in India.[67]

It is always difficult to get much idea of the volume of commercial credit. Commercial credit was in some ways the most influential element in foreign finance during the middle decades of the nineteenth century, and a series of estimates for the United States is given in Appendix IV below. Britain's contribution to the short-term financing of foreign trade during the 1830s ranged from 100 per cent for colonial trade to 33 per cent for Continental Europe. Chapman estimates 80 per cent as Britain's share of the North American trade, 90 per cent for South American, 95 per cent for Indian and Chinese, and 100 per cent for colonial.[68] But some sense of proportion is needed. The volume of capital engaged in short-term finance, important as it was in its effects, was never large when compared with capital invested long term. W. T. C. King, writing about the London discount market as it was in the middle of the nineteenth century, suggests the extent of the discount facilities of London (the Bank of England, banks and discount houses) to have been about £30 million.[69]

Arthur Bloomfield has made the most complete study of this subject, although unfortunately for a later period. His estimate for the outstanding volume of international commercial debt by 1913 was $2.9 billion (£580 million).[70] Short-term borrowing by governments on finance bills was also very considerable just before the First World War, as it had been half a century earlier. United States finance bills were placed, mainly in England and France, to the extent of $400–500 million during the stock market boom of 1906.[71]

As for long-term foreign finance, estimates are habitually inflated. Lenin thought that the foreign investment of France in 1913 was as high as 60 billion francs (£2.4 billion), whereas the consensus nowadays (itself rather too high) seems to be about 43 billion francs (£1.72 billion).[72] British investment overseas by 1914 is commonly estimated at about £4 billion; an alternative suggestion is £2.5 billion.[73] The much higher figures are distinctly implausible. They are unlikely to survive a current research project (by myself and Dr Rachel Whitehead) revaluing British portfolio investment, 1870–1914 – financed by the Social Science Research Council (UK) as a follow-up to an earlier article revaluing Britain's portfolio investment overseas prior to 1870. The earlier article indicates, in fact, that the volume of British portfolio investment overseas by 1870 was probably no more than half the £1 billion so widely accepted today.[74]

Nevertheless, it is possible to generalise. Foreign lending to the United States was 'negligible compared with the level of internal savings' by the end of the nineteenth century; it was of 'immense significance' in some areas (communications) and less so in others (risk capital for industry and funds for agricultural improvement); its chief role was to act, in some spheres, as the 'initial driving force towards capital formation'.[75] W. Arthur Lewis can think of 'no country, including Britain, Russia, and Japan, where foreign business did not play a major role in the initial stages of development, both by providing extra income, and also by imparting new techniques'.[76] And innovation – new techniques – was often the real point. There could be no question, John Knapp thought, of

> the very great importance of the contribution made to development by the movement to developing countries of entrepreneurs, civil servants, of skilled and unskilled workmen, and, not least, of ideas . . . These movements represented exports of knowledge, of enterprise, of labour, and, indeed, of national capital in a broad sense of the word.[77]

Knapp's distinction is worth making. 'National capital in the broad sense of the word' did not necessarily imply a cash contribution. British and French entrepreneurs and contractors took part, initially, in the construction of railways in most parts of the world. But it is unwarranted to assume that their compatriots actually *invested* in the lines 'in Bohemia, Austria, Hungary, and even in faraway Russia'.[78] Arthur Helps, in his biography of the English railway contractor Thomas Brassey, lists no less than thirty-seven Continental railway contracts undertaken by Brassey between 1841 and 1870,[79] for few of which sufficient evidence exists of participation by the British investor. The contractors themselves were often more substantial contributors to railway finance abroad than the private capitalists.[80]

Foreign entrepreneurs and contractors, in France, in Germany, in Russia and everywhere else, trained their (local) successors; so, indeed, did foreign capitalists. The point in so many places was not the shortage of capital, when the demand itself for capital was restricted, so much as the shortage of *risk* capital. The contribution of English investment to Ireland, for example, included its role in 'activating timid domestic funds', when 'many native investors lacked neither the capital nor the opportunity, but simply the will, to invest in Irish railways'.[81] British financiers and investors helped both to re-establish the credit of the government of France after Napoleon and to create, in the 1840s, an adequate climate for domestic railway investment. J. Pierpoint Morgan, whose operations began in foreign finance, developed his list of domestic savers and subscribers who were prepared to follow his judgement even where, normally, they would have been unwilling to trust the market. Morgan subsequently became 'the most successful mobiliser of [domestic] capital in American history'.[82] Morgan, with his experience of foreign finance, was creating confidence in the domestic investor and releasing large resources, just as Baron Stieglitz and his foreign friends, again starting from an international base, mobilised the domestic investor of Russia in the 1860s.

Governments (provincial and national) whose share in financing internal development is now much investigated, borrowed on uniquely favourable terms both at home and abroad.[83] Foreign finance thus found its way indirectly into domestic development. It enabled governments to realise their assets over a longer period, at more favourable rates. Fould, Oppenheim and Erlanger of Paris advanced the huge sum of £17.2 million to the government of Italy in May 1867 against the forthcoming disposal of Church property. The government had wanted to raise some £24 million, of which £6.8 million were already in the Minister's hands. But when it was found impossible to dispose of such a quantity of land at favourable prices, the remainder was obtained by discounting Church assets abroad.[84] Foreign finance was often employed by governments in competition with their own, domestic financiers. Release from the clutches of domestic usurers was a solid contribution of foreign finance, but it merely reflected the main attraction of borrowing abroad, that is, its cheapness by contrast with borrowing at home.

Fundamentally, however, the contribution of foreign finance was to release scarce domestic investment for productive employment, and nowhere more so than in the United States. Eli Heckscher, writing of Sweden in the nineteenth century, explained that Sweden borrowed abroad to finance her most capital-absorbing operations and thereby put domestic savings at the disposal of domestic business.[85]

It is, perhaps, too glib an assumption that foreign capital was critically important on the margin, certainly for the middle decades of the nineteenth century. Foreign finance accelerated existing trends. It provided access to entrepreneurial talents, to management and to engineering skills. It must often, in individual cases, have had more effect than its equivalent in domestic finance, if only because it was habitually better administered. But this is probably as far as one can go for the great majority of nineteenth-century economies. Railways – good, productive lines built step by step to meet demand – could normally find adequate capital at home. Foreign capital was imported, under government guarantee, to pay for unproductive 'political' lines, or to finance a war or suppress a rebellion. Until the last quarter of the nineteenth century, both government bonds and railway securities, the principal consumers of foreign capital, were *less* productive, pound for pound, franc for franc, dollar for dollar, than domestic investment; foreign capital was channelled deliberately into the kind of unproductive investment that could not be expected to attract the home investor.

This was no universal rule, as can be seen from the major part taken by domestic finance in so many unexpected quarters (government and railway) even during the period covered by this book. But at least it might suggest an answer to some of the questions that invariably arise. Given that foreign finance never reached the dimensions so often attributed to it, was it not, nevertheless, disproportionately influential? Is it the 'margin' that counts? Was foreign finance of 'critical importance' (during the period covered by this book) to the development of the economy? *Autres temps, autres mœurs*, but the answer could be 'no'.

Notes

1 Brinley Thomas, 'Migration and international investment', reprinted in A. R. Hall, ed., *The export of capital from Britain, 1870–1914* (London, 1968), p. 47.
2 A. Milward and S. B. Saul, *The development of the economies of Continental Europe, 1880–1914* (London, 1977), p. 493.
3 Joseph Lee, 'The provision of capital for early Irish railways, 1830–53', *Irish Historical Studies*, 16:61 (March 1968), p. 44.
4 Local financing of railway development is continually discussed in previous chapters, not least for the United States. Two valuable studies for Britain are Seymour Broadbridge, *Studies in railway expansion and the capital market in England, 1825–1873* (London, 1970) and M. C. Reed, *Investment in railways in Britain, 1820–1844: a study in the development of the capital market* (London, 1975).
5 M. C. Reed, *A history of James Capel & Co.* (London, 1975), pp. 37–8.
6 *The Times*, 25 April 1869, p. 10d.
7 Daniel Thorner, 'Great Britain and the development of India's railways', *Journal of Economic History*, 11:4 (Fall 1951), pp. 391–2. The best discussion of this policy, in the context of the contracts negotiated by the East India Railway and the Great India Peninsula Railway with the East India Company in 1849, is to be found in Thorner's book, *Investment in Empire: British railway and steam shipping enterprise in India, 1825–1849* (Philadelphia, 1950), pp. 119–82.
8 Peter Mathias, 'Capital, credit and enterprise in the Industrial Revolution', in his *The transformation of England: essays in the economic and social history of England in the eighteenth century* (New York, 1979), p. 104.
9 Jean Bouvier, *Les Rothschilds* (Paris, 1967 edn), p. 135.
10 Leland H. Jenks, *The migration of British capital to 1875* (London, 1971 edn) p. 131.
11 Ellis T. Powell, *The evolution of the money market* (London, 1915), p. 465.
12 ibid., p. 464.
13 Michael G. Mulhall, *Mulhall's dictionary of statistics* (London, 1884), p. 391.
14 *The Times*, 30 September 1867, p. 6d.
15 Quoted by Bouvier, *Rothschilds*, p. 190.
16 Bouvier, *Rothschilds*, p. 202.
17 Iván T. Berend and György Ránki, *Economic development in East-Central Europe in the nineteenth and twentieth centuries* (trans. New York, 1974).

18 I have suggested my reasons for saying this on several occasions, for instance, D. C. M. Platt, 'The national economy and British imperial expansion before 1914', *Journal of Imperial and Commonwealth History*, 2:1 (October 1973), pp. 3–14; *Latin America and British trade, 1806–1914* (London, 1972), Part I; and 'Dependency in nineteenth-century Latin America', *Latin American Research Review*, 15:1 (1980), pp. 113–30.

19 C. K. Hobson, *The export of capital* (London, 1914), p. 117.

20 Broadbridge, *Studies in railway expansion*, p. 173.

21 Thomas Tooke, *A history of prices*, Vol. VI (London, 1857), pp. 37–8.

22 G. R. Hawke and M. C. Reed, 'Railway capital in the United Kingdom in the nineteenth century', *Economic History Review*, 2nd ser. 22:2 (1969), p. 271.

23 A. G. Kenwood, 'Railway investment in Britain, 1825–1875', *Economica*, new ser. 32 (August 1965), pp. 320–1.

24 *Fenn on the Funds* (London, 1874 edn), p. vii.

25 Phyllis Deane and W. A. Cole, *British economic growth, 1688–1959: trends and structure* (Cambridge, 1967 edn), p. 273.

26 Mary B. Rose, 'Diversification of investment by the Greg family, 1800–1914', *Business History*, 21:1 (January 1979), p. 89.

27 The investors' guides of the day were clear upon this point. For instance, *Fortune's epitome of the stocks and public funds* (London, 1856 edn), p. x; Gresham Omnium, *A handy guide to safe investments* (London, 1854), p. 94; *Cassell's handbook of investments* (London, 1861), pp. 24, 39.

28 *The Economist*, 20 October 1866, p. 1219.

29 *The investors' guardian, almanack for 1869* (London, 1869), p. 7.

30 ibid., pp. 11–12.

31 A. R. Hall, 'A note on the English capital market as a source of funds for home investment before 1914', *Economica*, new ser. 24:93 (1957), pp. 59–63. He is referring in particular to the article by F. W. Paish, 'The London new issue market', *Economica*, new ser. 18:69 (1951), which claims that 'before 1914 the main business of the London new issue market was foreign investment' (p.2).

32 David S. Landes, *The unbound Prometheus: technological change and industrial development in Western Europe from 1750 to the present* (Cambridge, 1969), Table 4, p. 194.

33 Hartley Withers, *Stocks and shares* (London, 1910), pp. 327, 323.

34 Robert Lucas Nash, *A short inquiry into the profitable nature of our investments* (London, 1880), p. 50.

35 Hartley Withers, *International finance* (London, 1916), pp. 69–70.

36 *The Economist*, 21 October 1871, p.1274.

37 *Bankers' Magazine* (June 1859), p. 385.

38 R. Dudley Baxter, 'The recent progress of national debts', *Journal of the Statistical Society*, 37:1 (March 1874), pp. 5–7.

39 *Cassell's handbook of investments* (London, 1861), p. 48.

40 Robert Giffen, *Stock Exchange securities: an essay on the general causes of fluctuations in their price* (London, 1877), p. 160.

41 *The Economist*, 28 November 1868, p. 1355.

42 *The Economist*, 1 February 1868, p. 116.

43 Hobson, *Export of capital*, p. 232.

44 J. Horsley Palmer, *The causes and consequences of the pressure upon the money market* (London, 1837), p. 26.

45 Tooke, *History of prices*, Vol. II (1838), p. 148.

46 'The yield on investments', *Investors' Chronicle* (February 1900), p. 153.

47 *The Economist*, 11 July 1868, p. 79b.

48 *Report of the Royal Commission on the London Stock Exchange*: Parliamentary Papers, 1878, XIX, p. 272.

49 J. A. Hobson, *Imperialism: a study* (London, 1902), p. 86.

50 *Bankers' Magazine*, 21 (1861), pp. 281–2.

51 *The Times*, 11 October 1867, p. 6e.

52 *The Times*, 25 September 1868, p. 8f.

53 *The Times*, 15 April 1868, p. 7a.

54 W. P. Kennedy, 'Foreign investment, trade and growth in the United Kingdom, 1870–1913', *Explorations in Entrepreneurial History*, 11:4 (Summer 1974), pp. 423, 434.

55 Quoted by *The Times*, 18 May 1871, p. 10c.

56 Nash, *A short inquiry*, p. 32.

57 R. A. Lehfeldt. 'The rate of interest on British and foreign investments', *Journal of the Royal Statistical Society*, 76:2 (January 1913), p. 204. Lehfeldt published continuations of this article with data taking the story as far as the outbreak of the First World War: *Journal of the Royal Statistical Society*, 77:4 (March 1914), pp. 432–5, and 78:3 (May 1915), pp. 452–3. Leland Jenks agrees, in his article 'British experience with foreign investments', *Journal of Economic History*, 4: Supplement (December 1944), p. 69. Although Kennedy (note 54 above) describes Lehfeldt as a 'close, contemporary observer', he does not discuss these particular conclusions.

58 A. K. Cairncross, *Factors in economic development* (London, 1962), p. 42.

59 Estimate quoted by Berend and Ránki, *Economic development in East-Central Europe*, Table 5–1, p. 97.

60 ibid., pp. 97–8.

61 H. J. Habakkuk, 'Free trade and commercial expansion, 1853–1870', in J. Holland Rose, A. P. Newton and E. A. Benians, eds, *The Cambridge history of the British Empire*, Vol. II (Cambridge, 1940), p. 787.

62 Thorner, 'Great Britain and the development of India's railways', pp. 391–2.

63 W. J. Macpherson, 'Investment in Indian railways, 1845–75', *Economic History Review*, 2nd ser. 8:2 (1955), pp. 177, 186. Macpherson, however, acknowledges that Indians made an indirect contribution to the financing of their railways in the shape of taxes (the proceeds of which were employed to comply with the 5 per cent guaranteed by the government of India on railway capital).

64 Habakkuk, 'Free trade and commercial expansion', p. 790.

65 ibid. The figures seem implausible, but *The Times* believed that resident foreigners in India in 1871 held nearly three times as much of the public debt as natives, which may explain the popularity in India herself of such an unusually low-yielding security (*The Times*, 1 July 1871, p. 9f). Indian attitudes to investment and hoarding have been described by M. Mukherjee, *National income of India, trends and structure* (Calcutta, 1969), pp. 75–7; he reports that a sizeable part of net savings went into acquiring gold and silver, to the extent, he claims, (perhaps implausibly), of an average of 60 crores of rupees (£60 million) per annum, 1860–70. Latham adds that 'investment in the Indian economy would have been two-thirds higher if there had been no hoarding': A. J. H. Latham, 'Merchandise trade imbalances and uneven economic development in India and China', *Journal of European Economic History*, 7:1 (Spring 1978), p. 60.

66 *The Economist*, Commercial History and Review of 1880, 12 March 1881, p. 29.

67 *The Economist*, 5 February 1881, p. 164.

68 S. D. Chapman, 'The international houses: the Continental contribution to British commerce, 1800–1860', *Journal of European Economic History*, 6:1 (Spring 1977), p. 45.

69 W. T. C. King, 'The extent of the London discount market in the middle of the nineteenth century', *Economica*, new ser. 2:7 (August 1935), p. 326.

70 Arthur I. Bloomfield, *Short-term capital movements under the pre-1914 gold standard* (Princeton, NJ, 1963), p. 34.

71 ibid., p. 41.

72 Maurice Lévy-Leboyer, 'La Capacité financière de la France au début du

XXe siècle', in Lévy-Leboyer, ed., *La Position internationale de la France: aspects économiques et financiers XIXe–XXe siècles* (Paris, 1977), pp. 9, 32.
73 D. C. M. Platt, 'British portfolio investment overseas before 1870: some doubts', *Economic History Review*, 2nd ser. 33:1 (February 1980), p. 16.
74 Platt, 'British portfolio investment overseas', p. 13.
75 S. B. Saul, *Studies in British overseas trade 1870–1914* (Liverpool, 1960), p. 66.
76 W. Arthur Lewis, *The theory of economic growth* (London, 1955), p. 258.
77 John Knapp, 'Capital exports and growth', *Economic Journal*, 67 (September 1957), p. 433.
78 Rondo E. Cameron, *France and the economic development of Europe, 1800–1914* (Princeton, NJ, 1961), p. 78.
79 Arthur Helps, *Life and labours of Mr Brassey, 1805–1870* (London, 1872, pp. 161–6.
80 See, for example, P. L. Cottrell, 'Railway finance and the crisis of 1866: contractors' bills of exchange, and the finance companies', *Journal of Transport History*, new ser, 3:1 (February 1975), pp. 20–40, and Harold Pollins, 'Railway contractors and the finance of railway development in Britain'. *Journal of Transport History*, 3:1 (May 1957), pp. 41–51, and 3:2 (November 1957), pp. 103–10.
81 Lee, 'Provision of capital for early Irish railways', p. 63.
82 Lance E. Davis, 'Capital immobilities and finance capitalism: a study of economic evolution in the United States, 1820–1920', *Explorations in Entrepreneurial History*, 2nd ser. 1:1 (Fall 1963), pp. 94–5.
83 Nathan Rosenberg, 'Government and economic growth: the United States in the nineteenth century', *Third international conference of economic history*, March 1965, Vol. I (Paris, 1968), pp. 749–51.
84 *The Times*, 28 May 1867, p. 11d.
85 Eli F. Heckscher, *An economic history of Sweden* (trans. Cambridge, Mass., 1954), p. 211.

Appendix I

United States of America: Total Foreign Indebtedness (Public and Private), Direct Estimates (US$m.)

Year	*Quantity*	*Year*	*Quantity*
1821	30 [1]	1860	400[23]
1822	38 [2]	1863	200[24]
1837	150 [3]	1864	271[25]
	200 [4]	1865	320[25]
1838	110 [5]	1866	427[25]
	150–200 [6]		600[26]
1839	200 [7]	1867	519[25]
1843	197 [8]	1868	638[25]
	200 [9]		938[27]
1851	225[10]	1869	788[25]
1852	100[11]		900[28]
	300[12]		965[29]
1853	184[13]		1465[30]
	222[14]	1870	883[25]
1854	225[15]	1871	1047[25]
1855	230[16]	1872	1260[25]
	364[17]		1500[31]
1856	240[18]	1873	1393[25]
	500[19]	1874	1462[25]
1857	250[20]	1875	1000[32]
	300[21]		1489[25]
	400–500[22]	1876	1440[25]
			2250[33]

Sources: These are *direct* estimates. Overlapping *indirect* estimates (i.e. from the balance of payments) have been calculated by Douglass C. North, 'International capital movements in historical perspective', in Raymond F. Mikesell, ed., *U.S. private and government investment abroad* (Eugene, Oreg., 1962), p. 39, and by Matthew Simon, 'The United States balance of payments, 1861–1900', in National Bureau of Economic Research, *Trends in the American economy in the nineteenth century* (Princeton, NJ, 1960), p. 706. John J. Madden has collected together, with a critical commentary, a very wide range of estimates of American long-term indebtedness abroad, 1853–79, in his 'British investment in the United States 1860–1880' (unpublished Ph.D. thesis, University of Cambridge, 1957), pp. 391–408, Appendix 2.

1 *Niles Register*, quoted by Douglass C. North, 'The United States balance of payments, 1790–1860', in National Bureau of Economic Research, *Trends in the American economy in the nineteenth century* (Princeton, NJ, 1960), p. 623.
2 ibid., p. 623.

3 Messrs Marie & Kanz (New York), quoted by the *Bankers' Magazine*, 15 (May 1855), p. 290.
4 Comptroller of the State of New York, quoted by North, 'United States balance of payments', pp. 623–5.
5 *Niles Register*, quoted by North, 'United States balance of payments', p. 623 (it is my impression that this estimate did not include federal securities held abroad).
6 Charles J. Bullock, John H. Williams and Rufus S. Tucker, 'The balance of trade of the United States', *Review of Economic Statistics* (July 1919), p. 220.
7 President Jackson, quoted by Eugene Staley, *War and the private investor: a study in the relations of international politics and international private investment* (Chicago, 1935), p. 531.
8 Secretary of the Treasury, quoted by Cleona Lewis, *America's stake in international investments* (Washington, DC, 1938), p. 521.
9 US Department of Commerce, *Historical statistics of the United States: colonial times to 1970*, Vol. II (Washington, DC, 1975), p. 869.
10 *New York Times*, quoted by North, 'United States balance of payments', pp. 623–4.
11 *The Economist*, 23 April 1853, p. 462.
12 *The Times*, 10 September 1857, p. 8e (this was an estimate for *British* holdings).
13 Secretary of the Treasury, to 30 June 1853, quoted by *The Times*, 7 April 1854, p. 11a.
14 Winslow, Lanier & Co., quoted in Cleona Lewis, *The international accounts* (New York, 1927), p. 140.
15 *The Times*, 7 April 1854, p. 11a.
16 Messrs Marie & Kanz (New York), quoted by the *Bankers' Magazine*, 15 (May 1855), p. 290.
17 *Hunt's Merchant's Magazine* (December 1857), quoted by Bullock, Williams and Tucker, 'Balance of trade of the United States', p. 223.
18 Secretary of the Treasury, quoted by Margaret Myers, *The New York money market: origins and development* (New York, 1931), p. 36.
19 *New York Herald* (18 March 1857), quoted by Myers, *New York money market*, p. 37 fn 68.
20 *Hunt's Merchant's Magazine*, quoted by North, 'United States balance of payments', pp. 623, 625.
21 *American Railroad Journal*, quoted by North, 'United States balance of payments', p. 623.
22 *The Times*, 10 September 1857, p. 8e (these were estimates for *British* holdings alone).
23 Secretary of the Treasury, quoted by Bullock, Williams and Tucker, 'Balance of trade of the United States', p. 223.
24 Bullock, Williams and Tucker, 'Balance of trade of the United States', p. 223.
25 John J. Madden, 'British investment in the United States 1860–1880' (unpublished Ph.D. thesis, University of Cambridge, 1957), Table 24, p. 388.
26 Margaret Myers, *A financial history of the United States* (New York, 1970), pp. 289–90.
27 *Merchant's Magazine*, quoted by Matthew Simon, 'United States balance of payments, 1861–1900', in National Bureau of Economic Research, *Trends in the American Economy in the nineteenth century* (Princeton, NJ, 1960), p. 706.
28 *The Times*, 30 July 1869, p. 4a.
29 *Commercial and Financial Chronicle* (New York), quoted by *The Economist*, 24 July 1869, p. 871.
30 David A. Wells, Special Commissioner for the Revenue, quoted by Staley, *War and the private investor*, p. 531.
31 *Commercial and Financial Chronicle* (New York), quoted by Bullock, Williams and Tucker, 'Balance of trade of the United States', p. 225.

32 Leland H. Jenks, *The migration of British capital to 1875* (London, 1971 edn), p. 280.

33 Ernest Seyd, 'The rise in the price of silver, its consequences and their possible avoidance', *Journal of the Society of Arts*, 24 (10 March 1876), pp. 309, 311. Seyd's estimates were generally too high. Nor is it absolutely clear from the text whether this was an estimate for total foreign indebtedness or simply for federal indebtedness abroad. A separate, conflicting estimate for federal indebtedness in 1876 is cited in Appendix II.

Appendix II

United States of America: Federal, State and Municipal Indebtedness Abroad (US$m.)

Year	*Federal*	*State*	*Municipal*
1818	25.4 [1]		
1821	30 [2]		
1823	25.7 [3]		
1836		50 [4]	
1838		80 [5]	
		86 [6]	
1839		125 [7]	
1843		150 [8]	
1853	27 [9]	73 [9]	16.5 [9]
		111[10]	
1854		113[11]	
1856	15[12]		
1859	40[13]		
1860	30[14]		15[15]
1863	60[16]		
1864	111[16]		
1865	154[16]		
	320[19]		
1866	200[20]	150[19]	
	255[16]		
	350[19]		
1867	345[16]		
	500[20]		
	600[21]		
1868	425[16]		
	700[22]		
1869	512[16]	100[23]	7.5[23]
	800–1,000[24]		
	1,000[24]		
1870	518[16]		
1871	562[16]		
	845[25]		
1872	627[16]		
1873	643[16]		
1874	633[16]		
1875	623[16]	87[26]	
1876	600[27]		
	1,100[28]		

Sources:

1 Adam Seybert, *Statistical annals of the United States of America, 1789–1818* (Philadelphia, 1818), p.736.
2 ibid., p. 757.
3 'Statement of the amount of the public debt, held by foreign and domestic creditors, on the 31 December 1823', printed circular forwarded to Barings of London by a Philadelphia correspondent in 1824: papers of Baring Brothers & Co. Ltd., Public Archive of Canada, Ottawa, frame no. 60634.
4 Daniel Webster, speaking in the Senate, 31 May 1836, quoted by Douglass C. North, 'The United States balance of payments, 1790–1860', in National Bureau of Economic Research, *Trends in the American economy in the nineteenth century* (Princeton, NJ, 1960), pp. 623–4.
5 Margaret G. Myers, *A financial history of the United States* (New York, 1970), p. 119.
6 Deputy Garland, speaking in the House of Representatives in 1838, quoted by Dorothy Adler, *British investment in American railways, 1834–1898* (Charlottesville, Virginia, 1970), p. 83.
7 G. S. Callendar, quoted by North, 'United States balance of payments'. pp. 623–4.
8 US Congress, House Report, quoted by Adler, *British investment in American railways*, p. 10.
9 Secretary of the Treasury, quoted by *The Times*, 7 April 1854, p. 11a.
10 Winslow, Lanier & Co. (New York), quoted by Cleona Lewis, *The international accounts* (New York, 1927), Appendix A, p. 140.
11 *The Times*, 7 April 1854, p. 11a.
12 Secretary of the Treasury, quoted by North, 'United States balance of payments', p. 626.
13 *Philadelphia Public Ledger*, quoted by Adler, *British investment in American railways*, p. 24 fn. 128.
14 John J. Madden, 'British investment in the United States, 1860–1880' (unpublished Ph.D. thesis, University of Cambridge, 1957), p. 8.
15 ibid., p. 72.
16 ibid., Table 24, p. 388.
17 Cleona Lewis, *America's stake in international investments* (Washington, DC, 1938), p. 54.
18 *Commercial and Financial Chronicle* (New York), quoted by Henrietta Larson, *Jay Cooke: private banker* (Cambridge, Mass., 1936), p. 208.
19 Myers, *Financial history*, pp. 289–90.
20 Messrs E. & F. H. Geach (London), quoted by *The Economist*, 'Commercial history and review of 1866', 9 March 1867, p. 33.
21 *The Times*, 26 October 1867, p. 8e.
22 *Hunt's Merchant's Magazine* (October 1868), quoted by Charles J. Bullock, John H. Williams and Rufus S. Tucker, 'The balance of trade of the United States', *Review of Economic Statistics* (July 1919), p. 223.
23 Special Commissioner of the Revenue (David A. Wells), quoted by Lewis, *America's stake in international investments*, p. 523.
24 Report by Mr Francis Clare Ford, H.M.'s Secretary of Legation, on the Finances of the United States: Parliamentary Papers (United Kingdom), 1870, LXV, p. 843.
25 Messrs Jay Cooke, McCulloch & Co., quoted by *Fenn on the Funds* (London, 1876 edn), p. 470.
26 Madden, 'British investment', p. 71.
27 Secretary of the Treasury, quoted by Adler, *British investment in American railways*, p. 83.
28 Ernest Seyd, 'The fall in the price of silver, its consequences and their possible avoidance', *Journal of the Society of Arts*, 24 (10 March 1876), p. 311. He added that $400 million of this was held in Germany. His figures are absurd.

Appendix III

United States of America: Foreign Investment in Railway Securities (US$m.)

Year	*British*	*All foreigners*
1838		30[1]
1849		40[2]
1852	300[3]	
1853		52[4]
		70[5]
1854	90[6]	
1856		83[7]
1857	400[8]	
	400–500[9]	
1860	100[10]	135[10]
1861	100[11]	
1863	75[10]	95[10]
1866		50[12]
1869		243[13]
1870	195[10]	385[10]
	200[14]	
1874	535[10]	960[10]
1876	575[10]	375[15]
		500[16]
		965[10]

Sources:

1 Margaret G. Myers, *A financial History of the United States* (New York, 1970), p. 118.
2 Margaret G. Myers, *The New York money market: origins and development* (New York, 1931), p. 35.
3 *The Times*, 10 September 1857, p. 8e. The estimate was for British ownership of *all* classes of US securities, although these were mainly in railways.
4 Secretary of the Treasury, as of 30 June 1853, quoted by *The Times*, 7 April 1854, p. 11a.
5 Samuel G. Ward to Barings, 22 November 1853, quoted by Ralph Hidy, *The house of Baring in American trade and finance* (Cambridge, Mass., 1949), pp. 428–9, 605. Ward included in his total both railway securities and state bonds issued in aid of railways.
6 *Bankers' Magazine* (November 1854), p. 605.
7 Secretary of the Treasury, quoted by Albert Fishlow, *American railroads and the transformation of the ante-bellum economy* (Cambridge, Mass., 1965), p. 117.
8 C. K. Hobson, *The export of capital* (London, 1914), p. 128.
9 *The Times*, 10 September 1857, p. 8e. The estimate was for British ownership of US securities of *all* kinds, although mainly in railways.
10 John J. Madden, 'British investments in the United States, 1860–1880', (unpublished Ph.D., University of Cambridge, 1957), Tables 14 and 15, pp. 78–9.

11 Dorothy Adler, *British investment in American railways, 1834–1898* (Charlottesville, 1970), p. 24.

12 Myers, *Financial history of the United States*, p.289.

13 Special Commissioner of the Revenue (David A. Wells), quoted by Cleona Lewis, *America's stake in international investments* (Washington, 1938), pp. 522–3.

14 A. K. Cairncross, *Home and foreign investment, 1870–1913: studies in capital accumulation* (Cambridge, 1953). p. 183.

15 *New York Journal of Commerce*, 6 December 1911, quoted by Myers, *New York money market*, p. 296.

16 Adler, *British investment in American railways*, pp. 87–9.

Appendix IV

United States of America: Foreign Commercial Credit/Short-Term Finance (US$m.)

Year	*Amount*	*Year*	*Amount*
1836	85[1]	1857	150 [8]
	100[2]	1866–8	125 [9]
1837	30[3]	1869	150[10]
	60[4]	1869–70	150 [9]
	90[5]	1871–3	225[9]
1839	80–90[6]	1874–80	150[9]
1843	28[7]	1876	200[11]
1853	155[7]		

Sources:

1 G. S. Callender, quoted by Cleona Lewis, *America's stake in international investments* (Washington, DC, 1938), p. 13.

2 *Morning Chronicle* (London) and *New York American*, quoted by L. H. Jenks, *Migration of British capital to 1875* (London, 1971 edn), p. 87. Jenks describes this sum as 'the outstanding mercantile debt of the United States', which might imply the debt wherever incurred (e.g. on the Continent). In fact, he took the estimate from the *Morning Chronicle*, where the figure was for 'acceptances of the firms in the American trade at Liverpool and London'.

3 Contemporary estimate quoted by Margaret Myers, *The New York money market: origins and development* (New York, 1931), p. 66. As Myers explains, the estimate was set deliberately low in order to diminish the blame attached to the banks for their overestimation of credit.

4 Jenks, *Migration of British capital*, p. 86 (for which the same comment applies as for note 2 above).

5 US Department of Trade, quoted by the *Circular to Bankers*, 11 July 1845, p. 2. This was an estimate for the circulation of the credit of 'American' merchants, who might be US citizens or foreigners. The same figure is quoted by Margaret Myers from the *Democratic Review*, this time for the *total* amount of credit outstanding in the first part of 1837, just before the crash. She points out, however, that the *Review* was 'anxious for political reasons to magnify the amount, and discredit the Bank of the United States': Myers, *New York money market*, p. 66.

6 Callendar, quoted by Douglass C. North, 'The United States balance of payments, 1790–1860', in National Bureau of Economic Research, *Trends in the American economy in the nineteenth century* (Princeton, NJ, 1960), pp. 623–4.

7 Lewis, *America's stake in international investments*, p. 560.

8 Ezra Seaman (*Hunt's Merchant's Magazine*), quoted by North, 'United States balance of payments', pp. 623, 627.

9 John J. Madden, 'British investments in the United States, 1860–1880' (unpublished Ph.D. thesis, University of Cambridge, 1957), p. 156.

10 Lewis, *America's stake in international investments*, p. 560.

11 Ernest Seyd, 'The fall in the price of silver, its consequences and their possible avoidance', *Journal of the Society of Arts*, 24 (10 March 1876), p. 311.

Bibliography

Most economic histories pay some attention to international finance. This bibliography lists merely those books, articles and theses that have been found useful for the themes discussed.

Acworth, A. W., *Financial reconstruction in England, 1815–1822* (London, 1925).

Adler, Dorothy, *British investment in American railways, 1834–1898* (Charlottesville, Virginia, 1970).

Adler, John H., *Capital movements and economic development* (London and New York, 1967).

Anderson, B. L., 'Law, finance and economic growth in England: some long-term influences', in Barrie M. Ratcliffe, ed., *Great Britain and her world, 1750–1914* (Manchester, 1975), pp. 99–124.

Anderson, Olive, 'The Russian loan of 1855: an example of economic liberalism?', *Economica*, new ser. 27 (November 1960), pp. 368–71.

Anderson, Olive, 'Great Britain and the beginnings of the Ottoman Public Debt, 1854–55', *Historical Journal*, 7:1 (1964), pp. 47–63.

Anes Alvarez, Rafael, 'Las inversiones extranjeras en España de 1855 a 1880', in Pedro Schwarz Giron, ed., *Ensayos sobre la economía española a mediados del siglo XIX* (Barcelona, 1970), pp. 187–202.

Anes Alvarez, Rafael, 'El Banco de España (1874–1914): un banco nacional', in Tortella, *La Banca española*, Vol. I, pp. 107–215.

Artola, Miguel, ed., *Los ferrocarriles en España, 1844–1943* (Madrid, 1978), 2 vols.

Ayres, Henry, *Ayres's financial register of British and foreign funds, banks, etc. etc. for 1857* (London, 1857).

Bacon, Nathaniel T., 'Capital invested in the United States from abroad', *Yale Review*, 9 (November 1900), pp. 265–85.

Barker, Richard J., 'The Périer bank during the Restoration (1815–1830), *Journal of European Economic History*, 2:3 (Winter 1973), pp. 641–56.

Baxter, Robert Dudley, *National debts* (London, 1871).

Baxter, Robert Dudley, 'The recent progress of national debts', *Journal of the Statistical Society*, 38:1 (March 1874), pp. 1–20.

Berend, Iván T., and György Ránki, *Economic development in East–Central Europe in the nineteenth and twentieth centuries* (trans. New York, 1974).

Bigo, Robert, *Les Banques françaises au cours du XIXe siècle* (Paris, 1947).

Blackwell, W. L., *The beginnings of Russian industrialisation, 1800–1860* (Princeton, NJ, 1968).

Blanchard, M., 'The railway policy of the Second Empire', in F. Crouzet, W. H. Chaloner and W. M. Stern, eds, *Essays in European economic history, 1789–1914* (London, 1969), pp. 98–111.

Bloomfield, Arthur I., 'The significance of outstanding securities in the international movement of capital', *Canadian Journal of Economics and Political Science*, 6:4 (November 1940), pp. 495–524.

Bloomfield, Arthur I., *Short-term capital movements under the pre-1914 gold standard* (Princeton, NJ, 1963).

Blum, Jerome, 'Transportation and industry in Austria, 1815–1848', *Journal of Modern History*, 15:1 (March 1943), pp. 24–38.

Bouvier, Jean, *Les Rothschild* (Paris, 1967; first edn Paris, 1960).

Bouvier, Jean, *Le Crédit Lyonnais de 1863 à 1882. Les années de formation d'une banque de dépôts* (Paris, 1961), 2 vols.

Bouvier, Jean, 'Les Interventions bancaires françaises dans quelques "Grandes Affaires" financières de l'unité italienne (1863–1870)' in Bouvier, *Histoire économique et histoire sociale* (Geneva, 1968), pp. 181–92.

Bouvier, Jean, 'The banking mechanism in France in the late 19th century', in Rondo Cameron, ed., *Essays in French economic history* (Homewood, Ill., 1970), pp. 341–69.

Bramsen, Bo, and Kathleen Wain, *The Hambros 1779–1979* (London, 1979).

Broadbridge, Seymour, 'The early capital market: the Lancashire and Yorkshire railway', *Economic History Review*, 2nd ser. 8:2 (1955), pp. 200–12.

Broadbridge, Seymour, *Studies in railway expansion and the capital market in England, 1825–1873* (London, 1970).

Broder, Albert, 'Les Investissements étrangers en Espagne au XIXe siècle: méthodologie et quantification', *Revue d'histoire économique et sociale*, 54:1 (1976), pp. 29–63.

Brown, Arthur J., 'Britain in the world economy, 1870–1914', *Yorkshire Bulletin of Economic and Social Research*, 17:1 (May 1965), pp. 46–60.

Buck, N. S., *The development of the organisation of Anglo-American trade, 1800–1850* (New Haven, Conn., 1925).

Buist, Marten G., *At spes non fracta: Hope & Co. 1770–1815. Merchant bankers and diplomats at work* (The Hague, 1974).

Bullock, Charles J., John H. Williams and Rufus S. Tucker, 'The balance of trade of the United States', *Review of Economic Statistics* (July 1919), pp. 213–66.

Cairncross, A. K., *Home and foreign investment 1870–1913: studies in capital accumulation* (Cambridge, 1953).

Cairncross, A. K., *Factors in economic development* (London, 1962).

Callender, G. S., 'The early transportation and banking enterprises of the states in relation to the growth of corporations', *Quarterly Journal of Economics*, 17:1 (November 1902), pp. 111–62.

Cameron, Rondo E., 'The Crédit Mobilier and the economic development of France', *Journal of Political Economy*, 61:6 (December 1953), pp. 461–88.

Cameron, Rondo, E., 'L'Exportation des capitaux français, 1850–1880', *Revue d'histoire économique et sociale*, 33:3 (1955), pp. 347–53.

Cameron, Rondo E., *France and the economic development of Europe, 1800–1914* (Princeton, NJ, 1961).

Cameron, Rondo E., Olga Crisp, H. T. Patrick and R. Tilly, *Banking in the early stages of industrialisation* (New York, 1967).

Cameron, Rondo E., ed., *Banking and economic development: some lessons of history* (New York, 1972).

Canosa, Ramón, *Un siglo de banca privada (1845–1945); apuntes para la historia de las finanzas españolas* (Madrid, 1945).

Capefigue, J. B. H. Raymond, *Histoire des grandes opérations financières* (Paris, 1855–60), 4 vols.

Carlson, Robert E., 'British railroads and engineers and the beginnings of American railroad development', *Business History Review*, 34:2 (Summer 1960), pp. 137–49.

Caron, François, *Histoire de l'exploitation d'un grand réseau: la Compagnie du Chemin de Fer du Nord, 1846–1937* (Paris, 1973).

Carosso, Vincent, *Investment banking in America: a history* (Cambridge, Mass., 1970).

Carter, Alice, 'Dutch foreign investment, 1738–1800', *Economica*, new ser. 20 (November 1953), pp. 322–40.

Catin, R., *Le Portefeuille étranger de la France entre 1870 et 1914* (Paris, thesis, 1927).

Chandler, Alfred D., Jnr, 'Patterns of American railroad finance, 1830–50', *Business History Review*, 28:3 (September 1954), pp. 248–63.

Chandler, Alfred D., comp. and ed., *The railroads: the nation's first big business* (New York, 1965).

Chapman, S. D., 'The international houses: the Continental contribution to British commerce, 1800–1860', *Journal of European Economic History*, 6:1 (Spring 1977), pp. 5–48.

Chapman, S. D., 'British market enterprise; the changing role of merchants, manufacturers, and financiers, 1700–1860', *Business History Review*, 53 (Summer 1979), pp. 205–34.

Clark, Hyde, 'On the debts of sovereign and quasi-sovereign states, owing by foreign countries', *Journal of the Statistical Society*, 41 (June 1878), pp. 299–347.

Cleveland, Frederick A., and Fred Powell, *Railroad finance* (New York, 1912).

Cochran, Thomas C., 'Land agents and railway entrepreneurship', *Journal of Economic History*, 10: Supplement – The tasks of economic history (1950), pp. 53–67.

Cohen, Bernard, *Compendium of finance* (London, 1822).

Commerce, Journal of, and Commercial Bulletin, *A history of banking in all the leading nations* (New York, 1896), 4 vols.

Conant, Charles A., 'Securities as means of payment', *Annals of the American Academy of Political and Social Science*, 14:2 (September 1899), pp. 25–47.

Cooney, E. W., 'Capital exports and investment in building in Britain and the U.S.A., 1856–1914', *Economica*, new ser. 16 (November 1949), pp. 347–54.

Cope, S. R., 'The Goldsmids and the development of the London money market during the Napoleonic wars', *Economica*, new ser. 9:34 (May 1942), pp. 180–206.

Coram, T., 'The role of British capital in the development of the United States' (unpublished M.Sc. [Econ.] thesis, University of Southampton, 1967).

Corey, Lewis, *The house of Morgan: a social biography of the masters of money* (New York, 1930).

Corti, Egan C., *The rise of the house of Rothschild* (trans. London, 1928).

Cottrell, P. L., 'London financiers and Austria, 1863–1875: the Anglo-Austrian Bank', *Business History*, 11:2 (June 1969), pp. 106–19.

Cottrell, P. L., 'Investment banking in England, 1856–1882: case study of the

International Financial Society' (unpublished Ph.D. thesis, University of Hull, 1974).

Cottrell, P. L., 'Anglo-French financial cooperation, 1850–1880', *Journal of European Economic History*, 3:1 (Spring 1974), pp. 54–86.

Cottrell, P. L., 'Railway finance and the crisis of 1866: contractors' bills of exchange, and the finance companies', *Journal of Transport History*, new ser. 3:1 (February 1975), pp. 20–40.

Cottrell, P. L., *British overseas investment in the nineteenth century* (London, 1975).

Cottrell, P. L., 'La Coopération financière Franco-Anglaise, 1850–1880' in Lévy-Leboyer, ed., *La Position internationale de la France*, pp. 177–86.

Cottrell, P. L., *Industrial finance, 1830–1914: the finance and organisation of English manufacturing industry* (London, 1980).

Courtney, Leonard H., 'On the finances of the United States of America, 1861–67', *Journal of the Statistical Society*, 31:2 (June 1868), pp. 164–221.

Crammond, Edgar, 'British investments abroad', *Quarterly Review*, 428 (July 1911), pp. 43–67.

Cranmer, H. Jerome, 'Canal investment, 1815–1860', in National Bureau of Economic Research, Studies in Income and Wealth, Vol. 24, *Trends in the American economy in the nineteenth century* (Princeton, NJ, 1960), pp. 547–70.

Crihan, Anton, *Le Capital étranger en Russie* (Paris, thesis, 1934).

Crisp, Olga, 'Russian financial policy and the gold standard at the end of the nineteenth century', *Economic History Review*, 2nd ser. 6:2 (1953), pp. 156–72.

Crisp, Olga, 'French investment in Russian joint-stock companies, 1894–1914', *Business History*, 2:2 (June 1960), pp. 75–90.

Crisp, Olga, 'Russia, 1860–1914', in Cameron, ed., *Banking in the early stages of industrialisation*, pp. 183–238.

Crisp, Olga, *Studies in the Russian economy before 1914* (London, 1976).

Crouzet, François, *L'Économie britannique et le blocus continental 1806–13* (Paris, 1958), 2 vols.

Crump, Arthur, *The key to the London money market* (London, 1872).

Currie, A. W., 'British attitudes toward investment in North American railroads', *Business History Review*, 34:2 (Summer 1960), pp. 194–215.

Daumard, Adeline *et al.*, *Les Fortunes françaises au XIXe siècle: enquête sur la répartition et la composition des capitaux privés à Paris, Lyon, Lille, Bordeaux et Toulouse d'après l'enregistrement des déclarations de succession* (Paris, 1973).

Davis, Lance E., and J. R. T. Hughes, 'A dollar–sterling exchange, 1803–1895', *Economic History Review*, 2nd ser. 13:1 (1960), pp. 52–78.

Davis, Lance E., 'Capital immobilities and finance capitalism: a study of economic evolution in the United States, 1820–1920', *Explorations in Entrepreneurial History*, 2nd ser. 1:1 (Fall 1963), pp. 88–105.

Dewey, Davis R., *Financial history of the United States* (New York, 1922; first edn, 1903).

Donaghy, Thomas J., 'The Liverpool & Manchester Railway as an investment', *Journal of Transport History*, 7:4 (November 1966), pp. 225–33.

Dorfman, Joseph, 'A note on the interpretation of Anglo-American finance, 1837–41', Journal of Economic History, 11 (1951), pp. 140–7.

Doukas, Kimon A., *The French railroads and the state* (New York, 1945).

Dunham, Arthur L., 'How the first French railways were planned', *Journal of Economic History*, 1:1 (May 1941), pp. 12–25.

Dunham, Arthur L., *The industrial revolution in France, 1815–1848* (New York, 1955).

Dunning, John H., *Studies in international investment* (London, 1970).

Dúpont-Ferrier, Pierre, *Le Marché financier de Paris sous le Second Empire* (Paris, 1925).

Edelstein, Michael. *Overseas investment in the age of high imperialism: the United Kingdom, 1850–1914* (New York and London, 1982).

Emden, Paul H., *Money powers of Europe in the nineteenth and twentieth centuries* (London, 1937).

Epstein, E., *Les Banques de commerce russes: leur rôle dans l'évolution économique de la Russie, leur nationalisation* (Paris, 1925).

Falkus, Malcolm E., *The industrialisation of Russia, 1700–1914* (London, 1972).

Falkus, Malcolm E., 'Aspects of foreign investment in Tsarist Russia', *Journal of European Economic History*, 8:1 (Spring 1979), pp. 5–36.

Feinstein, C. H., 'Income and investment in the United Kingdom, 1856–1914', *Economic Journal*, 71 (June 1961), pp. 367–85.

Feis, Herbert, *Europe, the world's banker, 1870–1914: an account of European foreign investment and the connection of world finance with diplomacy before the war* (New York, 1965; first edn, New Haven, Conn., 1930).

Fenn, Charles, *A compendium of the English and foreign funds* (London, 1837, and subsequent editions).

Fetter, Frank Whitson, 'The Russian loan of 1855: a postscript', *Economica*, new ser. 28 (November 1961), pp. 421–6.

Fischer, Wolfram, 'The strategy of Public investment in XIXth. century Germany', *Journal of European Economic History*, 6:2 (Fall 1977), pp. 431–42.

Fishlow, Albert, *American railroads and the transformation of the ante-bellum economy* (Cambridge, Mass., 1965).

Fisk, Harvey E., *Our public debt: an historical sketch with a description of United States securities* (New York, 1919).

Fisk, Harvey E., *The inter-ally debts: an analysis of war and post-war public finance, 1914–23* (New York, 1924).

Fleetwood, Erin E., *Sweden's capital imports and exports* (Geneva, 1947).

Freedman, Joseph Robert, 'A London merchant banker in Anglo-American trade and finance, 1835–1850' (unpublished Ph.D. thesis, University of London, 1969).

Ford, A. G., 'The transfer of British foreign lending, 1870–1913', *Economic History Review*, 2nd ser. 11:2 (1958), pp. 302–8.

Fortune, E. F. Thomas, *Epitome of the stocks and public funds, English, foreign, and American* (London, 1796, and subsequent editions to 1856).

Fox Bourne, H. R., *English merchants: memoirs in illustration of the progress of British commerce* (London, 1866), 2 vols.

Fulford, Roger, *Glyn's, 1753–1953, six generations in Lombard Street* (London, 1953).

Garvey, G., 'Banking under the Tsars and the soviets', *Journal of Economic History*, 32:4 (December 1972), pp. 869–93.

Gayer, Arthur D., Anna Jacobson and Isaiah Finkelstein, 'British share prices, 1811–1830', *Review of Economic Statistics*, 22 (1940), pp. 78–93.

Gayer, Arthur D., W. W. Rostow and Anna Jacobson Schwartz, *The Growth and fluctuation of the British economy, 1790–1850: an historical, statistical, and theoretical study of Britain's economic development* (Oxford, 1953), 2 vols.

Gerschenkron, Alexander, *Economic backwardness in historical perspective: essays* (Cambridge, Mass., 1962).

Giffen, Robert, *American railways as investments* (London, 1873).

Giffen, Robert, 'Recent accumulations of capital in the United Kingdom', *Journal of the Statistical Society*, 41:1 (March 1878), pp. 1–39.

Giffen, Robert, *The growth of capital* (London, 1889).

Giffen, Robert, 'Accumulations of capital in the United Kingdom in 1875–85', *Journal of the Royal Statistical Society*, 53:1 (March 1890), pp. 1–49.

Gille, Bertrand, *Histoire économique et sociale de la Russie du moyen âge au XXe siècle* (Paris, 1949).

Gille, Bertrand, *La Banque et le crédit en France de 1815 à 1848* (Paris, 1959).

Gille, Bertrand, 'Investissements extérieurs et politique internationale (1815–1848)', *Bulletin de la Société d'Histoire Moderne*, 12th ser. 13 (1960), pp. 4–7.

Gille, Bertrand, *Lettres adressées à la maison Rothschild de Paris par son représentant à Bruxelles: crise politique et crise financière en Belgique, 1838–1840* (Paris, 1961).

Gille, Bertrand, 'Finance internationale et trusts', *Revue historique*, 127 (April/June 1962), pp. 291–326.

Gille, Bertrand, *Histoire de la maison Rothschild, des origines à 1870* (Geneva, 1965, 1967), 2 vols.

Gille, Bertrand, *Les Investissements français en Italie (1815–1914)* (Turin, 1968).

Gille, Bertrand, *La banque en France au XIXe siècle: recherches historiques* (Geneva, 1970).

Gille, Bertrand, 'Banking and industrialisation in Europe, 1730–1914', in Carlo M. Cipolla, ed., *Fontana economic history of Europe: the industrial revolution* (London, 1973), pp. 255–300.

Girard, Louis D., *La Politique des travaux publics du Second Empire* (Paris, 1952).

Girault, René, *Emprunts russes et investissements français en Russie, 1887–1914* (Paris, 1973).

Goldsmith, Raymond W., 'The growth of reproducible wealth of the United States of America from 1805 to 1950', in Simon Kuznets, ed., *Income and wealth of the United States: trends and structures* (Cambridge, 1952).

Gómez Mendoza, Antonio, *Ferrocarriles y cambio económico en España, 1855–1915* (Madrid, 1982).

Good, David F., 'Stagnation and "take-off" in Austria, 1873–1913', *Economic History Review*, 2nd ser. 27:1 (February 1974), pp. 72–87.

Goodrich, Carter, and Harvey H. Segal, 'Baltimore's aid to railroads: a study in the municipal planning of internal improvements', *Journal of Economic History*, 13:I (Winter 1953), pp. 2–35.

Goschen, G. J., *The theory of foreign exchanges* (London, 1861).

Gourvish, T. R., and M. C. Reed, 'The financing of Scottish railways before 1860 – a comment', *Scottish Journal of Political Economy*, 18 (1971), pp. 209–20.

Greenberg, Dolores, 'Yankee financiers and the establishment of trans-Atlantic partnerships: a re-examination', *Business History*, 16:1 (January 1974), pp. 17–35.

Gregory, Paul R., 'The Russian balance of payments, the gold standard and monetary policy: a historical example of foreign capital movements', *Journal of Economic History*, 39:2 (June 1979), pp. 379–99.

Grodinsky, Julius, *Jay Gould; his business career, 1867–1892* (Philadelphia, 1957).

Gross, N. T., 'The industrial revolution and the Habsburg monarchy, 1750–1914', in Carlo M. Cipolla, ed., *Fontana economic history of Europe: the emergence of industrial societies, Part I* (London, 1973), pp. 229–78.

Guyot, Ives, 'The amount, direction and nature of French investments', in Ernest M. Patterson, ed., *America's changing investment market* (Philadelphia, 1916), pp. 36–54.

Habakkuk, H. J., 'Free trade and commercial expansion, 1853–1870', in J. Holland Rose, A. P. Newton and E. A. Benians, eds, *Cambridge history of the British Empire*, Vol. II (Cambridge, 1940), pp. 751–805.

Hall, Alan R., ed., *The export of capital from Britain, 1870–1914* (London, 1968).

Hammond, Bray, *Banks and politics in America from the Revolution to the Civil War* (Princeton, NJ, 1957).

Hartland, Penelope, 'Private enterprise and international capital', *Canadian Journal of Economics and Political Science*, 19:1 (February 1953), pp. 70–80.

Hawke, G. R., and M. C. Reed, 'Railway capital in the United Kingdom in the nineteenth century', *Economic History Review*, 2nd ser. 22:2 (August 1969), pp. 269–86.

Hawke, G. R., *Railways and economic growth in England and Wales, 1840–1879* (Oxford, 1970).

Haywood, R. M., *The beginnings of railway development in Russia in the reign of Nicholas I, 1835–1842* (Durham, NC, 1969).

Hedin, Lars-Erik, 'Some notes on the financing of the Swedish railroads, 1860–1914', *Economy and History*, 10 (1967), pp. 3–37.

Helleiner, Karl F. M., *The imperial loans: a study in financial and diplomatic history* (Oxford, 1965).

Helleiner, Karl F. M., *Free trade and frustration: Anglo-Austrian negotiations, 1860–70* (Toronto, 1973).

Helps, Arthur, *Life and labours of Mr. Brassey, 1805–1870* (London, 1872).

Hidy, Ralph W., 'A leaf from investment history', *Harvard Business Review*, 20:1 (Autumn 1941), pp. 65–74.

Hidy, Ralph W., 'The organisation and functions of Anglo-American merchant bankers, 1815–1860', *Journal of Economic History*, 1: Supplement (December 1941), pp. 53–66.

Hidy, Ralph W., *The house of Baring in American trade and finance: English merchant bankers at work, 1763–1861* (Cambridge, Mass., 1949).

Hidy, Ralph W., and M. E. Hidy, 'Anglo-American merchant bankers and

the railroads of the Old Northwest, 1848–1860', *Business History Review*, 34:2 (Summer 1960), pp. 150–69.
Higgins, J. P. P., and S. Pollard, *Aspects of capital investment in Great Britain, 1750–1850* (London, 1971).
Hirst, Francis W., *The credit of nations, with special reference to the debts of Great Britain, Germany, France, and the United States* (National Monetary Commission, Washington, DC, 1910).
Hirst, Francis W., *The stock exchange: a short study of investment and speculation* (London, 1911).
Historical statistics of the United States, colonial times to 1970 (Department of Commerce, Washington, DC, 1975).
Hobson, C. K., *The export of capital* (London, 1914).
Homer, Sidney, *A history of interest rates* (New Brunswick, NJ, 1963).
Hughes, Jonathan R. T., *Fluctuations in trade, industry, and finance: a study of British economic development, 1850–1860* (Oxford, 1960).
Imlah, Albert H., 'British balance of payments and export of capital, 1816–1913', *Economic History Review*, 2nd ser. 5:2 (1952), pp. 208–39.
Imlah, Albert H., *Economic elements in the Pax Britannica, studies in British foreign trade in the nineteenth century* (Cambridge, Mass., 1958).
Izzo, Louis, 'Finances publiques et l'économie Italienne pendant les dix premières années de l'unité nationale (1861–1870)', *Third international conference of economic history*, Munich 1965, Vol. I (Paris, 1968), pp. 779–83.
Jagtiani, H. M., *The role of the state in the provision of railways* (London, 1924).
Jenks, Leland H., *The migration of British capital to 1875* (London, 1971; first edn, New York, 1927).
Jenks, Leland H., 'Railroads as a economic force in American development', *Journal of Economic History*, 4:1 (May 1944), pp. 1–20.
Jenks, Leland H., 'British experience with foreign investments', *Journal of Economic History*, 4:Supplement (December 1944), pp. 68–79.
Jenks, Leland H., 'Britain and American railway development', *Journal of Economic History*, 11:4 (Fall 1951), pp. 375–88.
Jensen, J. H., and Gerhard Rosegger, 'British railway builders along the lower Danube, 1856–1869', *Slavonic and East European Review*, 46:106 (January 1968), pp. 105–28.
Johnson, Arthur M., and Barry E. Supple, *Boston capitalists and Western railroads: a study in the nineteenth-century railroad investment process* (Cambridge, Mass., 1967).
Kellet, J. R., 'Glasgow's railways, 1830–80: a study in "natural growth"', *Economic History Review*, 2nd ser. 17:2 (December 1964), pp. 354–68.
Kennedy, W. P., 'Foreign investment, trade and growth in the United Kingdom, 1870–1913', *Explorations in Entrepreneurial History*, 11:4 (Summer 1974), pp. 415–44.
Kenwood, A. G., 'Railway investment in Britain, 1825–1875', *Economica*, new ser. 32 (August 1965), pp. 313–22.
Killick, J. R., and W. A. Thomas, 'The provincial stock exchanges, 1830–1870', *Economic History Review*, 2nd ser. 23:1 (April 1970), pp. 96–111.
Killick, J. R., 'The stock exchanges of the north of England, 1836–1850', *Northern History*, 5 (1970), pp. 114–30.

Kindleberger, Charles P., *The formation of financial centres: a study in comparative economic history* (Princeton, NJ, 1974).
King, W. T. C., 'The extent of the London discount market in the middle of the nineteenth century', *Economica*, new ser. 2:7 (August 1935), pp. 321–6.
King, W. T. C., *History of the London discount market* (London, 1936).
Knapp, John, 'Capital exports and growth', *Economic Journal*, 67 (September 1957), pp. 432–44.
Kravis, Irving B., 'The role of exports in nineteenth-century United States growth', *Economic Development and Cultural Change*, 20:3 (April 1972), pp. 387–405.
Kuznets, Simon, 'Foreign economic relations of the United States and their impact upon the domestic economy: a review of long-term trends', *Proceedings of the American Philosophical Society*, 92:4 (1948), pp. 228–43.
Kuznets, Simon, 'Long-term trends in capital formation proportions', *Economic Development and Cultural Change*, 9:4, pt II (July 1961), pp. 3–124.
Kuznets, Simon, *Capital in the American economy: its formation and financing* (Princeton, NJ, 1961).
Labouchère, G., 'Un Financier diplomate au siècle dernier. Pierre-César Labouchère (1772–1839)', *Revue d'histoire diplomatique*, 27 (1913), pp. 425–55, and 28 (1914), pp. 74–97.
Landes, David S., 'Vielle banque et banque nouvelle: la révolution financière du dix-neuvième siècle', *Revue d'histoire moderne et contemporaine*, 3:3 (July/September 1956), pp. 204–22.
Landes, David S., *Bankers and pashas, international finance and economic imperialism in Egypt* (Cambridge, Mass., 1958).
Landes, David S., *The unbound Prometheus: technological change and industrial development in Western Europe from 1750 to the present* (Cambridge, 1969).
Larson, Henrietta M., *Jay Cooke: private banker* (Cambridge, Mass., 1936).
Lee, Joseph, 'The provision of capital for early Irish railways, 1830–53', *Irish Historical Studies*, 16:61 (March 1968), pp. 33–63.
Lester, Richard I., 'An aspect of Confederate finance during the American Civil War: the Erlanger loan and the Plan of 1864', *Business History*, 16:2 (July 1974), pp. 130–44.
Lévy-Leboyer, Maurice, *Les Banques européennes et l'industrialisation internationale dans la première moitié du XIXe siècle* (Paris, 1964).
Lévy-Leboyer, Maurice, contr. and ed., *La Position internationale de la France: aspects économiques et financiers XIXe–XXe siècles* (Paris, 1977).
Lévy-Leboyer, Maurice, 'Capital investment and economic growth in France, 1820–1930', in Peter Mathias and M. M. Postan, eds, *Cambridge economic history of Europe*, Vol. VII pt 1 (Cambridge, 1978), pp. 231–95.
Lewis, Cleona, *The international accounts* (New York, 1927).
Lewis, Cleona, *America's stake in international investments* (Washington, DC, 1938).
Lida, Clara, and Iris M. Zavala, eds. *La revolución en 1868: historia, pensamiento, literatura* (New York, 1970).

Lyaschenko, Peter I., *History of the national economy of Russia to the 1917 revolution* (trans. New York, 1949).
McCloskey, Donald N., ed., *Essays on a mature economy: Britain after 1840* (London, 1971).
McCullough, J. R., *A statistical account of the British empire* (London, 1837, 1839), 2 vols.
McGrane, Reginald C., 'Some aspects of American state debts in the forties', *American Historical Review*, 38:4 (July 1933), pp. 673–86.
McGrane, Reginald C., *Foreign bondholders and American state debts* (New York, 1935).
McKay, J. P., *Pioneers for profit: foreign entrepreneurship and Russian industrialisation, 1885–1913* (Chicago, 1970).
Macpherson, W. J., 'Investment in Indian railways, 1845–75', *Economic History Review*, 2nd ser. 8:2 (1955), pp. 177–86.
Madden John, 'British investment in the United States, 1860–1880' (unpublished Ph.D. thesis, University of Cambridge, 1957).
Mallez, Paul, *La Restauration des finances françaises après 1914* (Paris, thesis, 1927).
Markwick, W. H., 'Scottish overseas investment in the nineteenth century', *Scottish Bankers' Magazine*, 27 (July 1935), pp. 109–16.
Michalet, Charles-Albert, *Les Placements des épargnants français de 1815 à nos jours* (Paris, 1968).
Michel, Bernard, 'Les capitaux français en Autriche au dèbut du XXe siècle', in Lévy-Leboyer, ed., *La Position internationale*, pp. 227–33.
Mitchell, B. R., *European historical statistics, 1750–1970* (London, 1975).
Moreno Redondo, Alfonso, ed., *El Banco de España. Una historia económica* (Madrid, 1970).
Morgan, E. V., and W. A. Thomas, *The stock exchange: its history and functions* (London, 1962, 2nd updated edn: London, 1969).
Mulhall, Michael G., *Balance-sheet of the world for ten years, 1870–1880* (London, 1881).
Mülinen, Comte de, *Les Finances de l'Autriche: étude historique et statistique sur les finances de l'Autriche Cisleithanienne* (Paris, 1875).
Murray, Andrew J., *Home from the hill, a biography of Frederick Huth, 'Napoleon of the City'* (London, 1970).
Myers, Margaret G., *The New York money market: origins and development* (New York, 1931).
Myers, Margaret G., *A financial history of the United States* (New York, 1970).
Nadal Oller, Jordi, 'La economía española, 1829–1931', in Moreno, *El Banco de España*, pp. 315–417.
Nadal Oller, Jordi, *El fracaso de la revolución industrial en España, 1814–1913* (Barcelona, 1975).
Nash, Robert Lucas, *A short inquiry into the profitable nature of our investments* (London, 1881; first edn, London, 1880).
Nervo, Baron Gonzalve de, *Études historiques. Les Finances françaises sous la Restauration, 1814 à 1830* (Paris, 1865–8), 4 vols.
Newmarch, William, 'On the recent history of the Crédit Mobilier', *Journal of the Statistical Society*, 21 (December 1858), pp. 444–53.
Neymarck, Alfred, *Finances contemporaines* (Paris, 1902–11), 7 vols.

Nolte, Vincent, *Fifty years in both hemispheres: or, reminiscenses of a merchant's life* (London, 1854).

Norman, George Wade, 'The future of the United States', *Journal of the Statistical Society*, 38:1 (March 1875), pp. 64–78.

North, Douglass C., 'International capital flows and the development of the American West', *Journal of Economic History*, 16:4 (December 1956), pp. 493–505.

North, Douglass C., 'The United States balance of payments, 1790–1860', in National Bureau of Economic Research, Studies in Income and Wealth, Vol. 24, *Trends in the American economy in the nineteenth century* (Princeton, NJ, 1960), pp. 573–627.

North, Douglass C., 'International capital movements in historical perspective', in Raymond F. Mikesell, ed., *United States private and government investment abroad* (Eugene, Oreg., 1962), pp. 10–43.

O'Brien, Patrick K., 'Government revenue, 1793–1813; a study in fiscal and financial policy in the wars against France' (unpublished D.Phil. thesis, University of Oxford, 1967).

Olmstead, Alan L., 'Investment constraints and New York City mutual savings bank financing of antebellum development', *Journal of Economic History*, 32 (December 1972), pp. 811–40.

Ouvrard, G.-J., *Mémoires de G.-J. Ouvrard sur sa vie et ses diverses opérations financières* (Paris, 1826–7), 3 vols.

Paish, George, 'Great Britain's capital investments in other lands', *Journal of the Royal Statistical Society*, 72:3 (September 1909), pp. 465–95.

Paish, George, *The trade balance of the United States* (National Monetary Commission, Washington, DC, 1910).

Paish, George, 'Great Britain's capital investments in individual colonial and foreign countries', *Journal of the Royal Statistical Society*, 74:2 (January 1911), pp. 167–200.

Paish, George, 'The export of capital and the cost of living', *Statist*, Supplement (14 February 1914), i–viii.

Palmade, Guy P., *French capitalism in the nineteenth century* (trans. Newton Abbot, 1972).

Pasvolsky, L., and H. G. Moulton, *Russian debts and Russian reconstruction* (New York, 1924).

Patterson, Robert T., 'Government finance on the eve of the Civil War', *Journal of Economic History*, 12:1 (Winter 1952), pp. 35–44.

Perkins, Edwin J., 'Financing antebellum importers: the role of Brown Brothers and Company of Baltimore' *Business History Review*, 45:4 (Winter 1971), pp. 421–45.

Perkins, Edwin J., 'Managing a dollar–sterling exchange account: Brown, Shipley & Co. in the 1850s', *Business History*, 16:1 (January 1974), pp. 48–64.

Perkins, Edwin J., *Financing Anglo-American trade: the house of Brown 1800–1880* (Cambridge, Mass., 1975).

Petit, Pierre, *La Dette publique de la Russie* (Paris, thesis, 1912).

Pintner, W. M., *Russian economic policy under Nicholas I* (Ithaca, NY, 1967).

Platt, D. C. M., *Finance, trade, and politics in British foreign policy, 1815–1914* (Oxford, 1968).

Platt, D. C. M., 'The imperialism of free trade: some reservations', *Economic History Review*, 2nd ser, 21:2 (1968), pp. 296–306.

Platt, D. C. M., 'Further objections to an "imperialism of free trade", 1830–60', *Economic History Review*, 2nd ser. 26:1 (February 1973), pp. 77–91.

Platt, D. C. M., 'The national economy and British imperial expansion before 1914', *Journal of Imperial and Commonwealth History*, 2:1 (October 1973), pp. 3–14.

Platt, D. C. M., 'British portfolio investment overseas before 1870: some doubts', *Economic History Review*, 2nd ser. 33:1 (February 1980), pp. 1–16.

Pollins, Harold, 'The financiers of the Liverpool and Manchester Railway', *Economic History Review*, 2nd ser. 5:1 (1952), pp. 90–7.

Pollins, Harold, 'The marketing of railway shares in the first half of the nineteenth century', *Economic History Review*, 2nd ser. 7:2 (1954), pp. 230–9.

Pollins, Harold, 'Railway contractors and the finance of railway development in Britain', *Journal of Transport History*, 3:1 (May 1957), pp. 41–51, and 3:2 (November 1957), pp. 103–10.

Powell, Ellis T., *The evolution of the money market, 1885–1915* (London, 1915).

Raffalovich, A., 'John Parish, banquier et négociant à Hambourg', *Journal des économistes*, 6th ser. (August 1905), pp. 197–210.

Ránki, György, 'Le capital français en Hongrie', in Lévy-Leboyer, ed., *La Position internationale de la France*, pp. 235–42.

Ravage, Marcus E., *Five men of Frankfort. The story of the Rothschilds* (London, 1929).

Raymond, A., 'Les Tentatives anglaises de pénétration économique en Tunisie (1856–1877)', *Revue historique*, 214 (July/September 1955), pp. 48–67.

Redlich, Fritz, *The molding of American banking, men and ideas* (New York, 1947, 1951), 2 vols.

Redlich, Fritz, 'Jacques Lafitte and the beginnings of investment banking in France', *Bulletin of the Business Historical Society*, 22:4 (December 1948), pp. 137–61.

Redlich, Fritz, 'Two nineteenth-century financiers and autobiographers: a comparative study in creative destructiveness and business failure', *Economy and History*, 10 (1967), pp. 37–128.

Reed, M. C., ed., *Railways in the Victorian economy: studies in finance and economic growth* (Newton Abbot, 1969).

Reed, M. C., *Investment in railways in Britain, 1820–1844: a study in the development of the capital market* (London, 1975).

Reed, M. C., *A history of James Capel & Co.* (London, 1975).

Reid, Stuart J., ed., *Memoirs of Sir Edward Blount* (London, 1902).

Rieber, Alfred J., 'The formation of La Grand Société des Chemins de Fer Russes', *Jahrbücher für Geschichte Ost Europas*, new ser. 21:3 (1973), pp. 375–91.

Riley, James C., *International government finance and the Amsterdam capital market, 1740–1815* (Cambridge, 1980).

Rosenbaum, E., and A. J. Sherman, *M. M. Warburg & Co., 1798–1938: merchant bankers of Hamburg* (trans. London, 1979).

Rozenraad, Cornelius, 'The international money market', *Journal of the Royal Statistical Society*, 63:1 (March 1900), pp. 1–40.

Rubinstein, W. D., *Men of property; the very wealthy in Britain since the Industrial Revolution* (London, 1981).

Rudolph, Richard, 'Austria, 1800–1914', in Cameron, ed., *Banking and economic development*, pp. 26–57.

Rudolph, Richard, *Banking and industrialisation in Austria–Hungary: the role of banks in the industrialisation of the Czech crownlands, 1873–1914* (Cambridge, 1976).

Salsbury, Stephen, *The state, the investor, and the railroad: the Boston and Albany, 1825–1867* (Cambridge, Mass., 1967).

Sánchez-Albornoz, Nicolás, 'El trasfondo económico de la revolución', in Lida and Zavala, *La revolución de 1868*, pp. 64–79.

Sánchez-Albornoz, Nicolás, *España hace un siglo: una economía dual* (Madrid, 1977 edn).

Schwartz Giron, Pedro, ed., *Ensayos sobre la economía española a mediados del siglo XIX* (Madrid, 1970).

Scott, J. D., 'Hambro and Cavour', *History Today*, 19:10 (October 1969), pp. 696–703.

Segal, Harvey, and Matthew Simon, 'British foreign capital issues, 1865–1894', *Journal of Economic History*, 21:4 (December 1961), pp. 566–81.

Seybert, Adam, *Statistical annals of the United States of America, 1789–1818* (Philadelphia, 1818).

Seyd, Ernest, 'The fall in the price of silver, its consequences and their possible avoidance', *Journal of the Society of Arts*, 24 (10 March 1876), pp. 306–34, and discussion in *Journal of the Society of Arts*, 24 (17 March 1876), pp. 345–66.

Simon, Matthew, 'The United States balance of payments, 1861–1900', in National Bureau of Economic Research, Studies in Income and Wealth, Vol. 24, *Trends in the American economy in the nineteenth century* (Princeton, NJ, 1960), pp. 629–715.

Simon, Matthew, 'The enterprise and industrial composition of new British portfolio foreign investment, 1865–1914', *Journal of Development Studies*, 3:3 (April 1967), pp. 280–99.

Simon, Matthew, 'The pattern of new British portfolio investment', in Adler, ed., *Capital movements*, pp. 33–70.

Skinner, Thomas, ed., *The stock exchange year-book for 1875* (London, 1875, and subsequent editions).

Smith, Walter Buckingham, *Economic aspects of the Second Bank of the United States* (Cambridge, Mass., 1953).

Sobel, Robert, *The big board: a history of the New York stock market* (New York, 1965).

Sontag, John P., 'Tsarist debts and tsarist foreign policy', *Slavic Review*, 27:4 (December 1968), pp. 529–41.

Steefel, Lawrence D., 'The Rothschilds and the Austrian loan of 1865', *Journal of Modern History*, 8:1 (March 1936), pp. 27–39.

Stern, Fritz R., *Gold and iron: Bismarck, Bleichröder, and the building of the German empire* (London, 1977).

Sterns, Worthy P., 'The international indebtedness of the United States in 1789', *Journal of Political Economy*, 6:1 (December 1897), pp. 27–53.

Sterns, Worthy P., 'The beginnings of American financial independence', *Journal of Political Economy*, 6:2 (March 1898), pp. 187–208.

Studenski, P., and H. B. Krooss, *Financial history of the United States* (New York, 1952).

Sturgis, Julian R., *From the books and papers of Russell Sturgis* (Oxford, 1893); Sturgis was a partner in Barings.

Supple, Barry E., 'A business élite: German–Jewish financiers in nineteenth-century New York', *Business History Review*, 31:2 (Summer 1957), p. 143–78.

Supple, Barry E., ed., *The experience of economic growth: case studies in economic history* (New York, 1963).

Sylla, Richard, *The American capital market, 1846–1914: a study of the effects of public policy on economic development* (New York, 1975).

Tallada Pauli, José María, *Historia de las finanzas españolas en el siglo XIX* (Madrid, 1946).

Tedde de Lorca, Pedro, 'La banca privada española durante la restauración (1874–1914)', in Tortella, *La Banca Española*, Vol. I, pp. 217–455.

Tedde de Lorca, Pedro, 'Las compañías ferroviarias en España (1855–1935)', in Artola, *Los ferrocarriles en España*, Vol. II, pp. 9–354.

Témime, Emile, Albert Broder and Gerard Chastagnaret, *Histoire de l'Espagne contemporaine de 1808 à nos jours* (Paris, 1979).

Temin, Peter, 'The Anglo-American business cycle, 1820–60', *Economic History Review*, 2nd ser. 27:2 (May 1974), pp. 207–21.

Thomas, Brinley, 'The historical record of international capital movements to 1913', in Adler, *Capital movements*, pp. 3–32.

Thorner, Daniel, *Investment in Empire: British railway and steam shipping enterprise in India, 1825–1849* (Philadelphia, 1950).

Thorner, Daniel, 'Great Britain and the development of India's railways', *Journal of Economic History*. 11:4 (Fall 1951), pp. 389–402.

Tilly, Richard, *Financial institutions and industrialisation in the Rhineland, 1815–1870* (Madison, Wis., 1966).

Tilly, Richard, 'The political economy of public finance and the industrialisation of Prussia, 1815–1866', *Journal of Economic History*, 26:4 (December 1966), pp. 484–97.

Tooke, Thomas, *A history of prices and of the state of the circulation during the years from 1793–1856* (London, 1838–57), 6 vols.

Tortella Casares, Gabriel, 'El Banco de España entre 1829–1929. La formación de un banco central', in Tortella, *El banco de España, una historia económica* (Madrid, 1970), pp. 261–313.

Tortella Casares, Gabriel, 'La evolución del sistema financiero español de 1856 a 1868', in Schwartz, *Ensayos sobre la economía española*, pp. 17–146.

Tortella Casares, Gabriel, 'Ferrocarriles, economía y revolución', in Lida and Zavala, *La revolución de 1868*, pp. 126–37.

Tortella Casares, Gabriel, *Los orígenes del capitalismo en España: banca, industria y ferrocarriles en el siglo XIX* (Madrid, 1973).

Tortella Casares, Gabriel, ed., *La Banca Española en la restauración* (Madrid, 1974), 2 vols.

Tortella Casares, Gabriel, 'La formación de capital en España, 1874–1914: reflexiones para un planteamiento de la cuestion', *Hacienda Pública Española*, 55 (1978), pp. 399–415.

Tortella Casares, Gabriel, 'El sistema bancario español en la segunda mitad del siglo XIX', *Dinero y crédito (siglos XVI al XIX)* (Madrid, 1978), pp. 221–38.

Tortella Casares, Gabriel, 'La economía española', in Tortella Casares *et al.*, *Revolución burguesa oligarquíe y constitucionalismo*, in M. Tuñon de Lara, ed., Vol. VIII, Histórica de España (Barcelona, 1981).

Trescott, Paul B., *Financing American enterprise: the story of commercial banking* (New York, 1963).

Truptil, R. J., *British banks and the London money market* (London, 1936).

Tyson, R. E., 'Scottish investment in American railways: the case of the City of Glasgow Bank, 1856–1881', in P. L. Payne, ed., *Studies in Scottish business history* (London, 1967), pp. 387–416.

Vamplew, Wray, 'Sources of Scottish railway share capital before 1860', *Scottish Journal of Political Economy* 17 (1970), pp. 425–40.

Vamplew, Wray, 'Banks and railway finance: a note on the Scottish experience', *Transport History*, 4:2 (July 1971), pp. 166–81.

Vamplew, Wray, 'The financing of Scottish railways before 1860 – a reply', *Scottish Journal of Political Economy*, 18 (1971), pp. 221–3.

Waís San Martín, Francisco, *Historia general de los ferrocarriles españoles, 1830–1941* (Madrid, 1974; first edn, Madrid, 1967).

Walford, Cornelius, 'Recent financial and taxation statistics of the United States', *Journal of the Statistical Society*, 26:2 (June 1863), pp. 154–67.

Walters, Philip G., and Raymond Walters, Jr, 'The American career of David Parish', *Journal of Economic History*, 4:2 (November 1944), pp. 149–66.

Weill, Georges, 'Le Financier Ouvrard', *Revue historique*, 127:1 (January/February 1918), pp. 31–61.

Westwood, John N., *A history of Russian railways* (London, 1964).

Whicker, E. R., 'Railroad investment before the Civil War', in National Bureau of Economic Research, Studies in Income and Wealth, Vol. 24, *Trends in the American economy in the nineteenth century* (Princeton, NJ, 1960), pp. 503–45.

White, Harry D., *French international accounts, 1880–1913* (Cambridge, Mass., 1933).

Williamson, J. G. 'International trade and United States economic development: 1827–1843', *Journals of Economic History*, 21:3 (September 1961), pp. 372–83.

Williamson, J. G., *American growth and the balance of payments, 1820–1913* (Chapel Hill, NC, 1964).

Wilson, Charles H., *Anglo-Dutch commerce and finance in the eighteenth century* (Cambridge, 1941).

Wolff, Otto, *Ouvrard, speculator of genius, 1770–1846* (trans. London, 1962).

Woodruff, William, *Impact of Western man, a study of Europe's role in the world economy, 1750–1960* (London, 1966).

Index

Appearing, as they do, so frequently throughout this book, Baring Brothers & Co., Limited, their senior partners (Thomas Baring and Joshua Bates), and their principal correspondents abroad (Hottinguer of Paris, Hope & Co. of Amsterdam, and their partners) are not indexed separately. Nor are the authors of books published after the First World War (other than Leland Jenks). All, however, are footnoted.

www.ingramcontent.com/pod-product-compliance
Lightning Source LLC
LaVergne TN
LVHW011127300926
849160LV00008B/553
* 9 7 8 1 1 3 8 8 7 9 8 1 2 *